After the Dust has Settled

Tom Ellis

bridge
books
Wrexham

After the Dust has Settled
First published in Wales in 2004 by
BRIDGE BOOKS
61 Park Avenue
Wrexham
LL12 7AW

© 2004 Tom Ellis
© 2004 Typesetting and design, Bridge Books

CIP Data for this book is available
from the British Library

ISBN 1-84494-013-6

Printed and bound by
Cromwell Press, Trowbridge

Contents

Acknowledgement

I wish to thank Alister Williams of Bridge Books for his professionalism. Whatever appeal the contents of this book may, or may not have, the quality of its production speaks for itself.

List of Illustrations

Hafod Colliery, the mine that has featured large throughout my life, where several generations of my family worked.

1. False Beginnings

I was born in Pant, then a hamlet between the villages of Rhos and Penycae, but now part of the growing urban sprawl connecting them. The parish boundary between the two villages was a small stream called the Afon Goch which ran through Pant alongside the old mill owned at one time by my great, great grandfather. My mother's family had lived near the Afon Goch for generations, although the stream itself had long since disappeared into a culvert so that it had become an invisible and merely notional boundary. Sometime after the First World War, however, the boundary reappeared in a more significant, if less tangible, guise as a linguistic divide between the two villages. When I was a small boy, Penycae children played in English and Rhos children in Welsh. Like the old Afon Goch, the language barrier separating them was measurable almost to a yard.

That fact influenced my childhood greatly because I chose, if that is the word, to play with the English speaking children of Penycae. I have been told that although I was a monoglot Welsh speaker at the age of three, I gradually lost my mother tongue as I ventured beyond our doorstep towards Penycae and by the age of six had acquired English in its place. The acquisition, partly the fruit of geography and partly of sectarianism, was to turn sour in the years ahead.

Soar, a Wesleyan chapel on the outskirts of Penycae, was my

maternal grandmother's chapel. Indeed, several of its pews were filled with three generations of our family, which also provided sundry lay preachers, deacons, organists, Sunday School teachers and Band of Hope organisers. In short we were 'pillars of the church', or in the Welsh idiom 'eight-inch nails of the cause'. My father's pedigree was less respectable. His father had played the trumpet in the Rhos Silver Prize Band, which practised with some devotion in the Coach & Horses, a hostelry located discreetly on the outskirts of the village. My father, however, was not only a teetotaller but a faithful member of Capel Bychan, a not unrenowned Congregational chapel at the far end of Rhos. My mother, following custom, became one of its members after marriage.

I had no doubt that my father's commitment to his chapel, despite or perhaps because of his pedigree, was one of conviction. I was less sure in my mother's case. She always claimed that her heart was with the Wesleyans in Soar, a rodomontade that I suspected was a result of the streak of contrariness in her nature. My doubts, however, might have been simply the consequence of my not knowing her well enough. She lacked my father's openness right to the end of her life, even to her close family. She surprised me, for example, when, a couple of days before she died, in pain and refusing pain-killing drugs as contrarily as ever, she expressed a wish to be buried from Horeb, the Wesleyan chapel in Rhos, not from Capel Bychan. If my father had not pre-deceased her, I suppose she would quietly have resigned herself to a Congregational funeral.

My parents had made their first home in Pant, a quarter of a mile from Soar but nearly two miles from Capel Bychan. It was thus inevitable that under the supervision of my grandmother, who lived next door, I attended Sunday School and the Band of Hope at Soar, no doubt partly for convenience but partly, I suspect, to my mother's sectarian satisfaction. I involuntarily lifted up mine eyes, so to speak, in the direction of Penycae and its non-Welsh speaking children.

My parents in old age.

A second misfortune augmented the Anglicisation process beginning to envelop me. The school nearest to Pant was a 'church school', that is to say an Anglican school, and it was there at the age of 3¹/₂ that I began my formal education. Unlike the two other schools in Rhos, its lessons were exclusively in English. The Anglican Church-in-Wales had been finally disestablished five years previously after a long campaign by the nation's nonconformist majority, but Wern School's ethos, faithfully reflecting Anglican attitudes, remained stubbornly anglophile and reluctantly Welsh. Indeed, had not the newly disestablished church chosen, rather presumptuously, to call itself 'The Church in Wales'? The school accordingly exuded a kind of missionary zeal for saving the natives.

A week or two after I had begun my first term at the school, the headmistress wrote to my parents asking them to speak English with me at home so that I might come to understand the lessons. They concurred unquestioningly and our hearth became an English speaking one except when neighbours called. It remained thus over the years, my brother and I speaking only English with our parents until their deaths, our father's at 89 and our mother's at 94. Rather surprisingly, my mother gradually became less fluent in Welsh, but my father remained equally comfortable in both languages, consequences, perhaps, of my mother's nervously private temperament and my father's extrovert Rhos sociability. My brother Ceiriog and I became monoglot English speakers. Ceiriog is nine years younger than I and was thus raised from birth as an English speaker speaking no Welsh. I do not know what Freudian complex made my mother choose a name for him so full of irony. In my own case, however, I had simply taken the first false step of my life and like thousands of Welsh men and women in similar circumstances, I was being tamely deprived of a national heritage, the seeds of which had already been planted. Despite the views of historians such as Dai Smith, who in his book *Wales! Wales?* applied an all-embracing reductionism to create a shallow definition of Welshness, I believe that such a deprivation and loss is profoundly damaging.

I have often wondered afterwards, from my late teens onwards, how it was that my father should so readily have failed to appreciate the importance of nationhood. I say 'my father' rather than 'my parents' because he was the one whom I would most have expected to appreciate the loss I was to suffer. My mother would have adopted a pragmatic attitude to the problem posed by the headmistress and, with little or no thought, would have accepted the request as an imperative stemming from someone of authority, although in later life, it has to be said, she was the one who defended Welsh political aspirations from the scorn heaped upon them by my father and others in the Rhos Labour Party. This later independence of mind was due partly to her increasing contrariness and more justifiably, partly to her cynicism about politicians, especially Labour ones. My father on the other hand, who was a thoughtful man but doctrinaire when young,

With two of my friends in Rhos. The open door of the cottage where I was born can be seen at the extreme left of the picture. It has now been demolished.

had been conditioned, like so many thoroughly Welsh miners of his generation and mine, by the internationalist pretensions of the British Labour Party. Meaningless slogans like 'Workers of the world, unite' had a resonance that deafened them to appeals for loyalty nearer home. Happily, by his late 70s, my father had come to see not only the hollowness of his objections to specifically Welsh political aspirations, but also the sheer bloody-minded English state nationalism of the Labour Party. We had always differed on the question of Welsh aspirations, yet during one of the last political discussions I had with him, he acknowledged that the Republic of Ireland would not have achieved, could not have achieved, its economic success had it remained part of the United Kingdom. It was a revealing admission, however, because despite his grasp of early twentieth-century Irish politics and the motivation of its leaders, it was the economics that had persuaded him; Irish nationhood could not be an end in itself.

It was my misfortune that neither of my parents saw the

importance of my native tongue, let alone my Welshness to my life. Nevertheless, having fortuitously been set on my fateful course by institutional religion, compounded by the refinements of local geography, I was blissfully unaware of my loss and my childhood passed happily and uneventfully. I recall little happening of importance, my memories being of trivial incidents such as the occasion when I was sitting in the front row of the 'babies' class at school playing with a wooden toy cow, which said "Moo" when I turned its head, surely my earliest memory.

I was ten years of age when there occurred two incidents, which heartbreakingly heralded my later coalmining career. The first was hearing, without comprehending, Emmanuel Griffiths, a neighbour in Pant who was a miner at Gresford colliery, saying to my father "You'll see, Bob, we'll all be blown to Gehenna one of these days." My father explained later Mr Griffiths's forebodings about the poor ventilation at the colliery and the presence of gas, as well as the meaning of the word 'Gehenna', Emmanuel Griffiths lost his life in the explosion.

The other related incident was hearing the milkman at our door early that terrible Saturday morning telling my mother that an accident had occurred at Gresford colliery. My father, who was at work at Hafod colliery, was captain of the Hafod rescue team and my mother knew that if the accident were a serious one, then the team would be called to it. As the news spread during the morning that there had been a major disaster, my mother became increasingly worried. Soon we heard that the Hafod team, along with rescue teams from the other collieries of the coalfield, had in fact been called to Gresford and that they were underground attempting to rescue hundreds of miners trapped after an explosion. Three members of the Llay Main rescue team lost their lives in the attempt. My mother, younger brother and I spent the Saturday at my grandmother's home. I was still awake when my father returned home late at night only to tell us that he had to be back at Gresford at six o'clock the following

Large crowds gather to await news from Gresford Colliery, September 1934.

morning to continue with the so far unsuccessful rescue attempt.

My father held a first class colliery manager's certificate — the youngest person then and, I believe, to this day to have passed the examination from the north Wales coalfield. When he returned to the colliery surface, the Chief Inspector of Mines asked his opinion of the underground situation. The Dennis district, where the explosion had been sparked, was an inferno and the air in the tunnels leading to the district contained a high proportion of deadly carbon monoxide — the rescue teams of course were wearing breathing apparatus. My father's opinion was that a second explosion could easily occur causing further loss of life. His advice was that the only sensible course of action was to seal both shafts at the surface, so that the fire would extinguish itself through lack of oxygen. The seals were put in place on the Sunday afternoon and attempts were abandoned at recovering what now would have been dead bodies. The following morning, a second explosion did in fact occur, which travelled along

My father (right), captain of the Hafod Colliery rescue team, prepares to enter the Gresford shaft in 1935.

the mine roadways and blew the seal off one of the shafts, sending a heavy steel girder hurtling through the air. The girder hit and killed a surface worker some yards away, thus bringing the total death toll to 266.

Some 40 years later, after the colliery had closed and the surface installations had been demolished, one of the pithead wheels was erected on a plinth as a memorial to the miners who had lost their lives. The local authority now owned the colliery site. A number of former Gresford miners, including myself, had sought to persuade the authority to let one of the headgears remain standing as a more fitting memorial and more visible acknowledgement of Wrexham's former dependence on coal. This could have been done without prejudicing the development of the site into an industrial estate, but the council rejected the proposal on the grounds that the cost of regularly repainting the headgear would have been prohibitive. I was even more dismayed at this astonishing reason than at the rejection itself. The memorial tablet, erected alongside the wheel some distance away from the colliery, was unveiled by the Prince of Wales and miners, by now much fewer in number, who had been employed at the colliery at the time of the disaster, were invited to attend the ceremony, as were local councillors and myself as the local MP. My mother was furious that my father did not receive an invitation, but he himself was unperturbed. Their respective reactions were in character.

My future occupation was hardly at the front of my mind at the time of the Gresford disaster, let alone the possibility of 'going down the pit', as the job was known in Rhos. I had enough to concern me preparing to sit the 'scholarship' less than a year later. I succeeded in passing the examination and, in September 1935, I became a pupil at Ruabon Grammar School. That change in my life was fateful in two ways. In the first place, it led to the second false step of my life but, on the other hand, provoked me into reversing the first false step. The provocation became stronger as I moved up through the school. I was unaware of it at first but, by the time I reached the fifth form, I had begun to feel the loss, not so much of my Welsh heritage as such — I became aware of that later on as I matured — but of my heritage as a Rhosite. The Welshman's love of locality was growing in me.

The sociology of Ruabon Grammar School was unusual, if not unique, when I became a pupil there. One half of the boys (it was a boys' school) were from Rhos and Ponciau (the West End of Rhos according to some) and the other half from the villages of Cefn Mawr,

The 'Scholarhsip Boy'.

Cefn Bychan, Acrefair, Rhosymedre, Ruabon, Johnstown and Penycae. The Rhos half was Welsh speaking, the other was made up largely of non-Welsh speaking boys, both Welsh and immigrants from England. The difference between the two groups was striking, with the Rhosites possessing the assertive self-assurance of their village. They tended to lead in all aspects of communal school life, in sport, the annual eisteddfod, drama, the occasional concert and more intangibly, in the easy naturalness of their intercourse with the teaching staff, a striking characteristic for that age of deference.

I hasten to disabuse readers who might think that the last paragraph is shameless boasting. It is not my intention to praise Rhos at the expense of its neighbours; I want simply to emphasise the undoubted fact that the place and its people, when I was a boy, had for better or for worse a distinctive character of its own. The fact is confirmed and to a degree explained by pointing out that the inhabitants of the surrounding districts were very ready and are so even to this day, to accuse Rhosites of bumptiousness; our response was to laugh at them and accuse them of envy.

A sense of the extrovert and self-assured Rhos temperament can be gained from an answer I once had from a friend of my father's who was a committed socialist. In the 60s when both he and my father were newly retired, they went together on a Russian holiday because he was anxious to see the May Day Parade on Moscow's Red Square. On their return I asked him for his impressions of Russia. He answered with conviction: "Tom," he said, "we have been misled about Russia, scandalously misled. I shall tell the people of Rhos." I would not want anyone to think that he was a stupid man. On the contrary, he was a leader of high standing in his community and an able man who successfully held an important position in the north Wales coal industry after nationalisation. His instinctive self-assurance, however, together with its inevitable accompanying naivety, faithfully reflected the temper of the village and its influence on his upbringing. One sees best, perhaps, the close relationship between self-confidence and naivety in the world of politics where 'strong' leaders habitually see complex problems in terms only of black and white. One thinks, for example, of Mrs Thatcher who rarely saw problems as multi-faceted and who prided herself on being a conviction politician, certain of her policy come what may. People who never see two sides to a problem are certainly self-assured and can be naive, especially when their vision is parochial as is so often the case.

Readers must forgive these digressions. I would not have dreamt of them, of course, when I was a new pupil at the Grammar School. What is interesting, however, is that I began subconsciously to sense what I could, without irony, describe only as a Rhos magnetism drawing me as I moved upwards through the school. Gradually I became aware of the rather special community I had inadvertently deserted and inexplicably began to feel a pride in its sometimes, no doubt, vainglorious attitudes. Yet I was not fully a member of that community nor of its junior branch at the Grammar School (I use the upper case since for Rhos people there was only one grammar school). The most obvious indication that I was not a member was the fact that a group of Rhos boys would never switch to the English language if I or any other non-Welsh speaking boy attached himself to the group. It was not a question of lack of courtesy; it would have been more that switching to English would have been an unnatural thing to do. It is easy to see how the village's cultural dissociation and Wrexham's curmudgeonly response arose.

By the time I was in the fifth form I regretted deeply that I spoke virtually no Welsh. In the first form, obligatory Welsh lessons had been held in two classes, 'Easy Welsh' and 'Mother tongue Welsh', In my first year I had been in the easy Welsh class, that is to say 'Welsh as a foreign language' (one sees how the school sensibilities produced the term 'Easy Welsh', a pre-war example of today's political correctness). It was the only formal education I ever received in my native language; in itself an outrageous state of affairs for the Welsh, as distinct from the British, educational system. The paucity of my knowledge at the age of twelve comes back vividly from another of those trivial memories of childhood. I recall at the examination after the first year having to add the missing word in the phrase "*yn ôl ac...*," the English equivalent would have been to complete the phrase 'to and ...' by adding the word 'fro', I failed to answer the question. At the age of 15 in the fifth form I determined to re-learn the language and remedy the first false step of my life.

I became a member of *Aelwyd yr Urdd*; there was a successful branch of that youth movement in Rhos, which I joined rather sheepishly because of my language inadequacies. I need not have worried; I soon got to know a warm-hearted crowd of young Rhosites, each one of whom was prepared to listen patiently to my pidgin Welsh. I was part of the boisterous, uninhibited society that was Rhos youth. During my three years of membership prior to entering university, I felt my Welsh steadily improving. Naturally, the foundations laid during my childhood up to the age of three were a help, but the most important thing was to live my life in the middle of a Welsh-speaking peer group and to absorb the language naturally and unconsciously. I have two memories, trivial yet again, but significant this time. I remember telling someone as I left the Aelwyd one night shortly after becoming a member, "I must go to *nol a bara* for *Nain*" (instead of saying in Welsh "I must go to fetch a loaf for my grandmother") and feeling a sense of shame at my linguistic inadequacy. But I also remember one of the members three years later correcting me as I mistakenly said in Welsh "I still have to go to Blackpool" when I meant to say "I've never been to Blackpool". The improvement in my Welsh is a measure of the three year gap between the two incidents.

The second false step of my life was to study chemistry for my higher school-leaving certificate and to graduate in the subject at University College, Bangor. The study of chemistry calls for some practical dexterity measuring out powders, distilling liquids, filtering residues and so on. I was no chemist for I always seemed to end up with a damp smudge on a piece of filter paper. To make matters worse, I found the long sunny afternoons cooped up in a laboratory burdensome, especially as the Welsh life of 'Top Coll', as we called the humanities block, was in its heyday. It was a privilege to be a student at the '*Coleg ar y Bryn*' in the golden age of its Welshness and I was loth to miss a minute of the activities in the 'Union'. This was the time when *Triawd y Coleg* — a trio of gifted students who acquired celebrity status singing their own compositions — was germinating before bursting into flower after the war.

After two years studying chemistry, before completing an honours degree, I was called for interview before a military panel named the Central Scientific and Technical Register. It was 1944 and D-day had passed. The panel decided that I was to go to Persia to work as a civilian in the oil industry. I refused and expected to be drafted into one of the forces. The panel, however, then decided that I should take up employment in an explosive works. Providence was smiling on me because the works to which I was sent was, of all places, at

The laboratory staff at Penrhyndeudraeth. I am seated in the centre.
Nona, later my wife, is seated at the front.

Penrhyndeudraeth, barely 50 miles from Rhos and in the heart of Welsh speaking Wales. I lodged with a widow who had two sons, the younger of whom was a six-year-old monolingual Welsh speaker. To all intents and purposes the community itself also was monolingual in Welsh. This was the period when I really had the opportunity of putting some 'polish' on my spoken Welsh. I spent three happy years in Penrhyn walking the mountains and beaches, alone at first but afterwards with a young woman who later became my wife. A memory of this period is of the two of us spending a beautiful August bank holiday on Black Rock sands at Morfa Bychan (today a kind of Welsh *Costa del Sol*) with not another soul in sight; there was something to be said for petrol rationing

Two years after my commencing work in Penrhyn, the chemicals company ICI purchased the explosives works from its previous owner. A new managing director, who was a native of Barry and a graduate of University College, Aberystwyth, arrived with his wife and children. His eldest daughter came to work alongside me as a laboratory assistant. We fell in love and, four years later, were married. The workings of providence transformed the second false step of my life into its greatest blessing.

I returned to Bangor in the autumn of 1947, ostensibly to spend two years reading for an honours degree in chemistry, but knowing full well that, however conscientiously I worked at the subject, I would never make a good chemist, my heart was simply not in it. Although I succeeded in graduating, I had already made up my mind to pursue a career in a very different industry.

My father was a coalminer at Hafod colliery, as had been my grandfather and, for all I know, his father before him. Hafod-y-bwch, to give it its full name, had been for almost a century the all-pervasive and baleful background to Rhos, its spoil heap reifying the image as it rose, like a threatening Vesuvius, from the lush Maelor plain at the bottom end of the parish. Talk at home turned daily about the pit, its activities and whimsies, its humour and malice, why such and such a district was on strike, how there had been a fall of roof at the bottom of Fox's Deep and, of course, the malignant conspiracies of the coal-owners providing validity for all manner of complaint.

My father had started work at Hafod at the age of 13 — it seems that pupils on passing a test were allowed to leave school at that age, although there was little employment awaiting them other than the pit and the brickworks. Indeed, over half a century later, I was charmed by the claim of an old miner, an innocent character that, on the day he was born in 1910, his father had gone immediately to see Ben Pritchard to put his name down for a job at Hafod. Mr Pritchard was the colliery under-manager. Hafod at that time had at least one thing in common with Eton College. My father, in due course, studied mining engineering at night school and gained his colliery manager's certificate when he was 23 years of age, the minimum age for sitting

Chaired Bard — I won the chair for writing a lyric poem on the theme 'Ar Frig y Don' (on the crest of the wave) at the Penrhyndeudraeth Youth Eisteddfod.

the examination. He was now the under-manager at the colliery. I felt a strong desire to emulate him and to become general manager of Hafod colliery, following in the footsteps of Johnny and Willy Jones, two legendary brothers who between them had managed Hafod colliery for over 40 years. Nothing could be nobler.

Once again providence smiled benignly. The Labour government nationalised the coal industry so that to contemplate a career in coal was less absurd than it would previously have been. Indeed it would be almost socially acceptable, or at least that was the rationalising behind my rashness. It meant, in the first instance, getting a job at one of the six local collieries, an easy thing although not commendable in the eyes of Rhos mothers who, to a woman, would still have urged their sons not to go 'down the pit' and secondly, attending night school to prepare myself adequately for sitting the colliery manager's certificate, a more difficult thing. It was necessary to have five years' practical experience underground before being allowed to sit the examination in Wigan, the nearest centre to our small coalfield where the examination was held. It would have surprised Lancastrians to know that the image of the town amongst the north Wales coalmining fraternity was that of a place lofty with academic distinction. To Rhosites just after the war, Wigan (or 'Wigeen' as we called it) was a vast examination hall and when the occasional privileged mother boasted that her son had gone to 'Wigeen', she meant that he was sitting an important examination.

As well as my family's mining tradition, there was another entirely different cause nurturing my romanticism. Like most children of mining families, I was brought up in an atmosphere of socialist rhetoric and soon learned the words of *The Red Flag*. My father was an active member of the Rhos Labour Party so that, at home, talk of the pit was accompanied by a party political descant, especially after I reached my middle teens and provided a reasonably adult foil for my father's fervour. The need to nationalise the mines had been confirmed in the communal mind by the Sankey Commission's report published after the First World War. My father and his colleagues preached the virtues of that report almost daily so that nationalisation had acquired a status akin to that of the Holy Grail in my mind. At the time of the 1945 general election when I was 21, the nationalisation of the mines had become a great banner unfurled before me, demanding that I follow it. How could I, the son of a miner and myself an enthusiastic socialist, refrain from taking part in this great socialist experiment pledged by the Labour Party and not help to realise the vision that had inspired me for so long. My romanticism would reach its full flowering in three years time, but in the meantime there was an election to be won.

There was another young Rhosite, Twm Dan Davies, who also was a chemist at the explosives works and together, with the brashness of our youth and upbringing, we had established a branch of the Labour Party in Penrhyndeudraeth twelve months before the election. During the summer of 1945 we campaigned hard for our candidate, Huw Morris Jones, a native of Talsarnau, just across the river Dwyryd from

Penrhyn, who later became professor of social theory at Bangor University. Public meetings were still in fashion and we had Jim Griffiths, T. E. Nicholas (*Niclas Y Glais*) and other well-known personalities to address crowded and enthusiastic meetings. We were, of course, on the verge of a political upheaval and it seemed at times that we could walk on water. The only failure was a meeting at Llanfrothen with me as the speaker because no one else was available that evening. I recall to this day my embarrassment, as it gradually dawned on me that it was my inexperience and immaturity which caused the audience of 50 or so villagers to show doubt about our policies as I laboriously expounded them. The election, of course, produced a great victory for Labour; I am still astonished, however, that I felt the loss of Merioneth to the Liberals more strongly than I did the joy of sweeping the country and gaining an overwhelming majority in the House of Commons — my inherent Rhos parochialism manifesting itself perhaps, rather like that of my father's friend on his return from Moscow.

By 1947, when at last the nationalisation of the mines had been accomplished, there was no doubt in my mind that my future was to be in that industry. The only problem would be the reaction of my future wife and my parents. What would they think of a young man, hoping to graduate with honours in chemistry, who proposed to work in the pit as a haulage hand, the lowest rung of the mining ladder he hoped to climb? My parents, of course, as every parent in Rhos would have done, had taken it for granted that one of the most important of their parental duties was to ensure that I would not have to earn my living in a coal mine. I need not have worried, however. After some hesitation, especially on my mother's part, they accepted, even if they did not understand, the conviction behind their wilful son's intention. As for my wife-to-be, we were head-over-heels in love and, thus, neither of us could make a mistake and, in any case as I told her, at least I knew that she was not marrying me for my money.

I sat my final examination at Bangor one Thursday morning in June and the following day went looking for work at Gresford colliery two miles from Wrexham. The clerk told me that Mr James, the colliery manager, would be interviewing men looking for work the following morning. Mr James was an unusual character, who put me off balance with his colourful language, although when I came to know him well later, I appreciated his humour and wisdom. My interview lasted no more than a few minutes, but I remember his asking me what I could do. When I replied "Anything," his swift response was that he was short of men who could do anything and that I was to go at once to the training officer to complete the necessary formalities and be signed on. By midday on that Saturday, I was a miner at Gresford colliery and had started on my career.

I chose Gresford as that was the Wrexham coalfield colliery furthest from my home and I would be fairly unknown there. I would not have to suffer the embarrassment of being an object of curiosity, a haulage hand with a degree in chemistry. My fears in this regard were confirmed a year later, when Richard Dimbleby visited Rhos with his radio programme *Down Your Way*, but more of that in the next chapter. For the moment I was pleased with myself and knew that I would never have made a good chemist but that I was sure to make an excellent coal miner.

2. First Steps

Men entering the coal industry to work underground for the first time had to undergo a short period of training designed to equip them with a knowledge of basic safety requirements, with the ability to recognise the more common dangers and with the competence to perform their own duties safely. This elementary requirement, introduced as a consequence of nationalisation, had superseded the previous common practice of sending a new starter underground accompanied by a workmate and expecting him gradually to acquire the skills necessary for his particular job. Accordingly, at eight o'clock one Monday morning in June, five new starters, of whom I was one, arrived at the training centre situated within the colliery's block of administrative offices. Eight o'clock was a civilized time at which to begin the day's work, a luxury that I appreciated during the three-week training period and was to lose at its conclusion.

The practice in the coalfield was to work three shifts, days, afternoons and nights, not one of which did I find ideal. The day shift began officially at 6.00a.m. but because twelve to fifteen 'ropes' were needed to wind the day shift down the shaft in batches of up to fifty men per rope, the first man-riding rope was wound at 5.30a.m. It was the custom that older men descended on that rope and younger ones on the last rope at 6.00a.m. At the end of the shift, of course, the reverse was the case, so the unwritten rule was that the elderly went down first and came up last, while the young bloods went down last and came up first. A problem common to all collieries at the end of a shift was that of controlling the number of unruly youths crowding the pit bottom to get on the cage for the first rope. Some years later, when I was assistant manager at Llay Main colliery, the problem on one occasion proved to be a severe test of my managerial resolve, as I shall explain in a later chapter.

I found the early start on the day shift irksome. I had always been a reluctant early morning riser, no doubt because I found it difficult to get to bed before midnight and the discipline of having to catch a bus at 4.45a.m. was a harsh one, especially during the winter; it was not until I became manager of my own colliery that I was able to enjoy the luxury of lying in bed each day until seven o'clock. Prior to that it so happened that I worked for most of the time on the day and afternoon shifts except for one short period on the night shift for six consecutive weeks immediately on returning from my honeymoon after a Christmas break.

On that fine eight o'clock morning in June, however, all five of us were wide-awake and eagerly anticipating collecting our lamps from the lamp room to go underground. It was not to be. Instead, we spent a dispiriting day sitting through a series of lectures in the training centre. We went home a little downcast and not much wiser, but a bit more apprehensive of what was before us. The following morning was sunny once again and this time we were not disappointed. The five of us, under the supervision of an instructor, were to visit the coalface used for training purposes. It was here that 'lads' (every haulage worker was a lad irrespective of his age) promoted from haulage work or other 'day-wage' work, were trained for the various types of coal face work. The face and its roadway, in which we were to spend that day and the following three weeks, were part of the 'deputy's district' used for training in general.

Gresford Colliery. This photograph was taken at the time of the disaster in 1934 but the colliery yard had changed very little by the time I began work here. Memories of the disaster were still vivid in people's minds.

My heartbeat quickened as I walked across the colliery yard from the pithead baths to the lamp room and then to the air-lock on the Martin shaft. There are at least two shafts to every coalmine, the downcast and the up-cast. Air for ventilating the mine is drawn down the one and along the roadways (tunnels) to the coalface and then back along the 'returns' or 'wind roads' to the up-cast shaft, which is connected by a 'fan drift' to a large fan housed near the shaft. To avoid short-circuiting the air current, an air-lock or large chamber encloses the mouth of the shaft. We approached the air-lock, trying to appear nonchalant as we passed some surface workers, while above our heads the two large winding wheels bearing the three inch thick steel winding ropes of the Dennis coal-winding shaft turned silently and smoothly on the massive pit head-gear, their spokes making a rhythmic pattern as they revolved in opposite directions in the sunlight, the cage of the one descending with its load of empty wagons and that of the other ascending with its 'paitches', as wagons full of coal were called. The deep throb of the powerful steam winding-engine played a kind of tympanic accompaniment in the background as it sent the cages hurtling up and down the shaft like a pair of enormous shuttles. The low hum of the fan joined in harmony and above its outlet, warm ventilating air condensed as it discharged from the mine to form billowing white clouds glistening in the sunlight. The air-lock itself, a forbidding metal structure ugly with rust and grime, seemed as if it housed a whole mysterious world of subterranean activity serviced by the awesome power I could see and hear all around me belching out clouds of steam and reverberating as if with the throb of distant thunder.

Looking back across fifty years, I believe that those few minutes walking to the Martin shaft at Gresford colliery for the first time were the most awesome of my life. I was dwarfed by the two winding-engine houses, the fan house, the power house, the row of a dozen Lancashire boilers, the colliery chimney vomiting its black smoke, the two head-gears with their spinning wheels and, in the background, the pit-head baths as a kind of last outpost of normal life which we had forsaken. The sun, however, was warm on my face and I thought rather sentimentally of my father fourteen years previously descending the same pit in such different circumstances. I was aware, above all, that somehow or other I was fulfilling my destiny in rejecting the clinical detachment of the laboratory for the rough warmth of the miner and his calling.

The first steel door of the air-lock clanged shut behind us and as the second door did the same a moment later, I felt for the first time the click in my ears as they adjusted to the change of air pressure, an experience which was to become so familiar a feature of my daily life. I was immediately in a new world, but I felt at home: everything was somehow more intimate, more personal and less daunting than I had expected. The throb and thrust of powerful machinery could no longer be heard, the treacly smell of oil and damp hung in the air, the banksman chatted unconcernedly in ordinary conversational tones with our supervisor, our electric hand-lamps glowed weakly in the semi-darkness and we waited our turn like old hands to get on the cage.

The cage was soon ready for us, so we formed a little queue as the banksman searched our pockets for contraband and received a tally from each of us to keep a record of the number of men underground. I stepped gingerly on to the cage and waited as everyone else came on board, the banksman closed both gates, one on the cage and one on the edge of the shaft, before ringing three on the bell as a signal to the winding-engine man that men were riding. The engine man acknowledged by ringing three back, the banksman rang two signalling to the engine man to start winding. This is it, I thought to myself and gripped the handrail overhead, a moment's pause and then, slowly at first but within seconds dropping like a stone, the cage and its load descended the 980 yards of the Martin pit. I gulped a breath of air and felt my stomach being left behind, the wind whistled past, the steel guide shoes at each corner of the cage squealed as they slid down the guide ropes and I wondered how on earth let alone in earth the winding-engine man could bring us to a halt before crashing into the girders lying across the pit bottom. Just as I was beginning to fear the worst, my knees suddenly buckled, the cage slowed and we landed on those girders as lightly as a feather. The ride had lasted over a minute and at one time we were descending at a speed of 60 miles per hour, but the whole operation was as smooth and certain as the swing of a pendulum.

The pit bottom was as I had imagined, a tunnel eight feet high and twelve feet across, well lit for some ten yards, then reaching into darkness from each side of the shaft, the air was warm and had the musty smell characteristic of a coalmine, motes glistened like micro-diamonds in the light and a few empty wagons stood on the narrow-gauge rail track waiting to be wound to the surface. Coal was not wound up the Martin shaft, which was used for off-shift man-riding and pit 'materials', the term for the multifarious tackle needed to work a coalmine. Apart from the six of us there were only two other men at the pit bottom, one of whom was the deputy (or fireman as he was called in our coalfield, but not to be confused with shotfirer) in charge of the training district, who had come to meet us. The other man was the 'hooker', responsible for loading and unloading the cage and for signalling to the winding-engine man.

There was a little light-hearted banter and we set off, Indian file, against a remarkably strong air current. Two rail tracks lying side-by-side on the uneven floor reached into the darkness ahead of us, with their steel haulage ropes resting on pulleys set a few yards apart in the middle of the tracks. Everything was covered with a thick carpet of fine stone dust spread deliberately, I learned later, to lessen the concentration of coal dust below the level necessary for propagating a slightly less disastrous and more localised methane explosion. As I was at the end of the Indian file, I walked in a cloud of dust raised by the men ahead of me. No one spoke except for an occasional comment from the fireman at the head of the procession. He explained that the training district was in an old part of the mine no longer used for coal production on a large scale and that the coalface to which we were heading was only a mile away. I consoled myself that I would not have to suffer the dust cloud for long. By this time, however, I was sweating profusely and, each time I licked my lips, found it necessary to wash my mouth with a sip of water from the three-pint tin hanging from my shoulder. It tasted warm and brackish.

The journey was beginning to seem endless and becoming more uncomfortable the further we progressed. The height of the road reduced to five feet or less and, here and there, wooden planks which were difficult to spot in the dim light of our lamps, stuck out from the roof and sides of the road, to provide obstacles against which I kept bumping my head. I had a headache and stiff neck, dust was everywhere, in my eyes, my nose, my throat, my clothes were wet with sweat and I could see ahead only with difficulty.

Years later, when I was accustomed to travelling underground in all kinds of difficult conditions, I enjoyed an unusual experience while travelling the return airway of Ifton colliery at the southern edge of the coalfield. I had gone to the colliery to see a new coal-getting machine at work and was accompanied underground by the manager, a Welsh speaker from the village of Gwespyr on the edge of the Flintshire coalfield. After we had seen the machine at work for some time, the manager, to my surprise, suggested that we should travel the three miles or so of wind road and return to the surface at the up-cast shaft. Ifton colliery had begun life at Bryncunallt near Chirk, but as the work of extraction followed the coal seams, first under the river Ceiriog and then further and further eastwards, the underground haulage costs rose to such an extent that the colliery company decided to sink a new coal-winding shaft at Ifton Heath near the village of St Martins in Shropshire. The two original shafts at Bryncunallt became up-cast shafts and the colliery took the name of Ifton colliery. I assumed that the manager was taking advantage of my visit to make an infrequent managerial inspection of the airway and I somewhat reluctantly agreed to his suggestion, suspecting that it would not be an easy journey. My suspicions were well founded for the roadway was not only hot and dusty, but for long stretches was not more than four feet high. It also had numerous examples of the problem common to most wind roads — broken planks projecting into the roadway. After travelling about two miles, during which I had been too polite to complain, the penny dropped. We reached a turn in the airway where a large notice board faced us bearing the newly painted words *'Croeso i Gymru'* [Welcome to Wales], I gave the manager ten out of ten.

But to come back to that first day travelling the return at Gresford colliery. After what seemed an interminable time we reached a doorway in the side of the road, which led, through a short connecting road and two more doors, to a haulage road. Wagons were being hauled along it, empties in-bye to the coalface and paitches out-bye to the Dennis pit bottom. The road itself was larger and in better condition than the return we had just travelled and the air was much cooler. In the distance two lights moved to and fro, signs of life and activity ahead. They were cap lamps worn by two lads working at a three-way junction. The main haulage road turned left to the district from which the drams of coal were coming and the smaller right hand fork turned off as a kind of tributary leading to the training face and the end of our journey. One of the two haulage lads was lashing and unlashing drams, empties and fulls, to and from the haulage rope running along one leg of the main road and the other lad was working similarly with the rope leading to the pit bottom. The unlashed drams ran swiftly and loudly down the track gradients as they rounded the bend of the junction so that one had to be wary as crossing the junction to the roadway leading to the training district.

The two lads were the first persons we had seen actually at work, indeed, apart from the hooker and the fireman, they were the first we had seen since getting off the cage at the pit bottom. One of the characteristics of work in a coalmine that I came most to appreciate was that a miner worked untrammelled by close supervision; he was expected to perform his duties using his own skill and discretion. In this respect, I suppose, a miner resembles a quarryman or farm worker, each having considerable discretion as a manual worker in the way he carries out his duties. The two lads we had seen, for example, would have been left entirely to their own devices for the whole of the shift, seeing no-one except the fireman making a brief statutory inspection once during the shift, or occasional visitors like ourselves going past on our own business. Both wore electric lamps in their helmets, very different from the electric hand lamps we were carrying and much more powerful and convenient. The colliery was in the process of converting to the new lamps, an early benefit of nationalisation and we who were under training were one of the few groups still using the old lamps. Within a few days, however, we too were equipped with the new ones. I had by chance begun work just in time to experience for a fortnight something of the old and, although I did not appreciate it at the time, this change, small as it was, was the harbinger of the technical revolution the industry would experience during the next twenty years.

We did not tarry at the junction because the fireman and supervisor were anxious that no one should be hurt by the drams careering round the turn, so we moved quickly down our road and almost at once came to the 'Meeting Station' which consisted of a notice board nailed to the side of the road with those words painted on it. A 'district' in a mine, or more precisely a 'deputy's district', consists of that part of the mine directly under the control of a deputy, or fireman as he was called in our coalfield. It could vary in size from a short length of roadway up to a large coaling district containing a mile or so of roadway as well as a coalface. The statutory requirement was that the fireman not only was able to inspect his district within 90 minutes, beginning and ending at the meeting station, but that in fact he did so at least once each shift. He was responsible for all the activity within his district as well as ensuring, for example, that no accumulations of methane gas occurred, that machinery was properly fenced, that samples of dust taken randomly from the roof and sides of roadways should contain a minimum percentage of inert stone dust, that the roof and sides of the coal-face and of the roadways were adequately supported, that supplies of water and other equipment for dust suppression and fire-fighting were available to a minimum standard, that a certain proportion of miners carried gas-testing lamps (the old Davy lamp) and so on. Since as many as a hundred men could be employed in a large district, the fireman's responsibilities were onerous. In due course I would shoulder the responsibilities and endure the worries of a fireman, but for the moment the novelty of being underground rendered insignificant any worries I might have had about the future. The training district comprised a short coalface some fifty yards long, served at each end by a roadway leading out respectively to the main intake and return airways. During the next three weeks we would be trained in haulage work, transporting coal from the face to the main haulage road and 'supplies' i.e. props, arches, bars, blocks, belting, pipes etc. along both roads to the face.

Trainee colliers filled (i.e. shovelled) the coal on to a face belt conveyor, which delivered its load on to the tail end of another conveyor running away from the face along the 'main gate', This conveyor in turn loaded the coal into drams (empty wagons) at a loading point a couple of hundred yards from the face. Our job was to provide a steady supply of drams and dispatch the paitches (filled drams) out-bye on their way to the main haulage road and the pit bottom. An endless wire haulage rope ran the length of the roadway from the loading point along each of the pair of rail tracks, its return pulley being fixed overhead in a horizontal plane about seven feet above the tracks a few yards in-bye of the loading point. The drams gravitated from one leg of the rope to be filled at the loading point and then gravitated out-bye to be attached to the other leg of the haulage rope. I found it difficult at first to attach the hook at one end of a heavy eight feet long chain to the coupling on the paitch, then lap the other end twice round the rope and lay the slack of the chain in its own hook before it was drawn taut as the haulage rope moved continuously out-bye at walking pace. The danger was of trapping fingers and indeed, for the first few days most of us trainees had blackened fingernails. We gradually became adept at the job, but none of us reached the standard of our instructor who liked to display his ability with some panache by 'lashing on' with one hand and to be sure, when he threw the end of the chain at the rope, the lash formed of its own as if by magic.

Our first day underground passed quickly. Within what seemed to be no time we were again going Indian file through the connecting doors into the warm and dusty return heading for the Martin pit bottom. Another thrill on the cage and then out of the air-lock half blinded by the dazzling sunlight into the everyday world we had left seven hours earlier. The sudden brilliance of daylight after I had been hours underground, even when the weather was wet and cloudy, never failed to thrill me throughout my time in the pits, but the effect that first sunny afternoon in June was overwhelming. We were stiff, tired and black, but we sang in the showers. I knew that I was not mistaken in my choice of career.

Within a month I had started proper work taking props, sand, boards, blocks, bags of cement, bricks, stone dust, arches, belting and other supplies to a large district working under the far boundaries of Wrexham Golf Club, $2^1/2$ miles from the pit bottom. Everything was transported along the return airways (or wind roads), some of which were in poor condition. I soon came to appreciate the resourcefulness of the mineworker. There were four of us in the team, the other three being old hands who made it clear to me, without actually saying so, that the day's supplies had to reach their destination and that the emptied drams had to be returned to the surface that day. If the amount of material happened to be less than usual and we were able to complete our work early, then so much the better; on the other hand if a journey of supplies came off the rails to become fast in the sides of a low and narrow roadway, then so much the worse. No one went home at the end of the shift unless the day's supplies had been delivered.

That we worked entirely unsupervised was an aspect of our work which made a great impression on me, the discretion given to us no doubt fostering the sense of responsibility within the team and its pride in, so to speak, delivering the goods. I gradually came to realise that the pride in his craft, which was a characteristic of the miner, stemmed partly from the considerable personal discretion he exercised in how he went about his work. It no doubt accounted for the influence of the pit on the character and temperament of every mining village, places which tended to be closed and self-sufficient societies built, if not always around an individual colliery, at least on coal mining. In Rhos everyone seemed to have a personal interest in the activities at Hafod colliery, the place of employment of half the men of the village and village talk seemed constantly to revolve around those activities. Indeed, one wag claimed that housewives shopping at the Co-op knew at once if the Meco-Mower had broken down, or that the Anderton shearer in 201s district had cleared a record 300 yards of coal in one shift. A drinker in a Rhos pub of an evening would scarcely see the bar for coal dust, unlike a drinker in, say, a pub in Dagenham who would be in no danger of being run over by a motorcar. Be that as it may, I found it congenial to know that officials not only assumed that, unsupervised, we would give of our best, but that they took it for granted that we possessed the resourcefulness to overcome difficulties without calling for outside help. I was happy in my work and confident that I had made the right choice of career.

A few months earlier I had become engaged to be married. Since I had been accused of rashness on announcing my choice of career, I felt it opportune to compound the rashness by binding myself incontrovertibly to a shared future. I married my wife, Nona, in the Holy Trinity Church at Penrhyndeudraeth three days before Christmas 1949 and took her home to be wife to a coalminer living in two rented rooms and a shared kitchen. My wages were five pounds fifteen shillings a week 'top of the bill', i.e. before the deduction of stoppages. We were not a wealthy family, a fact that has a part in a wry tale.

My parents-in-law lived at Penrhyn, not far from Portmeirion, Clough Williams-Ellis's celebrated Italianate village. As I recall,

My wife Nona and her Afghan Hound – Lia.

coalminers in the nationalised coal industry were granted a week's holiday with pay for the first time in 1949. The following year my wife and I took advantage of the break to spend the week at her parents' home. It happened that an exhibition of paintings by Welsh artists, which we visited more or less to pass the time, was being held that week at Portmeirion. It was the occasion when I felt for the first time the urge which has plagued me ever since in the form of a disease called 'collectivitis'. I fell in love with a painting in the exhibition the moment I saw it and without hesitation decided to buy it. It was then I discovered that my wife was made of sterner stuff than I. The price of five pounds was equivalent to a week's wages and her decision as the finance director of the partnership was final and irrevocable. The painting, to my everlasting regret, was left hanging. The painter was a comparatively unknown young man named Kyffin Williams. Twenty years later, however, after I had collected a large number of undistinguished paintings, a second great opportunity presented itself. And this time, despite my admiration and respect for Kyffin Williams, I felt that the opportunity was in some ways even more fortunate.

During the 60s and 70s I had for various reasons called occasionally on an acquaintance named Wynne Lewis who lived in a council house on the Adwy estate at Coedpoeth. Wynne was a crank, indeed he was extraordinarily eccentric. He had no furniture in his home except for two kitchen chairs, a small side-table, a kitchen stove and a mattress on the floor of one of the bedrooms. Heavy sacks were nailed to the windows so that no daylight entered the house. I took my wife to meet Wynne on one occasion when he offered her a cup of tea. After I had given him a shilling to get gas in the stove, Wynne went to make the tea. Ten minutes later he reappeared to offer the tea in a salmon tin. Wynne was decidedly odd, but he was also an unusually gifted artist. He had studied at the Slade School before the war and had been awarded the Prix de Roma. I said earlier that he had very little furniture, which was true, but he did have a large number of his own paintings stacked against the walls of every room, not unlike the stacks of books in the house of that renowned Welsh bibliophile, Bob Owen, Croesor. That was one reason why I visited him from time to time; I enjoyed looking at his paintings.

With one exception, Wynne never sold a painting: to do so would have been unprincipled he once told me. The exception was a still life in the style of Cézanne which was my favourite and which he offered me for fifty pounds some years later. I assumed that he was desperately short of money, but at the same time I was aware that he was doing me a great favour. I took advantage of the opportunity at once, of course and the painting hangs today in a prominent place in our house. That is not the end of the story, however. Three years went by and I had now become a member of parliament. One Sunday evening Wynne phoned agitatedly (from a call-box) to tell me in desperation that the Wrexham council housing manager was seeking an eviction order against him on the morrow for his having failed to pay his rent. Could I do something to help him? "I'll do my best," I answered, although I had no idea what precise action I could take other than to phone the housing manager and ask him if, in the almost certain event of the order being granted, he would take no action for a month so that I might explore ways of helping Wynne. He agreed readily.

In London the next day my secretary suggested that I should contact the Slade School — they might have a fund for helping impecunious artists. I phoned the principal, Sir William Coldstream and spoke to his secretary. Sir William would not be in his office until that evening, would I like to leave a message? When I explained the circumstances, she asked for the name of the former student and immediately expressed concern when I told her. "Oh dear," she said, "Sir William will be upset. He's sure to phone you when he comes in." I was intrigued, but I had to wait a while for an explanation. That

The Wynn Lewis oil painting.

evening a concerned Sir William phoned. After I had explained the situation he said that there was indeed a fund and that he would arrange to have the debt cleared forthwith and, moreover, the Slade fund would pay Wynne's rent henceforth. I was astonished, extremely grateful and very puzzled. When I asked Sir William to explain the remarkable generosity of his decision and he replied, "You must appreciate that Lewis is one of the most significant British painters this century" — I was even more astonished. I must add for the sake of balance, however, that I was disappointed to read Sir William's obituary in *The Times* some years later, in which his obituarist damned him with faint praise and questioned his judgement as an art critic. The obituary has not altered my regard for Wynne Lewis as a painter, nor of course for the painting hanging on our wall. Wynne died in the mid-90s. I do not know what has become of his paintings.

To return from the world of art to the less empyrian world of the pit and the early days of my career when I applied for and was granted a day-release from work each week to study mining at a very elementary level at the local technical college. I enjoyed the classes, especially the company of half a dozen high-minded young men who were 'going in for mining', as distinct from simply working commonly 'down pit', They tended to be in awe of me because they had somehow discovered that I had 'been to university', then still a comparatively rare phenomenon in our society. My embarrassment was made worse when I was obliged to explain my absence from the class the following week for the incongruous reason that I had to have a day off to attend the graduation ceremony at the university. The story spread and unfortunately coincided with a visit to Rhos by Richard Dimbleby who was recording interviews for his popular radio programme *Down Your Way*. I was an oddity, a graduate in chemistry working as a haulage worker at Gresford colliery — would I be prepared to take part in the programme? I have always been a sucker for flattery. The recording took place at our little cottage — we were moving up in the world — where at the same time Thomas Jones, known in Rhos as *Twm 'ffylau*, (Tom, the horses — his father had been in charge of the pit ponies at Hafod colliery) was interviewed as well. Tom was a character, who throughout the interview kept referring to Mr Dinglebody, much to everyone's amusement including Mr Dimbleby himself. He was well over the allotted span of three score years and ten and was being interviewed because of his role as trainer to the Rhos football eleven. Dimbleby asked him what was to account for his remarkable fitness at such an old age. "Deep breathing," replied Tom succinctly. I had my leg pulled for weeks after the programme, but I was more certain than ever of my ambition to be a colliery manager and of Hafod colliery in particular. My work as a haulage hand continued and after six months I began to think of the next step, that of gaining coal-face experience and becoming a collier, the aristocrat of the coalmine, clearing my stint daily on my own account.

3. The Coal Face

I had been employed as a haulage hand for ten months and was becoming anxious about getting coalface experience. It was important that I did so because I would not be permitted to sit the colliery manager's examination unless at least three of the stipulated minimum of five years' experience was experience of work at the coal-face (the requirement in the case of graduates in mining engineering was less stringent). The system at Gresford, however, was one of promotion by seniority from day-wage worker to trainee on the training face for a period of three months, following which the trainee became a 'stemmer'. Stemmers were face workers who, at the beginning of each shift, remained at the pit bottom until the last man-riding rope had been wound. They were then sent to fill individual vacancies caused through absenteeism. The job meant carrying one's tools — pick, shovel, axe, saw and sledgehammer — backwards and forwards to the pit bottom each day. It was naturally the aspiration of every stemmer to be allocated a permanent place with a set of established face workers, an aspiration which would not normally be achieved for a period of three or four years

In the normal course of things, I would not reach my turn to get on the training face for four or five years and, therefore, be unable to sit my manager's ticket examination for, possibly, another eight years.

That, I thought, was far too long an apprenticeship. Fortunately, however, the under-manager, who rather prided himself on being an intellectual concerned with things of the mind, sympathised with my ambition to sit the examination sooner rather than later. Moreover, I had also obliged him on a number of occasions by doing various odd jobs as a kind of all-purpose handyman, justifying, I suppose, the claim I had made to Mr James during that first interview. For example, I had done a three-week stint as the colliery weighman when the shift's regular weighman was taken ill at work. The job of recording the weight of the wagons of coal as they came off the cage and allocating the weights to the various sets of colliers whose set numbers were chalked on the wagons, was a responsible one which I had to undertake at a moment's notice.

As it happens, acting as weighman had been an interesting experience for a very human reason. I shared the cabin of the weighing machine with Richard Williams, the checkweighman employed by the colliers – a reification, so to speak, of the distrust with which the miner had long regarded management in the coal industry. Dick was a loveable old Rhosite (one of the small crew of Rhosites at Gresford) known to everyone in Rhos as 'Dick Amen', a nickname reflecting his obsessive tendency to respond to sermons from his seat in the front pew of the gallery at Seion Baptist Chapel by loudly proclaiming an approbatory seal of approval to each succeeding theological point. Conversation with Dick was a delight during the whole of my three weeks with him, especially when he related, as a kind of running commentary, the argument about the size of the congregation in Seion, revealing in so doing how his denominational loyalty sometimes led him along unexpected paths.

A fierce argument had broken out between Dick and a member of Capel Mawr, a large Presbyterian chapel, when Dick claimed and his adversary denied, that the congregation at Seion was larger than that at Capel Mawr. Dick related the cut and thrust of the argument for a whole week, living and reliving various aspects of it, until I could almost say who sat in which pew in Seion and implying that more pews were needed as a matter of urgency. The following Monday, Dick came to work full of himself. He had stood at the entrance to Capel Mawr from 9.30 until 10.05 on the Sunday morning, counting the congregation as its members entered for the morning service. He had now confirmed conclusively that Seion's congregation was by a large margin the bigger one. That confirmation, he said, softened his sense of guilt that, for the first time ever, he had arrived late at Seion for a service. The story was a delightful illustration of the combination of innocence, devotion and single-mindedness that made Dick Amen a congenial short-term fellow worker, but perhaps a burden as a fellow worshipper voicing his responses with unfailing regularity during services.

To return to my work underground and my anxiety about getting coalface experience, I pestered the under-manager with the claim that I had valid grounds for going on the training face ahead of my turn and without delay; an academic claim in more than one sense but which nevertheless persuaded him. I was instructed to present myself to the fireman of the training district on Monday morning and to bring a shovel, pick and sledgehammer with me. The weekend passed slowly, as had the one a year previously when I waited to begin work at Gresford colliery for the first time, until at last, at half past five on Monday morning I was on the first rope and on my way to my new place of work, carrying my clean new tools over my shoulder.

Two seams of coal were worked at Gresford, the six feet thick Main Coal and the three feet six inches Quaker. Winning the coal was like getting the meat out of a sandwich, the coal being the meat and the bread representing the various sedimentary rock formations above and below, such as sandstone, mudstone, shale and fireclay. The coal was extracted on a broad front called the coalface, which could be up to 200 yards in length. Steel props (in 1949) and occasionally wooden ones were set in rows at specified distances apart to support the roof where the coal had been extracted. As shift followed shift and more and more coal was won, the face advanced. The props in the row furthest from the face were withdrawn, allowing the roof to collapse into the 'waste', leaving some ten feet of roof still standing between the edge of the waste and the face itself. In that space two tracks were maintained, the first, between two rows of props, provided a path for a conveyor belt and the second, on the face side of the row nearest to the face, allowed the coal-cutting machine to travel along it as it undercut the face of coal.

The face was worked on a three-shift cycle. On the first shift colliers filled the newly cut and fired coal on to the belt conveyor, each man being responsible for clearing a six yard length of face to a depth of five feet (i.e. in the Main Coal; it was ten yards in the Quaker seam). After clearing a four-foot length of face he set a pair of props four feet apart in a line square to the face. The props carried a steel bar across their heads with a 'cleat' (a five to seven inches thick piece of wood) set between the prop and the underside of the bar. The idea was to get the thickness just right so that it took mighty blows with a sledgehammer to get the prop into a truly vertical position. A well-set prop would literally ring when struck and would be difficult to dislodge, whereas a poorly set one could be knocked out easily giving a dull thud in the process. The tighter the prop was set, the better was the mining practice. A collier in the Main Coal would ordinarily fill between twenty and twenty-five tons of coal and set five or six pairs of props and bars.

I recall the controversy, which arose when steel props were being introduced for the first time at Hafod colliery just before the war. They were unpopular with the colliers, especially in the thicker seams like the Main Coal and the Two Yard, because while there was no question that they provided better roof control, they were heavy and difficult to handle. A six-foot prop would weigh nearly a hundredweight; the steel bar, which had to be set above it, would weigh twenty-five to thirty pounds. To set the first prop under the bar, a collier had to rest the bar on his head against the roof, draw the prop towards him under the bar, insert the cleat, knock the prop nearly vertical and then hammer it home hoping that the cleat he had chosen was the right thickness to form a tight support. The argument that the Hafod colliers had used against the use of steel, or more correctly perhaps, the rationalising of their prejudice, was that wooden props creaked before breaking if a 'roof weighting' took place, thus giving the miner warning of impending danger. I followed the debate avidly as a fifteen-year-old schoolboy, although I suspected that the colliers' case was unconvincing. Enormous improvements were to take place in roof support methods following nationalisation, stemming primarily from the introduction of hydraulic supports based on the experience gained from the use of hydraulics for aeroplane undercarriages.

Two types of operation took place on the second shift of the cycle. One was 'turning over', that is to say dismantling the face belt conveyor, threading it through the row of props and rebuilding it in the new track, which had been cleared by the colliers. Usually three or four 'turnover men' were employed on this task. The second operation was 'packing', This involved first of all building 'packs' in the track vacated by the conveyor. Packs were walls about four yards long built from large stones taken from the waste, behind which rubble was packed as tightly as possible to the upper unbroken strata. The packs were built about twelve to fifteen yards apart with the intention of providing a measure of permanent support to the strata overlying that immediately above the coal seam and which had not collapsed into the waste but which cantilevered slowly downwards as the face moved away. When the packers had completed building the packs they withdrew the props and bars from that track, allowing the immediate roof, which tended to be fairly friable, to collapse and become the 'waste', The withdrawn supports were available for resetting on the next coaling shift. Usually two men would build two packs and withdraw supports from two lengths of waste.

On the third shift, a coal cutting machine cut out a slice of coal about six inches thick to a depth of five feet. The coal from the cut was churned out as slack and wooden wedges were jammed into the cut every four or five yards to provide temporary support for the cut coal. A coal cutter and his mate would cut the whole length of the face in the shift. Two or three 'borers' followed the coal cutter drilling holes into the face also to a depth of five feet and a couple of yards apart. Finally, a shotfirer would charge each hole in turn with explosive and fire the charge to loosen the coal ready for filling. To be a shotfirer, which was the lowest rung on the staff ladder, it was necessary to possess a fireman's (deputy's) certificate, obtained through passing a simple examination which involved estimating the percentage of methane gas in the air from the size of the cap of blue flame on the lowered yellow flame of an oil lamp (the traditional miner's Davy lamp). When gas was present at a concentration of one percent, the blue flame was just discernible, but as the concentration increased, so did the size of the blue flame to a height of about one inch at a concentration of five percent, at which point the mixture became explosive and blew the flame out. The examination also involved a knowledge of first aid, the ability to calculate the cross-sectional area of a tunnel of a given diameter (assumed to be circular) and the quantity of air flowing along it at a given speed. I recall a miner in his early forties, who was clearly baffled by the geometry, asking me when I was a pupil at the grammar school "What is this here pi?"

Another activity on the third shift was that of 'ripping' or advancing the roads, usually two roads one at each end of the face. That involved firing the rock above the seam to a height of about eight feet, building two packs from the rubble, one on each side of the road and setting steel arches a yard apart as the roadway advanced. In normal circumstances a team of three or four 'front rippers' for each road performed this work.

The face workers were the aristocracy of the pit, their work was heavier, more skilled, more hazardous and better paid — they earned twice the wage of a haulage hand. It was a substantial promotion, therefore, to get on to the face whether as packer, turnover man, cutter, front ripper or collier. The latter occupation was regarded as being the most prestigious, the collier being the grandee of grandees.

The training district lay to the east of the shafts and fairly near to the pit bottom. There were nine instructors on the face, each with a trainee under his care, but when I drew the attention of some of the trainees to the fact that this ratio compared more than favourably with that at Eton College where two or three pupils shared a tutor, I failed to strike a bell with my joke. The coal-getting cycle was carried out jointly by the instructors and the trainees and completed about once in a week. We worked on the day shift regularly, by far the most popular of the three shifts. The instructors were, of course, experienced face workers, all over fifty years of age, one or two over sixty and all having spent a hard-working life in the pits. Indeed, one of the most disconcerting things that I discovered was that at first I could not keep pace with my instructor who was 67 years of age and the oldest man on the face. Our productivity depended on sheer human effort and yet was no more than a quarter of the average for faces at Gresford. I began to doubt my ability to reach the physical standard normally expected of face workers. It was a time when there was a national shortage of fuel and miners were being urged to work ever harder, each pit boasting of its own 'stakhanovite' who filled an incredible tonnage and who was rumoured to earn an equally incredible wage, as well as making a paragraph in the local paper. Colliery managements basked in the reflected glory from the muscular exploits of their best men and at Gresford, were fond of boasting that their men would move Gresford colliery to Hafod if paid enough. The coal industry, which for a long time had had a dated view of life, was going through a kind of dinosauric last fling aimed at producing enormously muscular miners with huge arms and shoulders supporting tiny little heads. I sensed, one could hardly fail to do so, that this was quite unlike the enlightened management I had anticipated after nationalisation. It was an especially tragic irony that these management attitudes remained set during what was to be a period of brilliant post-nationalisation advance in engineering terms. I shall attempt a diagnosis of the condition in a later chapter.

My instructor, Peter Wilks, was a gentleman, a sidesman at his parish church and unquestionably a product of the Victorian age. His motto was the cliché 'A fair day's pay for a fair day's work', to which he introduced a note of originality by putting the emphasis on the work. We were on the face, he reminded me, to follow the fireman's instructions and no nonsense. He was of small build, taciturn, speaking in velvet whispers, almost always to reproach me for second rate work: "You had better do that again, or Dai the fireman will find fault with us." His professional standards, so to speak, were as high as those of any lawyer or doctor and most of all he was inordinately proud that in his late sixties he could 'still do a day's work'. To appreciate that this was no mean boast it must be remembered that, even on the training face, the work involved a much greater physical effort than would be expected of someone in our corpulent modern technological age. It might not have compared with building the pyramids, but it was certainly as demanding as driving the first canals.

Peter was very conscious that I was 'going in for mining' and the responsibility of guiding me along the paths of righteousness weighed heavily on him. Unfortunately, however, not everyone at Gresford, unlike some of the other pits, felt the same about aspirant mining engineers, as we shall see. Peter's mate on the training face was Ishmael, a totally different character. Ishmael was a big man, noisy, warm-hearted, open with everyone and inclined a little, perhaps, towards empty-headedness. More than anything I recall his hands, big as stone shovels (there were two sizes of shovel, coal shovels and stone shovels) with the miner's trademark of blue scars scattered generously across them. No one would accuse (the right word at Gresford) Ishmael of being an intellectual and his work was best measured by quantity rather than quality. He cherished his sledgehammer, his 'persuader' as he called it and believed that the only thing the pit understood was corporal might. Peter, always meticulous, tidied up after him.

We worked as a foursome for the three months, Ishmael and his trainee, Peter and I, until our training was completed. The face was a short one, fifty yards from rib to rib, as the ends were called. When we were on the filling part of the cycle it took the four of us two shifts to clear twelve yards and fill a little over forty tons of coal. This compared with two colliers on a normal Main Coal face doing the same work in one shift. Even so, at first I felt exhausted at the end of each shift. I found that the most demanding work was not shovelling but using the pick to bring down coal that had not fired well and was sticking to the face. My personal equation was that a quarter of an hour on the pick equalled two hours on the shovel.

I came to appreciate and admire Peter's economy of motion, not an ounce too much effort, not an inch too much movement, no feeling of rush or speed, only the smooth slide of his shovel into and out of the pile of coal, time and time again regular as a pendulum, the lifting at the last moment with the sudden turn of the wrist to deposit the coal precisely in the middle of the belt and not once turning his head over his shoulder to check the accuracy of the throw, muscles rippling across his sweaty back and the overall result manifesting itself as a steady inch by inch advance as the face was cleared.

We worked stripped to the waist in the heat and dust and I never lost my habit of drinking a mouthful of water from my tin every quarter of an hour, so that by snap time it was empty and I was cadging water from Peter and Ishmael. I sweated profusely and lost weight during each shift, a not unwelcome development. We worked well together as a team and gradually I found myself adapting to the work and, I like to think, acquiring some of the collier's skill. There was one matter, however, on which Peter and I disagreed during the whole of the time we were together. Rather pleasingly, it was an issue where Peter erred and I was whiter than white, or at least, less black. The bone of contention was spraying. Hand-held water sprays were provided along the face to lessen the make of dust, one of the more unpleasant aspects of the work. Peter's refusal to have the coal sprayed stemmed from his conviction that it was a waste of effort to "move water rather than coal". I was able to use the spray only on the rare occasions when Peter left the face briefly for the road-head to fetch cleats or blocks and other supplies.

When I had completed my training I began work as a stemmer. It was not long, however, when, courtesy of the considerate under-manager, I got a permanent place as a packer in a part of the pit known as the 'Slant', working afternoon and night shifts on alternate weeks. The face was about three miles from the pit bottom, but we rode for half the distance on a 'man-rider', a set of flat-topped wagons each fitted with a central plank for sitting on, drawn by a 'main and tail' haulage rope attached to each end of the set. The man-rider, nicknamed the paddy mail, had a top speed of only seven miles an hour, but one got the impression of great speed as it thundered along the narrow return airway. One had to keep one's arms and legs closely tucked in, because in places the paddy almost rubbed the sides of the roadway.

The 'wet bulb' temperature in my new district was in the high eighties Fahrenheit. It was thus much warmer than the training face, although not as warm as a district I got to know later at the neighbouring Llay Main colliery. There the wet bulb reached the dangerously high figure of 91 or 92 degrees. These temperatures were remarkably consistent, summer and winter, so that we wore nothing but shorts, helmet, socks and boots the year round. I gained a tacit advantage from the discomfort in that I have a natural tendency to sweat readily, a tendency which manifested itself more than ever, creating the impression of exceptional application. I took the line that it was a case of the least said, the better.

There were twelve of us in the set (team) working in pairs, each pair being responsible for a twenty-five yard length of face. I was fortunate to have Charlie as partner; he had two great qualities as a partner, physical strength and intellectual weakness. The latter enabled me to guide him in the best use of his strength without our ever having a disagreement. He was fond of 'going to the pictures' and he enjoyed subsequently relating the story. I recall one vivid account of a film with a title something like 'Beast from Ten Thousand Fathoms', in which the beast grabbed the girl in its claws and swallowed her whole. Charlie related the story with relish one snap time, concluding soberly, "Mind you, it was a little far-fetched".

The face was in the Main Coal. Sometimes the roof would collapse a little too freely into the waste, burying the back row of props up to their necks. That meant having to dig into the rubble to free the props sufficiently to be pulled out with a 'sylvester' (a hand operated high purchase pulling lever) and chain. I could never make up my mind whether this was better than having the roof stay up in cantilever over the waste. When that happened the face would occasionally 'take weight', the roof sitting heavily on the steel props, bending them into slender bows. It then required a great deal of hammering with the sledge to free the props and, sometimes, if the hammering was to no avail, the roof around the top of the props had to be picked away with a hand pick to free them sufficiently to be knocked out. I began to appreciate Ishmael's respect for his 'persuader' and to comprehend the importance of stamina as well as strength as essential requirements of a good face-worker. Gradually I adapted to the work and assumed that this would be my lot for the next two or three years

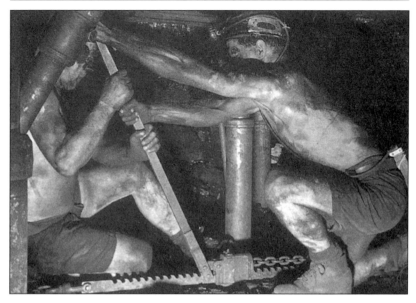

Packers withdrawing props from the waste.

while I was preparing for my examination. It was not to be.

I had been working as a packer for two months, earning a much better wage than previously. Everything seemed to be going along smoothly and I was happy with my situation until one fateful afternoon when a union official, unexpectedly and quite unusually, visited the face. I knew that something was afoot when he stopped to talk briefly and ask how long I had worked in Gresford and I half expected the note on my lamp the following afternoon telling me to see the under-manager. The union had lodged a formal complaint that I had been upgraded ahead of my turn. The under-manager was apologetic, saying that he had overreached himself and that although he could make a case justifying my promotion, he did not want an altercation with the union. He proposed to transfer me to work as a fireman's assistant.

I was disappointed and downhearted. Despite the fact that my new job, one specially created for me by the under-manager, would be interesting, it represented a possible setback in terms of sitting my examination: I was unsure whether I could still have claimed that I was getting coal-face experience. There was no uncertainty, however, about its effect on my financial position. My wife was now expecting our first child and we needed the extra cash. My plans had gone seriously awry and for some days I was in an anguish of indecision about what to do. To complicate matters, a post had recently been advertised as chemistry master at my old school and I had been urged by influential people to apply for it. After discussing the matter with my wife we agreed to postpone a decision until the coming Sunday while we brooded over it. Then, not for the last time during the next twenty years, providence intervened. I received a letter from the London headquarters of the Coal Board (I was surprised that I was not unknown in such high circles) explaining the Board's new scholarship scheme for mineworkers to study mining engineering and suggesting that I apply for a scholarship. I had been unaware of the scheme, which apparently, had just been announced.

The scholarships were tenable at universities offering courses in mining engineering; they were financially generous and included an allowance for a wife and children. Here was one of the advantages I had hoped for from nationalisation being realised, I said to myself in a mood of exultation as I contemplated the prospects of a professional grounding in my chosen career now potentially open to me. At the same time, I felt a tinge of shame at the doubts and despair, which had afflicted me during the past three or four days. I applied for a scholarship and within a month I was interviewed by an extraordinarily large panel of Coal Board officials at Wolverhampton — there were at least twenty people on the panel under the chairmanship of Sir Ben Smith, chairman of the West Midlands division of the Coal Board and former Minister of Food in the wartime government. One extraordinary question I was asked by a member of the extraordinary panel was to name another novelist who could be compared with Charles Dickens. I replied without hesitation: "Daniel Owen, another nineteenth-century writer who wrote half a dozen excellent novels in Welsh". The panel member nodded gravely. I must have satisfied the panel because in due course I was awarded a scholarship and in addition I was appointed a 'Directed Practical Trainee' under the direction of the Board's personnel department. The immediate result was that I would undergo practical training for a period of three months prior to the start of the university term. I spent the three months working as an assistant to Vincent Thomas, an electrician at Gresford who impressed me greatly. Some years later when I was manager of Bersham colliery I appointed Vincent to the post of Chief Electrical Engineer at that colliery. It was one of the best appointments I made, but it was not done without a struggle. The Area Electrical Engineer had a candidate for the post whom I also knew and we argued for several days about the respective merits of both before I finally made the appointment.

I applied for admission to the mining department at Nottingham University and was fortunate not only to be accepted, but also to be excused the first year of the three-year honours course by virtue of my already possessing a degree in chemistry. Thus on the 5 October 1950, I journeyed to Nottingham to become a student once again. On the same day my wife, who had been staying at her parent's home, gave birth to our first child at St. David's Hospital, Bangor. On my first morning at Nottingham I received a telegram informing me that I was a father as well as a student.

On looking back at the union complaint at Gresford, which led to my losing my job as a packer, I see it as a reflection of the differences between the culture at that colliery and those at other collieries in the coalfield. I am fairly sure that the situation would not have arisen at Hafod, Bersham or Llay Main, the three other pits at which I was employed at various times. Indeed, I would say that the union lodge

*Hafod Colliery, with (L–R), Back row: Jim Griffiths, Jack Jenkins, Harry Gittins
(Manager), Emlyn Read, -?-; -?-; -?-. Front row: William Tunnah (Overman),
Charlie Blaze, Lewis Williams, -?-; -?-; Les Evans (Penycae).*

committees at those collieries, even if they had not been glad of the
opportunity to support me in furthering a worthy ambition, which I
held in good faith, would at least have been sympathetic towards it
and would have resisted complaints about my being promoted out of
turn. It is hard to know why the differences existed. Gresford was by
far the most 'English' of the four collieries, not merely from the point
of view of language, but from a demographic standpoint. It was more
cosmopolitan, impersonal and fractious. It was not just simply that it
was border country with inherent long-standing tensions, but
something more makeshift; many of the pit's workers were migrants
who settled briefly in the Wrexham area, mostly in the town itself and
who sensed the anonymity and uncertainty of their society. The well-
to-do village of Gresford a mile down the road, from which the

colliery took its name, could in no circumstance be called a 'pit village' and the pit itself, perhaps for that reason, had acquired attitudes as perverse as its name. There was not a single Welsh speaker on the lodge committee.

The most Welsh speaking pit, Hafod, depended on Rhos for its workers. The tradition of son following father still carried residual leverage and indeed, the remnants of another more discerning tradition still lingered on, that of the elder son working in the pit helping to support the family while the younger son received an education as an escape route from it. There were at least three miners at Hafod on nationalisation, each of whom had a younger brother lecturing at a university: for example, Samuel Griffiths or *Sam Pwmp* as he was known had a professorial brother and was uncle to one of the most distinguished of British Egyptologists. Ninety per cent of the miners spoke Welsh, the language in which work was carried out. I heard from a witness who was present, of a visit to Hafod by an inspector of mines and of the subsequent altercation between him and my father. My father was speaking Welsh to a ripper when the inspector intervened to say "Don't speak that foreign language in my presence". My father responded in kind by saying "Listen mister, you are the foreigner here". The inspection was not a happy one. Bersham too had a good complement of Welsh speakers from the surrounding villages making up about a half of the labour force. As manager I communicated half the time in Welsh. Llay Main on the other hand was essentially English speaking, but had a not insubstantial minority of Welsh speakers. Indeed, one of the most pleasant surprises that I enjoyed when I first went there to work as assistant to the manager, was that a majority of the members of the lodge committee and all its officers were Welsh speakers.

4. College Days Again

Nottingham University had just moved from a site in the city centre to a new campus on its outskirts. I registered there as a mining student under Professor Hyndley, a well-known and respected figure in the mining world. His department had five members of staff, one of whom was a Welshman from Blaendulais bearing the indisputably Welsh name of Ieuan Handel Morris, although I was at first unaware of the fact. Second and third year students referred to him as Jimmy Proto and in my innocence I addressed him as Mr Proto, without realising it was a nickname bestowed upon him after his lecture on the 'Proto Breathing Apparatus'. At twenty-six years of age, I realised from that little contretemps that I was destined to play an avuncular role for my fellow students, all of whom had come to university straight from school and were more street-wise than I.

An intriguing result of my arrival at Nottingham was that, together with three other students, I obtained lodgings with a fortune teller. Her house near the market square had over its front door a large notice board proclaiming in literally and metaphorically colourful words: 'Madame Fuzzy, Clairvoyante, Palmiste and Advisor'. Her waiting room, especially on Saturdays, was often full of customers anxious to take a peep into the future. I recall opening the door one evening to a young married woman who confided in me that she was expecting a baby and was hoping that Madame could confirm that it would be a white one. Madame refused to tell me my fortune, a rebuff I considered with some misgiving, although I was reassured by her giving my wife the full treatment of crystal ball, cards and palm. Alas, neither my wife nor I remember the prophecies and we are thus unable to confirm whether they were realised. A policeman called once a year on a formal visit, according to Madame always on the night of a full moon, to satisfy the authorities that nothing untoward was likely to flow from Madame's mystic activities. He stayed for a cup of tea on the occasion when I was present and murmured for my benefit that Madame was a shrewd and sensible woman unlikely to cause anyone dismay. One of her most amusing traits, which gave constant pleasure to the four of us, was her sometimes bizarre misuse of words. When the Folies Bergère came to the Nottingham Playhouse, she preached us a sermon warning us against going to the show: "No-one goes there," she said, "except dirty old men spying on naked women through microscopes".

The mining course was non-specialised and included a number of subjects other than mining engineering itself, such as mechanical and electrical engineering, geology, applied mathematics and surveying. I found the variety congenial after the specialism which had characterised my chemistry studies. It may be that I am instinctively a generalist: to be sure, when I left the pit years later to be employed by the taxpayer at Westminster, I was happy to sail over deep waters without worrying unduly about their depths. Like Professor Pangloss, I was an assured professor of things in general. I enjoyed the mathematics course best and, indeed, the only academic achievement I still boast about, it being the only one on the list, was getting a mark of 148 per cent in the mathematics paper at the final examination. The instructions at the head of the paper were to answer as many of the twelve questions as possible and that full marks would be obtained for eight correct answers. I answered the twelve without difficulty in some two thirds of the allotted time.

During the Easter holiday each year the department camped at Llangollen, ten miles from my home, on surveying practice. We all attended two camps and sat a practical examination on the second one, carried out on the Vale of Llangollen Golf Club's attractive course, surely the most measured golf course in being. My two years passed quickly. I worked hard at my studies and during the summer holiday worked at Hafod colliery with a small set of men opening out a new face in the Quaker seam. The wages were a bonus and compensated for a scolding I received on one occasion from my father, the under-manager, for shoddy workmanship. A row of props we had set was not straight enough to satisfy him and although all the members of the team had set some of the props, it was I who received the reprimand. I consoled myself by thinking that the old boy was going out of his way to show the world and its wife that his son was not to have any favours.

At last examination time arrived and I succeeded in graduating and putting B.Sc.(Min.) behind my name. I also joined the Institution of Mining Engineers as a student member. I thought it would gratify an old friend in Rhos who assessed academic achievement by the number of letters behind a name, it certainly tickled my childish sense of humour, if I were to write to tell him that I now had 25 letters, B.Sc.(Hon.), B.Sc.(Min.)(Hon.), Stud. M.I.Min.E., behind mine. My friend died some years ago, but I am sure he would be ready to forgive me if he were with us.

One hurdle remained, the colliery manager's certificate of competency, which was the most important because without it I could not be a colliery manager. I needed a total of three years practical experience, a reduction from the former requirement of five years as a result of my having graduated in mining engineering. There was another year to go which I spent as a Directed Practical Trainee, an ugly and unimaginative title for what was in fact interesting and rewarding work. Like many training schemes, no doubt, it epitomised the platitude that what one got out of life depended largely on what one put in. I spent periods of up to two months each in various sections of the industry and realised that I could either sit back bothering no one and being bothered by no one, or I could make myself useful and find work accumulating mercilessly.

The National Coal Board was structured administratively into divisions, areas and collieries. The eight collieries of the north Wales coalfield constituted one area, which with four other areas in the Lancashire coalfield — Burnley, Wigan, St Helens and Manchester — comprised the Board's North Western Division. Divisional headquarters were in the centre of Manchester where I spent several weeks in the finance department acting as dogsbody to everyone. I learned more during that time about balance sheets, cash flow, capital and revenue codes, depreciation and other financial mysteries than I would have learned in years from textbooks. I saw the costing and sales figures, the turnover, the profits, or more often the losses, of all the division's collieries, some sixty or so, as they came in to be collated and found it fascinating to be an 'insider' seeing behind the workaday exterior that the collieries had previously represented. I had my favourites among them, in particular Cleworth Hall colliery at which I made an underground visit on one occasion, to find that several of the miners had relatives living in Rhos: their parents had migrated to Lancashire during the slump of the 20s and 30s. Many years later after being elected to the House of Commons I experienced a curious little episode. The Labour Party had lost the 1970 general election and Harold Wilson, now in opposition, had enough time to spare to welcome personally newly elected members of his party. He invited us, half a dozen at a time, for drinks in his room. My turn came along in due course and I was introduced to the party leader by the chief whip as a former colliery manager in the north Wales coalfield. "Ah," said Harold, "Let me see now: Bersham, Black Park, Gresford, Hafod, Ifton, Llay Hall, Llay Main and Point of Ayr," he announced triumphantly in alphabetical order. It was an impressive feat of memory from someone who had been a civil servant during the war gathering coal statistics. The question that came immediately to my mind, however, was who was supposed to be impressing whom, especially as Black Park, Hafod, Ifton, Llay Hall and Llay Main had closed in the meantime.

After the period in the finance department, I spent most of my remaining pre-examination time with the underground fitters at Hafod colliery, but the high point was a month at a French colliery in the Pas de Calais coalfield. The Coal Board had an arrangement with *Charbonnage de France* whereby young mining engineers exchanged visits to gain some experience of each other's coal industries. Thus, one sunny Friday afternoon in June I sailed from Newhaven to Dieppe. The ship was full of holidaymakers and I felt rather superior because I was not travelling frivolously but going 'on business'. I stayed the weekend at one of the *Sorbonne's* halls of residence with a young English speaking French engineer whom *Charbonnage de France* had provided to look after me.

We travelled on the Monday to the small mining village of Lievin where I met Pierre Auriol, the manager of the colliery at which I was to be based. He was a nephew of Vincent Auriol, the French President and had been educated at *L'École des Mines*, a prestigious French school comparable with, say, *L'École Normale Superieure*. M. Auriol was no exception among French colliery managers in this respect. The tradition was one to marvel at in the light of the educational standards of many British colliery managers: going to 'Wigeen' was a puny thing that I could only feel sheepish about. I stayed at the 'popot', as the small mess for unmarried engineers was called, where nine of us were in residence at the time and where the evening meal was a kind of ritual that began at 6.30p.m. to last for some three hours while the free-flowing wine lubricated conversation, which despite my rudimentary French I found stimulating.

The work underground was fascinating both in technical and human terms. I made an attempt each night to learn some new French words and at the end of the month I was able, with much gesticulation, to hold a rudimentary conversation in what was, I suppose, a kind of pidgin French. The most vivid difference between coalmining work in the two countries was a very human one. The staff of the pithead baths were women and each day while I was having a shower a young woman would appear to hand me a glass of beer. It was a disconcerting moment and not just in stepping out of the shower to avoid diluting the beer. The most dramatic technical difference was in the geology at the particular colliery. There the coal seams literally did a U-turn to fold over on to themselves and yet the coal was completely extracted, so that on one face props were set horizontally to act not only as roof/floor 'supports' but as perches for the miners working what was a vertical coal face.

I returned home at the end of the month to spend part of the time before my examination undertaking a ventilation network analysis at Hafod. A tunnel was being driven to connect two separate parts of the pit, which would affect the ventilation of each. The problem was to forecast the changes likely to affect individual faces on the completion of the tunnel in ten months time and to make arrangements for ensuring that the air quantities would be adequate for each face. I was fortunate to be able to use for the purpose a new analogue computer devised by researchers at my old department at Nottingham; the first time, I believe, it was used to make a forecast in practice.

This academic sally led appropriately, but with trepidation, to the visit to Wigan and the examination held in early November, the results of which would be published at the end of January. I remember clearly the thrill of receiving from the postman as he walked up the lane to our little cottage the envelope franked 'Ministry of Fuel and Power', The letter said that I had satisfied the examiners and that I would receive in due course an official certificate numbered 5631. The under-secretary advised me to keep the certificate in a secure place because if it were lost it would be extremely difficult to have it replaced. I had greater satisfaction from gaining my manager's certificate than I had from any other academic success. My one regret today is that I do not have my father's certificate numbered, I believe, 1127, which I loaned to Wrexham Borough Council who were organising an exhibition of mining artefacts. The certificate was lost.

The way ahead was now clear and accordingly I wrote to the coalfield's Area General Manager to tell him the good news and to ask for an appointment at a colliery as soon as possible.

5. Managing Men

In February 1953 I was appointed fireman at Bersham Colliery, a colliery employing 1,300 men situated on the outskirts of the village of Rhostyllen, three miles south of Wrexham town centre. I visited the pit on the Saturday morning prior to commencing work there on the following Monday, just as I had done on the Saturday before commencing work at Gresford. This time, however, the visit lasted longer and my interviews, especially the one with the under-manager, were a great deal more thorough. After arranging to have lockers at the pithead baths, two lamps from the lamp room, an electric lamp for illumination and an oil lamp for gas-testing purposes and receiving written authorisation from the colliery manager, Harry Lewis, to perform certain statutory duties as a mine official, I was interviewed by Tom Hunter, the under-manager. He described the district for which I was to be responsible on my shift and then lectured me for half an hour on what he stressed was my most important responsibility, my role in setting the wages of piece-workers.

The influence of the fireman on piecework wages was considerable, not only in controlling the amount of overtime worked, but more directly through the payment of 'allowances'. At the end of each working week the chargehand of a set of piece-workers would meet with the fireman to 'agree the allowances'. A set could be as few

*Bersham Colliery (originally known as Glanrafon Colliery) was opened in 1867
and was the last pit to close in the Wrexham area in 1986.*

as two men or as many as forty, depending on the nature of the work. The charge hands of large sets were invariably dominant characters but their negotiating styles varied greatly, ranging from the reasonable persuasiveness of mature men to the aggressive bluster of bullies. Agreeing the allowances was in essence a bargaining session with the chargehand demanding payments of allowances for 'standing time' when the belt broke on Tuesday, for the extra work clearing the fall of roof on Wednesday, for the additional timbering throughout the week at the downthrow fault on the face, for the water dripping from the roof and so on.

After reaching agreement on these often contentious matters, the fireman entered the figures into his 'wages book' ready for perusal, or more accurately, for intensive inspection the following morning, firstly by the overman, who almost instinctively would delete some of the payments and then by the under-manager. He in turn would invariably declare that the allowances were still excessive and did not accurately reflect the actual delays, extra work or inconveniences and would delete more of them. It was clear that the wages were influenced in part by the characters of the fireman and chargehand, but that ultimately they depended on the seemingly arbitrary decisions of the under-manager. The poor fireman, piggy in the middle, had the difficult task of attempting to reconcile the irreconcilable demands of management and workmen. If he were a good fireman, he would rely on his own assessment to provide as objective a measure of fairness as possible, not just for public-spirited reasons, but also to provide himself as piggy in the middle with a sustainable argument for rebutting the criticism by the overman that he would face at the start of the following week.

To make matters worse, allowances accounted for almost half the wage. Thus, when the miner received his wages on the following Friday, it was not unusual that they were a good deal less than he had been expecting. The system, common to all pits, was a disgrace, open to all kinds of abuse. It was clear, for example, that it was not necessarily the most deserving workers who received the best wages, but those whose chargehands could best wheedle or bully the fireman. The unfairnesses naturally led to dissatisfaction, which manifested itself in frequent small strikes by individual sets each week.

The under-manager, nevertheless, made his opinion clear in my interview that Bersham pieceworkers were being grossly overpaid by profligate firemen who scattered largesse indiscriminately in all directions and he warned me that he expected to see sensible accounting when he went through my wages book the following Saturday. It was an unnerving start to my managerial career, but I suspected, or at least consoled myself with the thought, which turned out to be well founded, that the under-manager was a fair-minded man and one who could be depended upon for support in difficult circumstances.

I was to be the fireman on the coaling shift in 24s district in the Two Yard seam. I realised that it was a privilege to be fireman on the most important shift of the three, but I gradually came to suspect that I was being nursed a little. Not only did the overman spend a disproportionate amount of his time in the district, but also the district itself was a comparatively easy one to run and the men were a notably level-headed and competent set of colliers. Coaling alternated between the day and afternoon shifts. I started on the Monday afternoon feeling very conscious of my responsibilities, hoping and praying that nothing would happen to cause difficulties. I should have known that it was too much to hope for. Coalmining, at best, is an uncertain business, the unexpected often happening, sometimes because of human error and sometimes because of the quirks of nature. Those quirks, incidentally, were largely responsible for the development of the unsatisfactory piecework payments system, a subject to which I shall return in a later chapter.

Difficulties soon developed on that first shift. The Two Yard seam had within it a band of fireclay seven inches thick some two feet from the floor. The seam was cut in that band of dirt, the cuttings being cast into the waste by a set of men following the cutting machine. The colliers on the following shift were thus presented with a face split into two halves, a 'bench' beneath and a 'wall' which had already been fired, above. That meant that the wall rested on the bench in large lumps, some weighing several hundredweights. It was an ideal proposition for the colliers as all they had to do at the start of the shift was to break the coal into smaller, but still large, manageable lumps and roll them off the bench on to the conveyor running alongside. It would have been an ideal arrangement but for one thing. The conveyor belt was not strong enough to deal easily with the weight of coal being loaded by 22 muscular colliers full of vim at the start of their shift. I had been warned that the secret was never to let the belt stop once coaling had started, not even for a moment or two. If it did stop, the colliers would keep on loading instinctively and would bury the belt even though they could see that it was stationary. It would then be difficult under its load to restart it. The face conveyor loaded on to the tail end of the main gate conveyor running from the face to load on to a third conveyor further out-bye which in turn loaded down a chute into empty wagons half a mile or more from the face. A stoppage anywhere along the chain, a wagon coming off the rails under the chute for instance, meant that the face belt had to stop.

We had been coaling for five minutes and the colliers were filling at peak rate. The river of coal falling from the face onto the main gate belt, like a black waterfall tumbling over rocks, was an enchantment to a young fireman on his first shift, anxious above all to see the face being cleared. I stood there, mesmerised, as the beautiful black river flowed into the darkness towards the pit bottom. I awoke abruptly. In an instant the river had frozen and before I could count three a mountain of coal had formed at the transfer point where the face belt loaded on to the now stationary roadway belt. "Hold the belt," shouted the nearest collier, but the belt attendant had anticipated him by half a second.

I phoned the loading point to find the reason for the stop, but while I was phoning, the main gate belt restarted. A lump of coal had been too large for the chute and had blocked it. I returned to the face transfer point where now there was trouble. The stop had lasted barely a minute, but the face belt, as I expected, was overloaded and would not start. It was slipping and squealing on the driving drums as they turned in the head, but the belt itself was not even inching along. The squealing continued for a few seconds until, suddenly and with a loud clack, the belt tore in half. The drums were now rotating effortlessly and quietly. "Broken belt," shouted someone and there it lay, sagging on the support rollers under its load, the tension released, at least from the belt. It had torn across its two-foot width inside the drive-head of the conveyor so that it was necessary, before being able to repair it, first to clear the small mountain of coal under which the head was buried. Only then could the two broken ends be withdrawn and fresh coupling joints put on. The belt then had to be uncoupled at the nearest joint up the face in order to re-couple the former broken joint, thread the new free end around the drive-head drums, draw the belt tight to the required tension and re-couple at the joint some yards up the face.

All this took over half an hour, the colliers meanwhile being idle the whole time except for the two or three actually repairing the belt. As the task of repair was nearing completion I travelled the face over the loose coal covering the belt to ask every collier, who had previously been loading the belt, now to unload it. There was some surly grumbling about working in vain and why couldn't the Coal Board buy some decent belting and so on, but I succeeded in getting the load lightened appreciably. Within three quarters of an hour of the stoppage occurring, the belt re-started. A bad start to the shift, I thought, but with a bit of luck we should catch up on lost time and clear the face by the end of the shift. I noted the length of the stoppage, anticipating an allowance claim at the end of the week.

Alas, one sin draws a hundred after it, or as the other more literally apposite Welsh proverb has it, the tighter the string the sooner it breaks. Ten minutes later the belt broke again, this time while running. It broke four times during the shift, as I dutifully reported in my end of shift statutory report when, nearly an hour and a half late, I reached the deputies' office on the surface. At the normal end of the shift there was still coal to be cleared. There was nothing I could do other than ask the colliers to work overtime, thus no doubt incurring the under-manager's displeasure. They did so to a man, clearing the face with the help of the packers and turnover men who had arrived for the night shift and who could not get started on their own work until the face was cleared. The commitment of the colliers was impressive, not simply that they worked overtime, but that they risked missing the last bus home. The colliery buses would have left to time, thus each man was dependent on public transport, a service that, in the environs of the colliery, ceased at around midnight. In the event, everyone caught his bus, some by very close margins. A few years later most would have had cars, as I found to my regret when I became manager at the pit and was obliged to lay tarmac over a lawn in order to provide a car park. I shall explain that regrettable circumstance in due course, but for the moment I can only say that I reported to my wife that it had been an unsuccessful first shift as fireman.

I soon discovered that being responsible for a coaling shift was also being responsible for the unforeseeable — one day broken machinery, the next day gas collecting on the rib, the following day a fall of roof and, the day after that, water breaking in and having to bribe the colliers with 'water money' while at the same time offering as small a bribe as I could get away with.

Whatever disadvantages a fireman's job had, monotony was not one of them — I never knew what to expect when I came to work. It struck me later that this unforeseeability might have been the reason why so many miners were superstitious. I have to admit though, that the platitude in Rhos and maybe in other mining villages, that a miner on his way to work on the morning shift would turn on his heels and 'play a turn' (i.e. have a day off) if he saw a strange woman, could have had other derivations. At the same time, miners were great optimists, who seemed in any adversity to be guided by a pragmatic acceptance of providence as a fickle lady who would in due course bestow her favours on them.

I had been fireman in 24s district for six months when I had a note on my lamp telling me to see the manager, Harry Lewis. It was good news. He was promoting me to be overman responsible for three districts in the Powell seam. Nine firemen would now be answerable to me and I would no longer have a direct relationship with miners. I would have to work through the firemen, my first experience of indirect management. The Powell seam was a more difficult one to work than the Two Yard, largely because it was much wetter. The under-manager suggested that I need not concern myself unduly with dust suppression measures, a humorous touch that reassured me I was on his wavelength. There was no shortage of other problems to concern me, however, not the least being that of maintaining the roadways in the seam in reasonable condition. The wet strata produced a combination of floor lift and arches sinking into the floor, so that the cross-sections of the road were constantly being reduced. When the headroom became too low, it was my responsibility to see that a set of 'back-rippers' was put to work to enlarge that section of roadway. The responsibility weighed heavily because there were not enough back-rippers for adequately maintaining the couple of miles of roadway involved. Often repairs of some sections of a roadway were postponed for too long, so that large lumps of coal on the conveyor belt began to foul the roof. My constant preoccupation was that of juggling the few sets of back-rippers between the sections of roadway most in need of repair. It was touch and go too often for comfort whether a district could continue to function, especially if a sudden 'weighting' occurred on a particularly bad stretch of road.

I recall one sad but droll occasion a few years later when I was manager at Bersham, which involved ease of access to and from a face in the Powell. One of the roadways had become so low that the only way in and out of the district was by belly-crawling along the conveyor for several yards. The belt, of course, had to be stopped for the purpose, normally at the beginning and end of a shift. The phone rang in my office one day shortly after the coaling shift had started work. "Ted Griffiths here boss," said the fireman (not his real name), "Jack Samuel (not his either) has had a heart attack and he's dead. I've got him here in the main gate but we've started coaling. Will it be alright if I leave him here till the end of the shift?"

"Bring him out at once," I replied, "or we'll all end up in the Old Bailey."

The fireman's anxiety to get the face cleared had overcome his common sense.

I was overman in the Powell seam for a little over a year, during which I came greatly to respect and admire most of the miners. Their comradeship was not sentimental humbug, but a sincere, if subconscious, expression of trust in and dependence on, each other. Indeed, were it not for their cheerful readiness to tackle unpalatable jobs, often in difficult circumstances, I doubt whether coal would ever have reached the surface.

The social climate that helped everyone to work instinctively as a team, notwithstanding the responsibilities borne individually by mineworkers, was one of wit and humour. From Harry Lewis downwards, we joked our way through difficulties and eased the tensions of challenging situations, with waggish, sometimes salty, remarks. Two occasions come especially to mind, the first when the coal cutter was buried under a large fall in the Two Yard. The overman, Lodwig Thomas, was a fastidious, somewhat prissy man, but no less an excellent overman for that. He was diffident, however, about breaking the news to the manager because the fall of roof was large enough to jeopardise the preparation of the face ready for the next coaling shift, with a consequential loss of output. Thus, on finally bringing himself to report the problem, he tried to lighten the gravity of his message by saying: "Don't you worry Mr Lewis, we know where the cutter is". The answer came in a flash: "Yes, and we know where the bloody *Lusitania* is, but we can't get her".

A more dramatic incident occurred just before Christmas one year when I was manager at the pit. While the first man-riding rope of the night shift was being wound at 9.30p.m., one of the guide ropes broke. There were four guide ropes to each cage, one at each corner, secured at the top and bottom of the shaft to prevent the cages twisting as they travelled through it. The winding-engine man sensed that something untoward had happened as the broken steel rope coiled down the shaft to sit heavily on one of the cages and he fortunately stopped his engine. It was, of course, a very serious incident as both cages were trapped in the 600-yard shaft. I arrived at the pit shortly before ten o'clock, a few minutes after the engineer and under-manager.

One cage carrying its full load of 30 men was trapped 200 yards from the surface, the other, carrying six elderly men, was 200 yards from the pit bottom. Bersham shafts were notorious for being wet; to be on the cage for half an hour, inspecting the shaft say, was to be soaked by the falling water as it dripped through the roof of the cage which was perforated to make the cage lighter. Furthermore, the weather was cold and Christmas-like, so that the trapped men were facing a very uncomfortable period waiting to be rescued, especially the older men on the lower cage on which the broken guide rope rested. The remaining underground workers were wound up in the much smaller cages of the other shaft.

After a brief discussion we decided to clamp the rope of the lower cage to the headgear, detach it from the winding drum and then wind the now free upper cage to the surface. It took an hour before the thirty young men could walk off their cage feeling cold, wet and relieved. In the meantime I had complied with the statutory requirement of informing the senior district inspector of mines of a serious incident and had also told my immediate superior. Within two or three hours it seemed as if the whole of the senior mining fraternity was present — divisional and area production directors, mechanical and electrical chief engineers, the Area General Manager, two inspectors of mines and so on. There were at least a dozen of the top brass assembled at Bersham Colliery.

In order to release the second cage, the 'pit men', a team of three men who were employed permanently on the night shift to maintain the shafts in good condition, were lowered on the now free cage that had been fitted with its special flat roof. From it they burned the coiled broken steel rope with an oxy-acetylene flame into handlable lengths for removal, descending slowly down the shaft a yard at a time until they were level with the trapped cage. Then at 3.00p.m. on the next day, the tricky job began of transferring the six men in mid-shaft from one cage to the other, an operation made all the more hazardous because of the men's ages and their, by now, weakened condition. At last came the signal to wind up the cage.

A large reception committee had lined up to meet the cage, composed of senior officials from the north Wales area and the north-western division of the NCB, together with reporters and cameramen of the local press. The first man off the cage, seventeen hours after getting on to it, was old Ned Vaughan, a character, 72 years of age, enthusiastic chorister at his local church, notable for the vigour of his language, tough as old boots and now soaked to the skin. He took a long look at the reception committee, doffed his miner's helmet and declared with feeling: "And a merry bloody Christmas to you all," only the word he used was a good deal stronger than bloody. It was the perfect response, the tension broke, we all laughed and the six were hurried away to a hot drink and an examination by the colliery doctor.

Much of the humour, however and perhaps the gentlest and best of it, was unconscious. My recollection of 'doing the books' on a Saturday morning, for example, is of a delightfully entertaining scene played out weekly in the overmen's room as we gathered to apply our red pencils to the clearly unjustified allowances entered by the firemen. There were four of us overmen at a large square table, always with a large fire in the room except in the hottest of heat waves. Tom Hunter sat with his back to the fire in pride of place as a kind of presiding deity. Facing him was dear old Llewelyn Jones, or *'Llew Snug'* as he was, for the most part although not always, affectionately called. Llew was a kind of lesser version of Ishmael of Gresford, his hands blue with the scars of a lifetime underground. His bete noir, just as Ishmael's would have been had he been doing the books, was precisely that of putting pencil to paper. .

I would watch, fascinated, as Llew went through the ceremonial ritual of preparing for the morning's intellectual exercise, first of all taking off his jacket and throwing it on the bench under the window, then stretching his arms, one at a time, far out in front of him in an excess of determination as he rolled up his sleeves, placing the all-important india-rubber in its niche on the table beside him, followed by the careful setting of his glasses on his nose, a couple of spits on his hands before grasping the small stub of pencil, a scratch or two on his forehead, a look of profound distaste at the books and to work. The cobbler to his last was not the guiding principle at Bersham on Saturday mornings.

Not all experiences were as happy, however. A much less agreeable one that I endured in the Powell seam turned out to be of crucial significance five years later when I was the newly appointed manager at Bersham. It led directly to an important early quarrel with my superiors at area and divisional headquarters. One of the Powell faces was being worked above Bersham Quaker 'deads' — that is to say, above an area of the Quaker seam, 40 yards below the Powell, from which the colliery had already extracted the coal. The Powell face was approaching the edge of the deads and after passing over them it would be in an area where the Quaker seam had not been worked. Face conditions had been reasonable while we were over the deads but as we came closer to their edge, conditions deteriorated rapidly and disastrously. Water flowed from the floor in little streamlets, the props sank into the ground, small falls of roof became a common occurrence and the working height of the seam reduced to between two and three feet as the floor heaved upwards. It took three months to advance the face ten yards, after which normal conditions were re-established, a distance that in normal circumstances would have taken little more than a week. I did not know then that I would experience the same phenomenon, only very much worse, in five years time. My experience as overman in the Powell seam of crossing our own Quaker deads, however, had seared itself to some purpose on my memory, as we shall see in a later chapter.

A year passed quickly. Then one morning, I received a message underground. I was to come at once to the surface and go to the Area General Manager's office at Llay, some eight miles away where Gordon Nicholls, the area manager, wanted to see me. I managed to beg a lift from one of the stores' lorries fortunately about to go to the central stores at Llay Main colliery and I arrived at the office an hour after receiving the message. I had not for one minute anticipated the good news. There were managerial changes taking place at Llay Main colliery and I was to report for work there on the following Monday as 'Assistant to the Manager', I had been working in the pits for seven years and now I felt I was beginning to get somewhere. That evening, my wife and I got a baby-sitter and went out to celebrate.

6. Mechanisation and Industrial Relations

Despite the seeming importance of its title, no formal authority was in fact attached to the job of Assistant to the Manager. I was keen, therefore, to ascertain what precisely were to be my duties. David Holmes, the colliery manager at Llay Main was not at the colliery when I called there on the Saturday morning and the only information I could get was a curt reply from one of the two under-managers, who told me that Mr Holmes would be in his office at eight o'clock on Monday morning. Responsibility for the extensive underground workings at Llay Main was divided between two very different under-managers, the one extrovert, large and loud, the other introvert, placid and quiet. When the manager was away, the former acted as his deputy.

The welcome he gave me was less than warm and I sensed that I would have to be careful not to tread on his toes when performing my duties, whatever they turned out to be, in his part of the pit. I surmised that it would be difficult to establish a positive role for myself without affronting his dignity or challenging his position as a man of long experience enjoying unquestioned authority. Nevertheless, since it was clearly important that I should have such a role, I pondered long on the difficulty during the weekend without getting anywhere near to an answer.

We had moved as a family, now with two children, to a new home in Wrexham, but we were still without a car. I caught the only colliery bus scheduled for the morning run and arrived at the pit at a quarter to five on the Monday morning. There was nothing to do while waiting for a first meeting with my new manager but kick my heels, wander about the colliery surface and drink tea in the canteen. Mr Holmes' welcome was much warmer than had been that of the under-manager and, better still, he outlined the solution to the problem I had been pondering to little effect over the weekend. He explained that a major development was scheduled for completion at the pit bottom during the summer holidays in ten weeks' time and that the preparatory work was running seriously late. I was to be responsible for the development and I was to concentrate exclusively on it. He added cryptically that I was to accept orders from no one but him.

He did not offer an explanation why the work was behind schedule, but after I had inspected the plans and seen the preparatory work that had been completed, I realised that the senior under-manager, whose responsibility it was, had been less than attentive in overseeing the work. The suspicion dawned on me that the many blunders, which had occurred in the work so far, were the reason for my abrupt transfer from Bersham to Llay Main. I would have been less than human not to feel a degree of pride in the trust being vested in me by the Area General Manager, but looking back today over nearly half a century, I wonder at my youthful enthusiasm for shouldering a very heavy, specific responsibility without for a moment contemplating the possibility of failure. Nor, such is the self-assurance of youth, did I doubt my ability to establish a working relationship with the under-manager.

One little occurrence that morning gave me great pleasure, although I knew at the time that my reaction was childish. David

Llay Main Colliery in the 1950s. This was the deepest mine in Wales, if not Britain — Nº 1 Pit was 1,009 yards deep.

Holmes told me that he had arranged an office for me next door to his own office and I was sufficiently immature to feel self-important when I saw the words 'Assistant to the Manager' painted on the door. It was later that I realised his action had been done deliberately to establish a relationship of implicitly equal standing between me and the two undermanagers, who in fact were obliged to share an office in a less prestigious part of the office block.

Llay Main — the name was a result of combining that of the village of Llai with that of the Hickleman Main Colliery Company, the original owners — was a larger and more modern pit than Bersham. It employed 2,200 men and had been producing coal since 1922. Everything about it was big, the shafts were wide and deep, the coal-winding one at 1,009 yards was one of the deepest, if not the deepest, in Britain, two large cages carrying 50 men on each of two decks reached a top speed when winding coal of nearly 80 miles an hour, the power house was large enough to meet the electrical needs of a small town, extensive surface buildings included features of a settled community. Indeed, two of those features were quite unexpected. The first was the pub, possibly the only licensed house, or more accurately licensed cabin, on a colliery yard in Britain. Alas, it closed shortly before I arrived. A less appealing feature was the mortuary. As I recall, no one lost his life at Llay Main during the three years I was there (a very different story from Bersham as we shall see), but the pit's record before the war was a sobering one. The refrain in Wrexham at that time was "Join the navy and see the world, join Llay Main and see the next."

The pit bottom development was one of mechanising the loading of the cages and reducing from twelve to three the number of men employed on the process, a saving of 18 men on the two coal-winding shifts. The preparatory work, which had begun three months previously was difficult to carry out as it had to be done without disrupting the existing working arrangements. Locating the sites for the new machinery, setting their levels and fixing the gradients of the new rail network prior to installing the hydraulic machinery during the holiday break, so that full and empty wagons would gravitate smoothly from point to point over a length of 50 yards on each side of the shafts was a fairly complex task calling for considerable accuracy of measurement. It was something of a shock, therefore, to discover that much of the work done during the three months did not conform to the plan. There were ten weeks to go before the changeover, but much of that time would have to be devoted to correcting work wrongly done, raising and lowering foundations, sometimes moving them completely, widening the roadway in the appropriate places, all to be ready for the track and machinery installation in August.

At home that night, I contemplated the task ahead through rose-tinted glasses, a temperamental quirk of mine that served me well on many occasions. I saw mainly the advantages of my new job — a specific task with a specific deadline, a free hand at tackling it and a team of hand-picked men working three shifts, seven days a week. I lived at my work during that short summer, sometimes being underground for fifteen hours at a time, but deriving great satisfaction as the job began to conform to plan and catch up on the timetable. Most satisfying of all was seeing the enthusiasm of the team develop slowly but surely to reach full pitch at the time of the actual installation during the summer break. For the most part the job was an engineering one, measuring and levelling, mixing concrete, setting foundations ready to receive machinery, connecting electrical and hydraulic cables and so on. It was satisfying work, but even more satisfying was the creation of a committed team from the many differing characters engaged on the job, each contributing to the full his own particular skills. I knew that I would never make a first class engineer as such, no more than a first class chemist, but that was never my ambition. I wanted to be a good manager, able to lead a team. Even so, in a perverse sort of way I almost enjoyed the crises, the false warnings and the disappointments that in a practical engineering sense seemed to be a permanent feature of the work. On the Monday morning after the holiday, however, as the miners returned, the thrill of seeing the new arrangements working smoothly was a more than generous repayment for the difficulties and hard work of the previous weeks.

I had been at Llay Main for ten weeks and had been no further underground than the pit bottom. I did not even know the firemen, let alone many of the 2,000 miners. I decided, therefore, to spend a week or two just visiting the districts — about twenty of them — and gain a superficial understanding of the pit, its geography and its culture. I met the seamy side of that culture when I protested to a collier at the inordinately foul language he was using loudly amongst a group of his fellow workers.

"I wasn't speaking to you," he replied caustically.

"A self-respecting man wouldn't speak to a dog like that," was my response and I sensed the approval of his workmates. The most striking physical difference between Llay Main and Bersham was the underground temperature. It was unbearably hot in the districts furthest from the pit bottom where temperatures over 90 degrees Fahrenheit were not unusual, so that merely walking along the dusty roadways was a burden. One face, the furthest of all from the pit bottom, was being worked beyond Gresford parish church. A pillar of coal some 200 yards square had been left as a support beneath the church and the face was being worked along the fourth side of the pillar furthest from the pit bottom. Since the seam dipped in the direction of the church, the face was some 1200 yards below the surface, the deepest face in Wales I suspected and surely the hottest.

A fortnight passed as I familiarised myself with the pit, pondering yet again what role to adopt. The answer once more came, as I should have expected, from Mr Holmes, who entered my office one afternoon as I sat at my desk twiddling my thumbs — an office, incidentally, with no papers on its desk, nor any sign of real office work having taken place — to say that he had a new job for me and a difficult one. "I want you to sort out the wages," he said rather sheepishly and half apologetically.

There were two problems with the wages at Llay Main, one in respect of pieceworkers and the other to do with applying the five nationally agreed different wage rates to men on 'day work', i.e. men being paid a fixed wage, or datallers as they were called. The first problem had arisen because of the difference of attitude of the two under-managers; the second through sheer negligence. The wages of pieceworkers in the two parts of the pit reflected the characters of their respective under-managers, the one tending to permit generous allowances and the other tending towards miserliness. The unfortunate consequence was that wages for the same job were higher in one part of the pit than in the other. This, naturally, created a great deal of resentment among those who were less well paid and resulted in numerous minor strikes taking place. Each Friday there were strikes and threats of strikes from various sets and on one or two occasions during the past year or two, all the pieceworkers in one half of the pit had been on strike for a day. It had been agreed at the time of the most recent strike just before the summer holidays that the average earnings in the two halves would be the same. And that was the task now falling on my plate, apparently as one of the 'odd jobs' that Mr Holmes had spoken about when he first welcomed me to Llay Main.

The same system of piecework payment operated at Llay Main as at Bersham and indeed at all collieries. Pieceworkers were paid according to a mixture of out of date piece rates and a ragbag of allowances, prejudices, browbeating and arbitrary managerial decisions. The problem of establishing a measure of fairness in the payment of wages throughout the pit was compounded by the fact that the day-wage workers were mostly wrongly paid. In principle this second problem was a more straightforward one, although even more difficult to resolve in practice. The wage rates of datallers were governed nominally by a national agreement establishing five grades of pay according to the degree of skill required for the job. Unfortunately, of the nearly 1,000 daily paid workers, some 70 per cent were on too high a grade, 10 per cent were too low and 20 per cent were graded correctly.

It was evident that 'sorting out the wages' was a job requiring the wisdom of Solomon, the patience of Job and the persuasive skill of Queen's Counsel. Nevertheless, after a preliminary meeting with the lodge officials of the union, I started on the task of dealing with this second part of the problem feeling reasonably hopeful. As for the first part, David Holmes had expressed his confidence in me at an earlier meeting when the under-managers were present, declaring pointedly and in unambiguous terms that I was to brook no interference from anyone. I was aware, of course, of the potential resentment of the under-managers at my authority to override their decisions regarding allowance payments and I was equally aware that the union would probably object to any meaningful reforms I wanted to introduce in relation to day-wage payments.

My initial meeting with the three lodge officials, however, was made easier in that all three were Welsh speaking. The discussions, therefore, were conducted in Welsh and, consequently, more frank and friendly than they might otherwise have been, although I find it difficult to explain why this psychological quirk should be so. My main argument in the case of the day-wage workers was that if it was right to raise the wages of workmen who were wrongly underpaid under a national agreement to which the union was party, then it was equally right to reduce the wages of those who were wrongly overpaid. Furthermore, local union officials had a responsibility, just as I had, to see that the agreement was implemented correctly. It was easier to persuade the three officials of the validity of this argument than it was those workmen who faced a reduction in their wages but, gradually, conceding a little here and insisting rather more there and dealing with small numbers of individuals at a time, the discrepancies in day-wage payments began to reduce in number. I became acutely aware that, without the courageous leadership of the three union men, it would have been extremely difficult to reach a position of paying wages honestly according to the national agreement.

The problem of pieceworkers' wages was more difficult to deal with in that there was no clear principle that could be followed reasonably objectively. It would have been easy, of course, simply to increase the allowances in the less well paid part of the pit, but that would have resulted in a significant overall increase in earnings per manshift at the colliery, a statistic that was scrutinised more carefully than others by the divisional board at its monthly meeting, mainly because wages costs constituted some forty per cent of total costs. The only practical way to deal with the problem was arbitrarily to reduce the allowances permitted by the benevolent under-manager, to do a Tom Hunter on his books so to speak and to allow a compensating increase in those of the grudging under-manager. At the same time it was important that the overmen should gain the impression that I was being even-handed in dealing with the books from both parts of the pit. It was also important, of course, not to go too far at any one time in cutting allowances. To familiarise myself with the detail of the myriad allowances at play meant making a careful comparative study of the wage make-up of over one hundred sets of workers, a tedious task which I undertook mostly at home after my normal day's work. In the meantime my personal relationship with the under-managers was under some strain as I overruled some of their arbitrary decisions with what appeared to be equally arbitrary decisions of my own. I spent several hours each week over a period of two years on the wages exercise and I learned more from it about the difficulties of the art of persuasion than in the whole of the rest of my working life. At the end of the exercise, however, I felt some pride that wages at Llay Main were being paid more honestly and fairly than at its beginning and that the job had been done with the minimum of industrial unrest. A few years later, when I was manager of my own pit, I attempted with some success to remedy the systemic weakness in the payment of piecework common to the whole of the coal industry. I shall describe the attempt in a later chapter.

The lesson I learned above all others from the Llay Main experience was the key role character plays in a good leader, whether manager, union official, teacher, politician or anyone else. The three union officials, with whom I had been working, especially on the day-wage exercise for which they had a specific formal responsibility, were all men of character. One in particular was a natural leader of exceptional quality. Ernie Griffiths, a native of the nearby village of Treuddyn, was known at Llay Main as 'Walloper' on account of his fondness for generous measures of beer. His word was his bond and I witnessed several furious arguments between him and his more intractable members when he insisted that he was acting fairly despite their protestations to the contrary. Ernie was killed in a motorcar accident some years later at a time of crisis for Llay Main when his leadership would have been invaluable. My most cherished memory of him, however, was of his speech of welcome to Lord Robens, the chairman of the Coal Board.

Lord Robens was making his one and only visit to the coalfield and a rather grand reception had been arranged to which a hundred or so representatives of the north Wales coal industry had been invited. Walloper, who had been asked to make a formal speech of welcome, began by saying how much he appreciated the opportunity of warmly welcoming Mr Lord Robens and continued for ten minutes with frequent references to his "very good friend Mr Lord Robens" and to "dear Mr Lord Robens" (on one occasion he said, "*fy hen gyfaill annwyl Mr Lord Robens*" — which rather pleased me). To its credit, the assembled company remained throughout the speech as gravely sober as a conclave of cardinals, but the dam burst when Lord Robens began his response with "Call me Alf".

Shortly after I had begun work on 'sorting out the wages', an important engineering development occurred. The coalfield had its first experience of the technological revolution that was completely to transform the industry, at least in an engineering sense. It was a development that would prove to be an Indian summer for the British coal mining industry. The first attempt at mechanised mining in the north Wales coalfield was at Llay Main and to my great satisfaction David Holmes decided that it was to be my baby. It turned out to be a sickly child, if not quite stillborn.

It might perhaps not be inappropriate here to outline some historical aspects of the coalmining industry in Britain. The management of the industry had for a very long time been an uninspired one. The failure to invest in technological research and development during the industry's golden age up to the First World War had resulted in its being unable to compete in a global market from the 1920s onwards. The main reason for the failure was not shortage of finance — the Rhondda Valleys after all had been the Abu Dhabi of their day — but one of culture. Management clung to the dangerous Victorian belief in permanence, everything remaining immutable — buildings were to last for ever, processes were to be unchanged, conventions frozen, societies and empires inviolate. Coalmining thus continued to depend on the muscular efforts of hundreds of thousands of miners. At the same time, the need to reduce production costs in order to compete in an increasingly open world market became ever more pressing and since wages made up a very large proportion of those costs, management's policy for survival was to reduce wages. The 'sliding scale' came into being, tying wages to the price of coal on the market. The consequence of this emphasis on wages rather than on research and development was inevitable. Productivity remained at a low level. Production methods in 1947 were essentially those of 1914. It is true that the coal cutter and the belt conveyor had been developed, but their overall effect was marginal, barely meeting the natural increase in costs over time inevitable in an extractive industry. Cost cutting rather than technical innovation led ultimately to the disaster at Gresford, where the ventilation inadequacies of a 'modern' colliery which did not even have a properly constructed surface airlock over the up-cast shaft were a disgrace.

A radical change of policy followed nationalisation in 1947 when the Coal Board established an engineering development department. In conjunction with private engineering companies the department developed a range of revolutionary machines for getting coal, one of which — the meco-mower — arrived at Llay Main in 1955. I looked forward eagerly to the opportunity of working in the vanguard of the revolution about to take place, although I did not know at the time that the meco-mower — my baby — would prove to be a failure. It was supplanted a few years later by the Anderton disc-shearer, an entirely different machine that within a decade had become universally successful in engineering terms. It was a crushing irony that this British development should prove ultimately fatal to British coalmining as mining engineers across the world exploited the machine to the full, while short sighted and perverse British attitudes on the part of both management and union stultified its potential at home.

At Llay Main we had a number of difficulties with the meco-mower as a coal-getting machine. It was not robust enough for its purpose and numerous mechanical breakdowns kept occurring. Each breakdown meant a loss of output, a fundamental sin in a coalmine and as I was in charge of the mechanised mining project, I found myself having to answer time and time again for the loss. To redeem myself I spent more and more time nursing my baby until I was able to recognise the least change in the sound it made as it cut through the coal and know when it showed signs of labouring. This was the time, I suppose, when I came nearest to being truly an engineer.

It was not the machine as such that was the biggest problem, however, despite the breakdowns. There was no avoiding the fact that we were working in a coalmine and that the main problems were those presented by mother nature, chiefly that of keeping the roof under control. The seam behaved as though it objected to the new method of working, so that the roof conditions deteriorated seriously despite the greater density of support being applied. There was a plague of falls of roof, an interesting consequence of which was the division of opinion among the face workers, the younger ones in favour of the machine even with its difficulties and older ones against. The young contingent laid the blame for the falls of roof, without justification it has to be said, on poor craftsmanship by the older men, who in turn, although reluctant to accept the new system, seemed almost to welcome the opportunity of displaying their ability to secure the sometimes frightening cavities in the roof. They surpassed themselves in tackling large falls which at first sight seemed impossible to clear in less than a week, but which in fact were cleared in a matter of hours. There was no question that it might have been lack of effort or competence on the part of the face workers that the meco-mower failed.

An important lesson I learned during this period and one that accorded with my naturally optimistic temperament was that things are never quite as bad as they sometimes seem. The lesson proved to be especially salutary during my first years as manager of Bersham colliery, when I sometimes felt that providence was conspiring to put every obstacle in my path to prevent my succeeding as a manager.

It became obvious at last that the meco-mower experiment was a failure, that it should be brought to an end and that the machine should be withdrawn. I confess that I was not disappointed to be rid of it and that I was happy with the thought that, at least, I had by now established my presence at Llay Main sufficiently well to fulfil the role of assistant to the manager meaningfully in the general running of the pit. A second technological development, which I adopted as yet another baby of my own, was methane drainage. The practical experience I gained in that field was to prove invaluable as well as profitable when I became manager of Bersham colliery some time later, a colliery where gas was more of a problem than at Llay Main. There was one incident, however, which on looking back at it, I now realise that I was seriously at fault in naively overreaching myself to bring it about. The incident provided me with a direct personal challenge that could have gone disastrously wrong and which had nothing to do with mechanised mining except perhaps in the sense that the new cage-loading system at the pit bottom contributed to circumstances that, together with my ineptitude, gave rise to the incident.

A tunnel, a mile and a half long, ran from the pit bottom marshalling area to a junction serving several districts. Large drams of coal, each holding three tons, were hauled by rope from the various districts to the junction, where they were formed into trains of fifty drams for hauling by electric locomotive to the pit bottom. At the end of a shift, miners gathered at the junction to await a train of empty drams specially provided for man-riding to the pit bottom. Each dram held up to eight men, thus when the train arrived at its destination, nearly 400 men disembarked, some while the train was slowing to a halt and made a frantic rush for the cage. It was clear that sooner or later someone would be hurt.

Foolishly I decided to stop the dangerous practice on my own account, without formal authority and without serious thought about the consequences of my action. There was no hope, of course, of halting the reckless rush of hundreds of men merely by putting up an arm like a policeman controlling traffic, I would simply have been swept off my feet. There was nothing for it other than to wait until the vanguard of men had filled the cage for the first man-riding rope and then, with my fingers crossed, order them off the cage on to the empties side of the pit. I had instructed the hooker not to signal the cage away until I had given him a sign. On my ordering the men off the cage, however, no one moved. The danger I had failed in my naivety to appreciate now loomed before me. A stand-off between the men on the cage and me, let alone the 300 men waiting impatiently for man-riding to begin, meant that I would finally have to climb down and lose whatever authority I presumed to possess. In some desperation, therefore, I spoke directly to the three or four men at the front of the cage, hoping to influence them with arguments about the reasonableness of my action and threatening to hold the cage for an hour or more until they complied with my instruction. After a short pause and to my great relief, the first man walked off the cage and was followed by the others, one behind the other like sheep. I then allowed the cage to be filled by the men still waiting on the fulls side. The gamble had paid off, but only just and I have to admit that it was not one I should have taken. I subsequently had notices posted prohibiting running and stipulating fines for those caught doing so. More importantly I had barriers built with which to control the rush of men. I lectured the pit bottom firemen on their responsibilities and for a week or two made a point of being present at the end of all three shifts. A tradition of discipline was gradually established to everyone's benefit.

I cringe today as I recall my foolhardiness. In the event I succeeded in my aim largely through a fortuitous coincidence. The first man to come off the cage had appeared before the 'absentee committee' a fortnight previously, when I had rebuked him harshly for his frequent absence from work. It is more than possible that the memory of the interview and of the sanctions, with which I threatened him, had established a personal contact between us and influenced him into obeying my order at the pit bottom. Chairing the rather ambiguously named absentee committee was another of the odd jobs I had been given. In the early 50s there was a national shortage of fuel and as a consequence absenteeism in the mines was a subject of public interest. The response of most collieries to the problem was to establish committees composed of management and union representatives charged with the task of interviewing men persistently taking time off work. At Llay Main the committee met once a fortnight to interview half a dozen offenders at each meeting, trying through a mixture of appeals and threats to get them to attend their work regularly, but with little success I fear. The proverbial answer to the question "Why do you work only on four days each week?" was "Because I can't afford to work on three". There were, however, moments of light relief. One man appearing before the committee for the umpteenth time gave as an excuse that he had a stomach ulcer and he clapped his hand to his side to emphasise the seriousness of the complaint.

"Look here," I said to him, "the last time you were here a month ago, the pain was on the other side".

"Well yes," he replied, "that's it you see. The doctors can't pin my ulcer down".

I had been Assistant to the Manager for over twelve months and had been fully occupied with duties ranging from mechanised mining to sorting out the wages, chairing the absentee committee, dust suppression, methane drainage and so on, down to trivial but time consuming tasks like organising the coal field's annual first aid competition. I was so busy that I had not given serious consideration to my formal position on the staff of the colliery. The good news, when it came, was all the sweeter for being unexpected. I received a letter from the secretary to the Divisional Board offering me the post of Deputy Manager at Llay Main colliery with a formal standing second to the manager and deputising for him in his absence. It was a substantial promotion and I was naturally delighted, although apprehensive of the reaction of the under-managers. I need not have worried. Both accepted the situation, not least I suspect, because both were in any case approaching retiring age.

My work did not change appreciably, but my salary increase was substantial and enough to purchase a second-hand car. I met the union officials for discussions much more frequently and significantly extended my experience of industrial relations, sometimes attending meetings arranged at area level. I remained at Llay Main for another two years. Then came the news that Harry Lewis, manager of Bersham colliery, was retiring because of ill health. His job was advertised; I applied for it and was fortunate enough to be appointed. Thus in May 1957 at 33 years of age, I became a colliery manager, if not at Hafod, my village pit and my prime aspiration, then at least at one which was a good second-best, namely its next-door neighbour at Bersham.

7. My Own Pit

I came back to Bersham after being away three years and found the colliery little changed. Bersham was a difficult pit, gassy, wet, faulty, brittle roofs, roads squeezing under roof pressure and floor lift and above all few reserves of coal. It seems odd that a coalmine should be desperately short of coal, but that was the unfortunate situation. The pit had been sunk in 1867 and, from the 1920s onwards, there had been little investment to open up new reserves. Consequently the pit was scratching for coal in the most unlikely places, small pockets between two faults, for example, in areas which had been abandoned half a century previously and which promised a productive life for a new face of only two or three months. A high proportion of the workforce was employed driving roadways to reach these pockets scattered across the colliery take — not the most profitable of activities at a colliery. Nor were the new faces profitable when finally in full production. On one occasion during my early years as manager, it was necessary to open a face in the Quaker seam a mere 36 yards long. As the seam itself was barely a yard thick, the face was doomed from the start to make a heavy loss and be a drain on the colliery's overall performance.

Five seams were being worked concurrently, a sure sign of the lack of long-term investment. They were, in ascending order, the Main

Coal, the Crank, the Quaker, the Two Yard and the Powell. The Crank, an 18-inch seam that in normal circumstances no one in his right mind would have dreamed of exploiting, was being worked because there was simply no other reserve available in more profitable seams. It astonished me and was a tribute to the face workers, that they were managing each working day to turn over a face 180 yards long and only two feet thick (the coal seam was undercut in the fireclay floor to a thickness of six inches). Simply to crawl on one's belly along the face after it had been fired was an achievement in itself. The galling paradox gnawed at the back of my mind that two excellent seams, some would say renowned seams, the Ruabon Yard and the Wall and Bench, remained unexploited across the whole colliery take. Indeed, had not Ruabon Yard coal from the neighbouring Hafod colliery been supplied for many years to Queen Victoria during the latter part of her reign? The two seams existed in pristine condition at Bersham because they were a hundred yards deeper than the Main Coal, the seam to which the shafts had been sunk. No development had taken place to reach them.

Not unexpectedly, the colliery was losing large sums of money. In the early and mid-1950s, however, there was still a fuel shortage so that the emphasis was on immediate production at almost any cost, profitability counted for little. Despite its technical shortcomings I was thrilled to have my own pit; there was also the added pleasure, parochial as it was, of being amongst my own people — a substantial proportion of the miners were Rhosites. Indeed, on my very first morning as manager I experienced a typically Rhos-flavoured contretemps, which gave me much pleasure and not a little embarrassment. I answered as manager to John Kerr, agent for three collieries, Hafod, Ifton and Bersham. On my first morning we went underground together to visit a district in the Main Coal. As we approached the face along the wind road, we came across Joe Griffiths, or Joe Harriet, as he was familiarly known, spreading stone

The shearing end of an Anderton Disc Shearer at Bersham.

dust. I was 33 years of age and I had known Joe, who was approaching 70, for over twenty years.

"Hello Mr Griffiths," I said, "how are you?"

"Oh hello Tom," he replied, "It's nice to see you down here".

To me his greeting was natural and friendly, but John Kerr did not think so.

"Show a bit of respect for your new manager and call him Mr Ellis," he told Joe Harriet curtly.

"Well Mr Kerr," replied Joe equally curtly, "I call you Mr Kerr and Tom I call Tom, but I have more respect for him than I have for you," and he turned peremptorily to his work to bring the exchange to an end.

Joe Harriet retired about a year later and, on his last day, called at my office to present me with a gift. We were both fond of poetry and we had many chats about matters poetic when I came across him underground. He enjoyed reciting *englynion* (four line epigrammatic verses in a Welsh strict metre). His customary greeting would be "What do you think of this?" and he would recite an *englyn* and then take advantage of the opportunity to discuss its merits. His gift was appropriate although a little trite perhaps in that it was a copy of a book familiar to many Welsh children called *Beirdd Ein Canrif* [Poets of our Century]. Joe had written the following on the frontispiece — I give a literal translation:

> *This book was presented to Brother Tom Ellis, Pant,*
> *By a friend as a signification and sign of appreciation*
> *Of the above Brother's Tendencies of Mind towards the literature*
> *And the poetry of Wales. I hope that the reading of it*
> *Will deepen and strengthen his affections to love Wales and*
> *Her language at all times. April 1958.*

I thanked him for his friendly gesture, but I was tickled when I looked more closely at the book at home that night and saw the words 'Denbighshire Education Committee: Rhos Central School' stamped on the inside back cover. I still have the book.

The Joe Harriet episodes, of course, were not representative of the mainstream Bersham culture (in its broadest sense), but they would hardly have occurred at Llay Main and would have been impossible at Gresford. They could have occurred quite easily at Hafod.

I spent my first week or two as manager familiarising myself with the colliery's paper work, its finances and costs, wages trends, short term planning proposals, accident rates, stores requisitioning and so on. I was soon reminded, however, that mining was a practical calling, often dealing with the unexpected and dangerous. The phone rang at home in that harsh tone it seemed to adopt for the early hours when one was in bed and which I became too accustomed to and to dread over the years. The message was serious. Geoff Williams, a 28-year-old front-ripper was buried under a fall and the situation was not hopeful. I dressed, rushed to the colliery, changed into pit clothes and spoke to the district deputy on the pit phone. Men were clearing the fall, which was a large one, to try to reach the young man, but there was no sound from him and the prospects were bleak.

I had arrived at the colliery at the same time as the under-manager. Together we went underground to walk the two miles to the face and arrived just as Geoff Williams' body was being dragged out of the rubble. It seemed as if he had been killed the moment the fall had occurred three quarters of an hour earlier. Everyone was quiet and his workmates went mechanically through the process of putting the body on a stretcher and covering it with a blanket. I ordered six men to start on the sad journey to the pit bottom, four carrying the stretcher at a time. The under-manager and I remained at the road-head for a quarter of an hour, making arrangements to have the rubble cleared and the roof cavity secured and we then started on the journey back to the pit bottom.

We caught up with the stretcher party not far from the pit bottom where the colliery doctor was waiting. There was nothing he could do other than confirm that Geoff Williams was dead, but I thanked him for coming to the colliery so quickly and for going underground. The Coal Board employed a full-time doctor in each area. We went to the medical centre on the surface where an ambulance was waiting to take the body to the mortuary. I phoned the coroner's officer at Wrexham police station and arranged to complete the necessary formalities later that morning. The most difficult task, of course, was to break the news to the widow. Fortunately, the colliery nurse had arrived (colliery nurses were another innovation following nationalisation) and together we went to deliver our sad message. The nurse stayed with the widow while I knocked up some neighbours who were her friends and we then returned to the colliery.

This was the first fatal accident to occur at Bersham while I was manager and it happened a fortnight after I had been appointed.

There had been no fatality there for a long time, but during the next five years there were to be another five, three of them to firemen whom I naturally knew well and all except two from falls of roof on the face. Of all the vicissitudes that I experienced as a colliery manager, these were the ones that floored me completely. I felt at one stage that providence was conspiring against me to make me the most unfortunate colliery manager in Britain. I came to dread hearing the phone ring when I was at home and my wife began to worry about my peace of mind, a worry that led in due course to a rather delightful story, which I shall tell later.

That morning, however, as well as seeing the coroner's officer, I notified the local inspector of mines, whose responsibility it was to enquire into the circumstances of the accident, ascertain whether negligence was a contributing factor and draw whatever lesson he could. The colliery continued to work as usual, a change from the pre-war Rhos tradition when Hafod 'played a turn', i.e. did not work for a day after a fatal accident. Such accidents naturally weighed heavily on my mind, each leaving its own scar.

About a month after the accident when I was beginning to find my feet as manager, the issue of the Powell seam arose, the only satisfactory outcome of which was the opportunity in due course to make the empty boast "I told you so," although in fact I did not succumb to that temptation as the situation spoke eloquently for itself. One of the faces in the Powell seam was approaching Plas Power Quaker seam deads. Plas Power was a colliery four miles from Bersham, which had closed in the 1930s. The pit was full of water; indeed, to my astonishment the shafts were still open, guarded by a ramshackle fence, which any young child could have broken through and the water could be seen some 15 feet below their rims. I estimated that there would be about 1500 feet head of water in the Plas Power Quaker deads bordering onto Bersham's take. The plan I inherited at Bersham was to work the Powell seam, lying 40 yards above the

Quaker, across those Plas Power deads. The first of the Powell faces was already advancing towards Plas Power and was expected to cross the edge of the deads in seven months time. The big attraction was an area of Powell coal still remaining in the Plas Power take, a reserve of coal, which Bersham desperately needed.

I knew from my previous experience as overman in the Powell seam, however, that there would be a serious risk of an inrush of water making mining conditions extremely difficult as the face crossed the edge of the Quaker deads. The difficulties that had arisen at Bersham when the Powell face crossed the edge of its own Quaker deads would be trivial in comparison with what could now be expected because of the head of water at Plas Power. It was not unthinkable that millions of gallons of water could break through to jeopardise the whole colliery. I believed that at best the loss of the Powell seam in the Plas Power take would be the likely consequence, whereas that area could be exploited safely by driving two tunnels across the edge of the deads and developing faces at a safe distance past them in the new take.

I informed the planning department at Llay that I intended to halt the Powell face fifty yards short of the Plas Power deads, then to drive two tunnels to a point fifty yards past the edge of the deads and reopen the face. The operation would take about four months, but of course, in the meantime there would be a loss of output of 200 tons each day. The planning department disagreed with my proposal and over the following week or two the disagreement developed from being a mildly courteous one, to being a mildly acrimonious one, but ending as a blazing row. Finally a meeting was arranged at my office attended by seven members of the area staff, including the Area General Manager, the Area Production Director, the colliery agent, the head of the planning department with two of his staff and the Area Safety Officer. It was a meeting I shall never forget. I argued for more than an hour against the area plan, quoting my experience as overman four years previously without success. I then played what I thought was my trump card by pointing out that it would be illegal to do what the area planning department wanted. Regulations made under the Mines and Quarries Act prohibited mine workings wider than twelve feet from approaching within forty yards of an area known or suspected to contain water. The shaft section at Bersham showed the Powell and Quaker seams to be just under forty yards apart. The head of the planning department, however, asserted entirely without justification in my opinion, that their distance apart at the point of crossing was forty yards six inches. I said that his argument appeared to be a sophistical splitting of hairs. At this point, Gordon Nicholls, the Area General Manager, must have realised that I was determined not to implement the area plan and said that the only way forward was for him to give me the written instruction that the Act permitted him to do. "Who precisely takes responsibility is not the point," I responded bitterly, "but now that we've reached this stage, then I will comply with the area plan," and on that note of reluctant compromise, the meeting ended.

It had been an extremely difficult hour, especially for a young whippersnapper of a colliery manager of barely a month's standing. The meeting seared itself indelibly on my mind and looking back over nearly half a century, I wonder that I managed to remain so obdurate. The meeting, however, contributed more than a penny's worth towards upsetting my peace of mind; I felt a loss of self-confidence for weeks before the buoyancy of youth restored my customary sense of optimism. The only immediate comfort I was able to gain after losing the day was from the unequivocal support of my under-manager when I gave him an account of the meeting.

As the Powell face steadily approached Plas Power during the following months, I prepared anxiously for the worst. In the context of dealing with an inrush of water the layout of the pit was unfortunate as the pit bottom was, so to speak, in a saucer. The roadways from the shafts rose gently at a gradient of about 1 in 20 for about a hundred yards before forking in different directions to follow gradients in the Main Coal. The exception was 'the Brake', a tunnel of 700 yards rising steeply to the Powell seam from the rim of the 'saucer' close to the shafts. The return airway from the Powell followed a level course to break into the up-cast shaft about a hundred yards up from the shaft bottom. Near the pit bottom there was a 'lodgement' capable of holding 10,000 gallons of water, or in other words just over three hours make of water pumped from the various districts. In the lodgement were three pumps, each with a capacity of 100 gallons a minute. Water was in fact pumped continuously up the shaft at a rate of 50 gallons a minute to be discharged into the Black Brook, a small stream flowing past the colliery. If the make of water were to exceed the capacity of the pumps, the pit bottom would, of course, flood and trap anyone working in-bye in the districts.

I explained my anxiety to the colliery engineer and asked him to have the pumps thoroughly overhauled and then to measure the maximum flow that could be pumped with the three pumps working simultaneously, something that had never previously been tried. The figure turned out to be 250 gallons a minute.

It was odd how serious incidents seemed always to occur at weekends and it was so this time. The phone rang shortly after midnight on the Monday morning, inducing that empty feeling in my stomach once again. I was half expecting an inrush of water, of course, although it actually happened three days earlier than I had forecast. Bert Gittins, the night overman, was on the line and when I heard his voice and realised that he had come to the surface to speak directly to me, I knew that something very serious indeed had happened.

"There's a river flowing down the Brake," he said, "you had better come here quickly".

There was only a skeleton staff at work on the Sunday night shift, so the fireman had not begun his opening inspection of the Powell district ready for the Monday morning shift. He had seen the water running down the Brake and had called the night overman.

Within half-an-hour, the overman, the under-manager and I were paddling through water on our way to the face. There the source of the water was clear. The Powell seam was a little less than four feet thick, but that morning the floor had risen to within a foot of the roof and water was welling out of scores of fissures in the floor. There was no question that it was Plas Power water, nor was there a question that the face was lost and I was fairly certain too that the roadway would be closed before very long, a matter of a few weeks at best. My main concern, however, was for the rest of the pit and the possibility of the pit bottom being drowned. The day shift of about 300 men would be descending at half past five, when a decision would have to be made whether they should go to their places of work or go home. The three of us returned to the bottom of the Brake and built a makeshift dam to channel the water into a short iron pipe. After an hour's work we had a reasonably effective dam diverting what I estimated as half the total make of water into the pipe. It filled a bucket held at the end of the pipe in about three or four seconds and I was able to make a rough calculation that the total flow of water was about 40 gallons a minute. At least, I said to myself, we have some sort of objective measurement and if the flow continues at that rate, it will be safe for everyone to go to his work, except of course, those employed in the Powell.

I decided to meet the day shift at the pit bottom as they came off the cage, explain the position and correct any misleading rumours likely to be circulating on the surface and reassure everyone that it was safe to go to his work. I was confident that the lodgement pumps could deal easily with the water. The men accepted my account of what had happened and although some of them expressed concern, they all went to their districts dutifully. At five past six every man was underground and on his way to work, except the Powell workers for whom the under-manager was making emergency arrangements after they had collected their tools from their doomed district. I returned to the bottom of the Brake where the night overman was still measuring the flow of water.

Matters were not as simple as I had hoped. It was a bitter disappointment and a considerable worry to hear that the flow had increased. At nine o'clock there were 70 gallons a minute coming down the Brake and I began to be seriously worried. It would take at least two hours to contact and recall everyone to the pit bottom and be certain that no one was overlooked. Although there would be ample time if the flow of water increased gradually as it was doing so far, the situation would be very different if a really large inrush occurred suddenly. I discussed the possibility with the under-manager and we agreed a figure of 100 gallons a minute as a benchmark. If the flow reached that figure, I would give instructions to withdraw everyone out of the pit except those men installing additional pumps to pump water if necessary out of the pit bottom saucer into those districts running to the dip.

The next few hours were the most anxious I have ever experienced. I had sent a message by my clerk to my immediate superior but so far there had been no response. The flow gradually increased until at the end of the afternoon shift it had reached a figure of 90 gallons a minute (we had by then installed a V-notch to improve the measuring arrangements). I went home at midnight, tired and worried and slept fitfully to be woken at six o-clock by the phone, when for once it was a pleasure to hear it ring. I had arranged to be called the moment the flow reached 100 gallons a minute, otherwise not to be phoned until six. The flow had remained constant at 90 gallons a minute and quite extraordinarily, it stayed at that figure during the whole of the rest of my time as manager of Bersham. Work continued as usual in the other parts of the pit, no- one making the least protest at having to go to his place of work during the crisis.

We had lost not only the Powell face itself, but a large area of coal in the Powell seam, a loss that seriously affected the performance of the colliery over the long term. In the short term, it took several months to open a replacement face in another seam; meanwhile the profit and loss account, never a healthy one, worsened seriously and I began to ask myself how long the colliery would continue in operation. One important result of the crisis on me personally was the change in my feelings towards the industry's senior management. No one came to the colliery for three days after the crisis was over and there was no discussion, either immediately or indeed ever, on the events that had led up to it. The silence was deafening. As I said earlier, I refrained from saying, "I told you so," partly because I had no formal opportunity of doing so and partly out of scorn. My earlier scepticism about the quality of the coal industry's management grew deeper and my self-confidence was correspondingly strengthened.

The world continued to revolve, however and gradually the prospects, although still gloomy, began to brighten a little; output grew slowly and everyone became more cheerful. I had noticed on other occasions how a pit became more chirpy as its men realised that it was doing well, not least of course, because the conditions of work improved, as did the wages. We were on the verge of turning a corner at Bersham, at least in the context of our low expectations, when cruel providence struck yet again. This time, although the blow was similar in kind to that which struck the Powell and worried me seriously for a day or two, its effect was nothing like as devastating.

It was another inrush of water, more sudden and certainly more unexpected than that in the Powell seam. Fortunately, the water was not from Plas Power but from an area of Quaker deads of our own. We were driving a gently dipping tunnel over 1,000 yards long to an area of coal under Erddig Hall, the celebrated mansion on the outskirts of Wrexham. The tunnel had reached a point below an area of deads abandoned in 1910, which were assumed to be dry. As usual, trouble began at a weekend. There were early indications on the Friday when the dayshift fireman reported at the end of his shift that a few drops of water were falling from the roof at the face of the tunnel, but adding that they were nothing to worry about. I felt uneasy, nevertheless and later that afternoon decided to have a look at the place. I could not have timed my visit better because when I arrived, the fireman and tunnellers were beginning to get alarmed at the quantity of water pouring from the roof. The flow increased rapidly, until suddenly, like a trap door being released, a rush of water and rubble flooded the floor to a depth of over a foot. In moments it had reached our knees and we were obliged to retreat and leave the tunnelling machinery to drown while we rushed out-bye to make arrangements for pumping the water through the fire fighting range to the pit bottom lodgement. Within three hours we had the arrangements working, but the water was now only 600 yards from the entrance to the tunnel.

We pumped throughout the Friday night, all day Saturday and were still retreating on the Sunday morning although not as fast as at first. On the Sunday afternoon the edge of the water was 200 yards from the mouth of the tunnel and the situation was becoming desperate. Then for the first time a note of hope was sounded as a tunneller shouted "I'm sure it's going back". It was difficult to judge, so I chalked a benchmark on the rail track at the water's edge and walked the short distance to the pit bottom office to pass the time. Ten minutes later, wonder of wonders, the water had retreated a yard into the tunnel. Within an hour we were galloping along at 50 yards an hour and it was clear that the make of water had ceased.

The crisis was over and the Monday morning shift would go to work unaware of the drama which had been played out over the previous forty-eight hours. I gave a sigh of relief, swore that if ever I went to another pit, it would be a dry one and went home to a more comfortable bed than the oak chair in the pit bottom office on which I had snatched an occasional forty winks during the past couple of days. I had decided not to notify my superior of the incident, the most intriguing aspect of which for some of us, especially one or two older men who could remember the person concerned, was later to find in the midst of the rubble, a wooden prop with the initials 'A. P.' carved neatly upon it. They stood for Abraham Pemberton, a highly respected resident of Rhostyllen who had been a fireman in the Quaker seam fifty years previously. It was the custom then for the firemen to carve their initials on newly set roof supports as a kind of certification, both of the workmanship and of their own assiduity in making inspections.

About three years later the last in the sombre series of fatal accidents happened. It was the one I felt most personal responsibility for and my feeling of guilt was irrationally compounded by the fact that it occurred shortly before Christmas while I was at a dinner party in a Chester hotel given by the Area General Manager for his senior staff. Technical developments had proliferated in the mining industry, in particular the Anderton shearer had come into common use. This was a machine which had at one end a large drum, three feet in diameter and two feet deep, studded with tungsten carbide picks. As the machine travelled along a steel chain conveyor, which had superseded the old belt conveyor, the drum rotated and bit into the coalface to load the sheared coal onto the conveyor as slack or small coal. In principle, the longer the face the more profitable it became. In practice, however, to work effectively the chain conveyor was limited to a length of about 200 yards. The common tendency, therefore, was to plan faces of that length.

In due course a shearer arrived at Bersham for use in the Quaker seam, the only suitable area of coal available at the time. This seam was overlain with a bed of fairly brittle mudstone twelve feet thick, overlain in turn by a massive sandstone bed about fifty feet thick.

Long experience at Bersham had shown that if a Quaker face were limited to a little over 100 yards long, then the sandstone was sufficiently strong to span the face without sagging and hence the mudstone remained comparatively unbroken and reasonably easy to support. If the face were much longer, the sandstone sagged and bore heavily on the mudstone, which then tended to crack and make the setting of roof supports more difficult and dangerous. To open a face 200 yards long would be asking for trouble.

Another squabble thus broke out between the planning department and me, but this time, much to my regret, I gave in too readily and agreed to a 200-yard face. My self-confidence had not yet recovered from the trauma of the earlier row, the series of fatal accidents that seemed to be dogging my managership and calamities like the most recent inrush of water, so that I lacked the resolve strongly to challenge the planners. I knew that they would support without question the received wisdom of long faces, no matter how mistaken and inappropriate it was for Bersham.

A face 200 yards long was thus opened and the shearer installed. Roof difficulties began once the face had advanced a little over 100 yards. Within a fortnight it was more a stone quarry than a coalface. Falls of roof became routine and conditions were extremely dangerous. I decided therefore to shorten the face to 100 yards and informed the area production director that I was not prepared to ask men to work for an indefinite period in such conditions and that in any case coal production would be hopelessly unrewarding. He came to visit the face the following morning, significantly staying on it for only a few minutes and agreed that it should be shortened. I gave instructions to do so at once. That evening, when I was in Chester, a fall of roof buried and killed the fireman. Once again long distance management was at fault, but this time I shared the guilt because of my lack of backbone.

Those early years as manager were difficult and painful. The argument about the Powell seam, two inrushes of water, one of which had been potentially calamitous, several fatal accidents, monthly interviews with the Divisional Board in Manchester who were highly critical of the pit's performance, continuing prickly relations with Llay and numerous wages disputes at the pit, arising essentially from the mining difficulties, all had their effect. Bersham was far from being a bed of rose petals for one to lie on who was having his first experience as colliery manager. I spent long hours at the pit and even at home, often late at night, the phone would ring remorselessly with all kinds of bad news. There was only one habitual phone conversation with the colliery, which paradoxically cheered me up. I made arrangements with Bert Gittins, the night overman, to phone me each night at half past ten to give a picture of the position. Almost invariably the conversation began with my asking: "How are things tonight Bert?" Equally invariably Bert would reply in a sepulchral tone, no matter what the circumstances, "Black!" Gradually, as I became aware of his temperament, his reply became less disconcerting and with my sense of humour tickled, I found it provided me with a sense of perspective.

Looking back on that period, I see why my wife began to urge me to take up a hobby. The pit was weighing far too heavily on my mind and I needed something to make me forget it occasionally. She suggested that I should take up oil painting and join a class at the Wrexham technical college. I was lukewarm about the idea, but at last, after nagging me for twelve months, she finally persuaded me to enrol. As things turned out, the colliery problems were easing, the whole nature of the work was changing for the better and the psychological burden was about to lighten, although I did not realise it. I purchased the necessary tackle, brushes, palette and oils and comforted myself with the thought of painting a beautiful, nude, young woman who would be my model. At the first lesson the tutor placed two apples and a banana before me and said, "Let's see what you can make of those". I persevered for a term and finally succeeded in producing a painting of the steps leading from the bottom of Yorke Street up to Temple Row and the east end of Wrexham Parish Church. I felt proud and compared myself to Monet, whose style I had surely captured.

It was my custom to arrive at the colliery at half-past seven each morning, spend a couple of hours reading the firemen's statutory reports for the previous 24 hours, deal with other paper work and speak to the under-manager in his office underground. Then, at half past nine, before changing into my pit clothes, I usually had half an hour in Les Rogers' office, the colliery mechanical engineer, where three or four of us gathered for coffee. They were, of course, all well aware of my hobby, as I had frequently explained how the inspiration would surely lead in time to my painting a masterpiece. Now, with the view of the Yorke Street steps an accomplished fact, I announced with pride that the painting had been completed successfully in the style of Monet. The coffee crew were generous in their congratulations and envious that they too did not have the creative gift enabling them to transcend the drudgery of their daily work.

The following Saturday evening, my wife and I happened to call at the Four Crosses pub between Bwlchgwyn and Maes Maelor. To my surprise, half the lounge had been converted into an art gallery in which several paintings by local artists were hanging for sale.

"Providence has brought us here tonight," I said to my wife. Her instant response was "Don't talk rubbish," and looked rather doubtfully at me. However, when I went to buy drinks at the bar, I could not resist telling the publican that I, too, was a painter in oils.

"Well why don't you bring one of your paintings here," he replied, "I'll be happy to hang it for you".

I let the "one of your paintings" go uncorrected and two days later took the masterpiece to the Four Crosses. "How much do you want for it?" asked the curator, as I had begun to see him.

"What do you suggest?" I queried diffidently.

"What about five pounds, four for you and one for me when it's sold," he said.

I agreed at once and looked on in admiration as he hung my painting on the wall.

The following morning at coffee, I mentioned casually that I had embarked on a new part-time career as a professional painter in oils and that I was fairly sure there would be a substantial demand for my work as it gradually became recognised. I explained that my first painting for sale could be seen at the Four Crosses gallery, but that anyone who would like to see it should not delay as it could easily be sold quickly. During the following weeks I became a regular at the Four Crosses, but was disappointed at each visit not to see a little red star at the side of my painting denoting 'SOLD', The coffee crew showed much interest and kept asking had the picture been sold? I kept replying confidently that a knowledgeable collector would come along, see the painting and snap it up. Time was passing, however and the crew now asked how was business? I was beginning to run out of credible excuses; I had already explained that the painting was a little avant-garde and that it was only when a really knowledgeable person came along who appreciated the work, that one could expect a purchase. Then, one unforgettable summer evening, my wife and I called at the pub for the hundred and first time and I stood transfixed. There it was, with a coruscating little star alongside winking benignly at me. There were a few people in the lounge and once again I couldn't resist proclaiming to the world and his wife: "Isn't that a brilliant painting that's been sold?"

"In my opinion," said my wife equally loudly, "whoever bought that wants his head examining".

"You're absolutely right madam," said a cheeky little so-and-so who was sitting nearby. I wasn't brave enough to argue, so I retreated to the bar to claim my fee. At coffee the next day, I was chuffed to

My masterpiece, 'in the style of Monet'!

inform the chaps, not without a touch of pride, that the painting had been sold.

"Some lucky fellow has had a bargain" I proclaimed and sat back basking in their congratulations and pontificating on some of the more obscure aspects of the oil painter's art.

Two months had gone by when Les Rogers invited my wife and me to dinner one Sunday night with others of the coffee crew and their wives. After chatting for a while it was time to eat. We entered the dining room and the truth hit me hard in the eyes. There it was, my masterpiece, in pride of place above the mantelpiece. From the hilarity that broke out I realised there had been a conspiracy to cut me down to size and that Les had purchased the painting. Everyone was in the conspiracy, even my wife.

That is not the end of the story, however. One evening forty years later, my wife and I were chatting nostalgically about past times. She mentioned the painting and how, for years, she had regretted that I had sold it. I did not know its present whereabouts but there was a ray of hope. Les had died a widower without close family, but I knew some of his close friends who might know where the painting now was. On my third phone call I struck gold. Yes, he had the picture and he would be happy for me to have it. Through his kindness it now hangs in our drawing room reminding us of happy days and dear but mischievous old friends. No one is prouder of it than my wife, I am not burdened with worries, nor do I paint any more.

8. Change of Key

After five difficult years as manager, years of turmoil, tragedy and worry, a change of key gradually took place in my managerial activity. I did not at first appreciate that the change was happening, but gradually, almost without my knowing, I began to respond to a psychological release as the more positive and constructive opportunities of management presented themselves. The release had a cumulatively beneficial effect, which led to a significant change in my managerial style. That in turn changed my relationship with my superiors at Llay and Manchester.

During my early period as manager I had been responding to events beyond my control, most often practical mining problems, some unforeseen, some anticipated, but all nerve-wracking. For almost the whole of the time I had been engaged in crisis management, seeing myself the victim of an obdurately malign providence and feeling more and more powerless and apprehensive. The experience was not one to foster self-confidence, nor did it stimulate the will to develop a new management style different from the traditional one prevalent throughout the whole of the mining industry.

I suppose the turn for the better came providentially. Unexpected occurrences became less frequent and two or three years passed, if not imperturbably, then at least without serious upset. It might have been that the painting too had its beneficial effect. Who knows? The upshot was a period of reasonably routine activity and the opportunity to set my own agenda rather than having to respond frantically to the latest calamity. It was odd, however, that I, who had never claimed great practical engineering competence, nor displayed much enthusiasm for machines and the like, should have embarked on an engineering development as the first step towards putting my stamp on the pit. I decided to introduce a comprehensive scheme of methane drainage.

Bersham was a gassy pit. An explosion had occurred there at the end of the nineteenth century in which nine men, including the manager, a Mr Pattison, were killed. Gas continued to be a serious problem over the years and was a matter of concern when I became manager. At the time, the new technique of methane drainage was in its infancy, a technique with which I had been involved at Llay Main, although without the resources fully to take advantage of it. The technique consisted of drilling holes into the strata to a depth of twenty yards above and below the coal seam at about fifty yard intervals. Steel pipes were cemented into the mouths of the holes and coupled to a pipe running out-bye to a suction pump situated in a main return airway. Over time we extended the suction pipe up the shaft so that the pump discharged the gas into the air. The cost of the operation, although substantial, was within the limit allowed at the colliery manager's discretion, but there was some massaging of the figures to keep within it.

The reason for the introduction of a methane drainage scheme in the first instance, of course, was to lessen the concentration of gas in the ventilating air underground, especially near the coalfaces. There were legal requirements prohibiting certain activities at specific concentrations of gas; for example, if gas were detected at any concentration, however small, either in the general body of the air or in fissures in the strata, shot-firing was prohibited; if the concentration in the general body of the air reached $1^1/4$ per cent, the electricity supply had to be switched off; and if it reached $2^1/2$ per cent, all men had to be withdrawn from the district. The struggle to maintain the concentration below $1^1/4$ per cent was unremitting and was always more difficult when the barometric pressure was low. Visiting inspectors of mines were extremely vigilant at testing for gas and ensuring that the regulations were complied with, a responsibility that bore heavily on the firemen. Gas, being lighter than air, tended to accumulate in roof cavities and sometimes when the barometer was low, a return airway would have several sheets of brattice cloth hanging along its length to divert the air current into the cavities and disperse accumulations of gas. The inspectorate, incidentally, made frequent visits underground, sometimes averaging one visit each week. I invariably accompanied an inspector on his visit, often at considerable inconvenience, as the visits were never announced beforehand.

An interesting little incident involving an inspection took place one afternoon when the Area General Manager was paying me a rare visit at my office. Keith Folwell, the newly appointed manager of Llay Main colliery phoned wanting to speak to the Area Manager, a man for whom I came in due course to have a high regard. A Mr Cauldwell, H. M. Inspector of Mines, had made an underground inspection at Llay Main and had been very critical of numerous minor breaches of the safety regulations, that he had uncovered. He had insisted that coal production should cease until all the contraventions had been put right, a task that had taken several hours and had ultimately resulted in the loss of a day's output from the particular coalface. The colliery manager was now phoning his superior, essentially "to cry on his shoulder". The interest for me in the episode was the effect the tale of woe had on the Area Manager. His response was "We must take a strong line with Cauldwell". It was an emotional and, as I thought, typically English reaction to what was a set of straightforward breaches of the regulations, a factual circumstance to which the remedy could only be an equally factual and dispassionate practical correction. The incident registered in my subconscious mind ready to be recalled in future dealings with my Coal Board superiors if necessary.

We experienced some early success with the methane drainage scheme. Within six months it had been introduced into every district and produced better than expected results. From then onwards, the only costs were those of maintaining a small team to carry out the work and of purchasing a few materials such as pipes, cement, drills and bits. Of course, no-one had thought of making a profit from the venture. That idea surfaced at coffee one morning when someone remarked that it was a shame to be wasting 'all that gas', The gas being released into the atmosphere averaged about 90 per cent pure methane, although the figure could vary slightly by increasing or decreasing the suction of the pump. Someone suggested that I should meet the manager of the local Wales Gas Board at Wrexham with a view to marketing the gas. Fortunately the structure of the gas industry at the time was appropriate for such a local venture; if the suggestion had been made ten years later, *ceteris paribus*, it is doubtful that it would have borne fruit.

When the gas industry was nationalised in 1948, twelve regional gas boards were set up, each one having considerable autonomy, being responsible for all its activities under the loose guidance of a Central Gas Council. The Wales Gas Board was one such board, which, under the inspired leadership of its chairman, T. Merfyn Jones, became one of the most effective, if not the most effective and certainly the most innovative of the gas boards in Britain. Wales Gas was the first to build a grid, a network of pipes connecting gasworks across Wales. The other gas boards followed a few years later to take advantage of imported liquid petroleum gas and then North Sea gas that became available in 1968. The Welsh network, however, existed in the early 60s. Furthermore, Merfyn Jones had established a management structure in which the managers of the dozen or so gas 'undertakings' scattered across Wales were permitted a great deal of discretionary authority. John Lloyd, the manager of the Wrexham undertaking, not only had that authority, but also was blessed with the imagination and determination to use it to some purpose. He was prepared to exploit the gas grid.

Les Rogers and I went to meet Mr Lloyd who received us warmly. We met on a number of occasions and finally agreed in principle that the Wrexham Gas Undertaking would purchase methane gas from Bersham colliery. A number of technical requirements had to be met such as, on the part of the pit, the gas would be supplied at a guaranteed level of purity (allowing a small variation), the daily supply would not fall below a stipulated figure and so on and, on the part of the gas undertaking, would construct a pipe line from Bersham to Marchwiel (the site of the gas works), it would accept all the gas that was offered and was to maintain the gas pressure at a specific figure, again with a small variation.

The talks had taken place without the knowledge of the Coal Board's area management, thus giving me the childish pleasure of breaking the news, firstly to the marketing department at Llay and secondly to the legal department at Manchester. I asked the departments to open formal negotiations with the Wrexham Gas Undertaking with a view to agreeing a price on the gas and to concluding a formal contract. Their reaction was churlish, especially that of the marketing department, as was that of the production department when it was informed: a number of area and divisional officials complaining that I should have discussed the matter with them before meeting a representative of the gas undertaking. I responded by saying that the scheme would have been stalled between a number of committees had I done so, depriving the colliery of desperately needed income for an unnecessarily long period.

Within three months we were selling large quantities of methane gas at a price of 4.1 pence per therm. Unfortunately for Mr Lloyd and Bersham colliery, North Sea gas became available in large quantities in the early 70s, at a price of a little over a penny a therm. Bersham's contract with the Gas Board was terminated for reasons which, as I had by then left the coal industry, were unclear to me. I suspected that the sales of gas ceased because of the intransigence of the marketing department, which was not prepared to lower the price to a figure comparable with or lower than that of North Sea gas. The marketing department, during a period of shortage of fuel, had for a long time been in reality less of a marketing department and more of an allocation department. As the fuel situation improved, the department seemed unable to adapt itself to the old idea that the customer was boss.

The basic reason, possibly a subconscious one, why I had not mentioned to my superiors the idea of selling gas to the Gas Board, was my desire for independence. During my first five years as manager I had lost confidence in the Coal Board's management, not so much on engineering grounds, although some catastrophic mistakes had been made, but more in the reactionary attitude of the industry's management *per se*. I regarded many senior managers as relics of the Victorian age although I would have been hard pushed to present a detailed list of the changes I wanted to see in their management style. I had the opportunity to think seriously about that particular problem some years later when I attended a course at the Coal Board's staff college. I saw much more clearly then the reforms that were needed in the management of the industry: in the meantime, however, I was responding more instinctively than intellectually in my dealings with my superiors, often being unable to present a reasoned argument for some of my managerial decisions. I was angry at the reactionary behaviour of management in general, especially now that the industry had been nationalised and when one could have expected a symbiotic relationship working for good between workman and manager. I kept referring in a somewhat woolly manner to the notice which had been posted at every pithead in 1947: "This colliery is managed by the National Coal Board on behalf of the people". Admittedly it was a fairly meaningless notice, even as a factual statement of ownership, but it clearly implied a background, which required radical change in the style of the industry's professional management.

One trivial incident, which grew into a series of trivial incidents, illustrated the problem clearly. It was a good example of the pettiness, which I found stupid and repugnant and which was the antithesis of good management practice. In 1954, pithead baths, a canteen and an office block were built at Bersham to form three sides of a square. Within a year or two the square had become a depository for all kinds of rusty machinery, parts of wooden structures and other materials and was typical of most colliery yards in its unnecessary ugliness. I decided to clear the site and turn half of it into a lawn, partly to prettify the place and partly to inculcate a regime of tidiness in the main colliery stockyard. Within twelve months there was an attractive little lawn in front of my office barely thirty yards from the headgear itself. There was also a good deal of favourable comment by the mineworkers.

In the summer each year the Divisional Production Director ventured from his Manchester office on a sort of royal progress around his territory, visiting two or three pits each day. Mr Glossop was a 'practical man', as he frequently reminded everyone, one of the old school who made a point of calling a spade a spade and who prided himself on his decisiveness, with little concern for its effect on the feelings of his subordinates. One bright summer's day it was Bersham's turn to receive him and I looked forward to discussing a number of important issues with so senior a figure.

The first thing Mr Glossop saw as he got out of his chauffeur-driven car was the lawn. He seemed to take leave of his senses and started on a long rant about my wasting the Coal Board's money on an attempt to turn Bersham into a holiday camp. There was no wonder, he said, that the level of output was unsatisfactory, what with a harebrained manager in charge and all manner of tomfoolery being practised. He continued in this masterful vein for ten minutes, brushing aside all my efforts to explain my reasoning. I was stunned, not just by his intemperate outburst, but also by his refusal to let me try and justify my actions. His visit was from my point of view a most unfortunate and unsatisfactory one and left me feeling very depressed, but Mr Glossop had undoubtedly had great satisfaction in putting me in my place. The advice I received from my father later that evening was, "Pay no attention to him".

The following year, when the note came to say that Mr Glossop would be making his yearly visit in three days' time, I prepared for his visit with a little joke that I hoped he would appreciate, even if not quite as much as the coffee crew, to whom I had recounted the events of the previous year. I asked Les Rogers to send someone to purchase a deck chair, which on the morning of the visit I placed on the lawn with the word 'MANAGER' printed in large letters on its back. Providence helpfully conspired to produce a beautifully sunny day. Mr Glossop's reaction was even more extreme than that of the previous year and I had to suffer another angry sermon. To me, however, the most remarkable thing about his outburst was that he had failed to appreciate that the whole thing was a joke. His sense of being a 'practical man' had overcome his sense of humour, let alone his common sense.

Some years passed before the third in the series of trivial incidents happened, but this time I penetrated into Mr Glossop's character more deeply and exposed him for what he was. We had bought a piece of land adjoining the colliery tip (which was already far too high) to provide additional tipping space and were thus about to start burying a field of green grass. I decided to remove the top soil and spread it on that part of the existing tip facing the village of Rhostyllen. The only reason for doing so was to try and make the tip less ugly for the villagers who looked out on it from their homes. We made terraces, spread soil and planted tree saplings. As things turned out the experiment was not wholly successful, although today the bottom two thirds of the tip is covered with dense foliage and the view is much improved as travellers through Rhostyllen can see for themselves.

When Mr Glossop came on his visit after the terraces and the planting had been completed, we had the same old pantomime — I ought to be concentrating on making money from the pit, not wasting it and so on. I remembered my father's advice and let the sermon go by over my head. Three months later the tragedy of Aberfan happened. One of the consequences of the disaster for the coal industry was the holding of a number of conferences, at which the management of tips, safe practice and so on, were discussed. The day of our conference in Manchester arrived and I was shocked, in view of my experience with the terraces, to see that Mr Glossop was the main speaker. It was an even greater surprise, however, to hear him boasting that under his direction it had been the custom in the division to guard against the slipping of tips. "For example," he said, "at Bersham, near Wrexham, we have built terraces and planted trees on the spoil heap". I was sitting in a row near the front and when I caught his eye, I gave him a wink!

It might not be inappropriate here to refer in passing to the report of the Aberfan Commission of Inquiry under the chairmanship of Lord Justice Edmund Davies. Paradoxically the report's recommendations reflected the very weakness from which the coal industry suffered, namely outdated and reactionary management. The Commission fell into the same trap as that which had shackled the industry in the first instance and which had been the ultimate cause of the disaster. The management culture in the coal industry was what has become known as mechanistic management. Its characteristics are authoritarianism, hierarchy and bureaucracy, hallmarks inherited from the Victorians. Those characteristics, in essence, were the reason why the workmen on the Aberfan spoil heap continued to tip waste even though the risk of a collapse had become evident to them. Indeed, spoil heaps lower down the valley had in fact slipped and buried the highway to a depth of several feet; local residents were holding public meetings to protest at the tipping practice.

The key question, to which the Commission did not give a satisfactory answer, was why the Coal Board's local management had not used its imagination and authority to make better arrangements for the disposal of pit waste, especially in view of the previous incidents of spoil heap collapse. The Commission failed to provide the answer because it looked at the circumstances of the disaster with a legal mindset, the law itself being authoritarian, bureaucratic, hierarchic and static, or in other words dependent on precedent in its quest for legal certainty. For the uncertainties of an innovative industry, which mining had become, the Commission's approach was inappropriate. Its report thus made matters worse in that its recommendations tended to justify the inappropriate management culture prevalent in the industry. For example, the Commission emphasised the need to strengthen the formal lines of communication between the various levels of management from the headquarters in London down to the pit in the valley. In reality, the problem was that the lines already were too formal, bureaucratic and strong. They were such that they stifled local initiative and limited the freedom of local officials to act according to their own judgement. As a consequence the system was unable to cope with the technical innovations that had become a recent feature of the industry and the response of those in a position to know what was happening on the ground was inadequate.

In the case of Aberfan, it was no longer dry rubble that was being tipped, but wet slurry and no-one locally had the self-assurance, firstly to allow his imagination its full scope and secondly to take decisive action accordingly. People at the pit no doubt expected a decision from above, perhaps after the problem had landed on Lord Robens' desk. The Commission's report justified that expectation.

An important consequence of the coal industry's managerial attitudes was its failure to reform an archaic system of calculating pieceworkers' wages, an entrenched misfortune I have mentioned previously. In the industry's infancy, mining methods were simple and involved small teams of workers, often a father and son, each working in its own wicket at the coal face, the father cutting the coal by hand and the son loading the cut coal into tubs brought to and from the wicket by a 'putter', usually a young boy paid by them. The couple's weekly output was fairly constant and thus, once a price had been agreed, a direct link existed between wage and output. Gradually the size and complexity of coalmines grew until several thousand men could be employed at one mine, thirty or more colliers could be employed as a set filling coal from one face and a dozen faces could be competing with each other to get their coal to the surface and to the weighing machine. Often a set's output could vary substantially from week to week and in extreme circumstances the output from a coalface could halve or double according to a number of geological and engineering factors. It was hardly practical, of course, to halve a man's wages one week or to double it the next. Thus the practice developed of paying or not paying allowances to dampen the weekly variation of wages.

In the early days the practice was legitimate and could be justified, but over time it became corrupt in two ways. Firstly it was open to subjective assessment and thus to abuse leading to disagreement and dispute. Secondly it led to the phenomenon of 'wages creep' and to attempts by management to halt the creep, with consequential long term effects on industrial relations, effects which the more idealistic of us had not anticipated once the industry had been nationalised. Colliers' wages doubled in the fifteen years after 1947, not that the increase was bad in itself, indeed a large part of it was due to reasons extraneous to mining. The problem was that the increase took place often without changing the formal contract under which the pieceworker was paid, such as the price per ton or per yard. Consequently, half a pieceworker's wage was composed of allowances, which were conceptual payments, not based on any objectively measurable criterion. They depended on the persuasive powers of the deputy and the chargehand of the set of pieceworkers. The original function of a legitimate dampening factor on fortuitous fluctuations in a man's wage had become a contentious lottery, which was threatening to become anarchic. It is not an overstatement to claim that the seeds borne by the allowance system fructified in due course into the bitter fruit, firstly of two leaders, each deserving of the other, in the persons of Ian MacGregor and Arthur Scargill and then finally of nemesis at the hands of Mrs Thatcher.

The provocation that prompted me to tackle the problem of piecework payments at Bersham was the number of small strikes that were happening continuously. It was the same old story each time — face conditions are difficult and the allowances are not sufficient to compensate for the difficulties. Sets of men came knocking on my door each Friday after getting their wage packets, often several sets queuing up to voice their complaints forcibly, the more hot-headed men among them bellowing loudly to vent their anger and threatening to strike. Occasionally a set of men would carry out the threat and refuse to go to work on the following Monday and demand a meeting with me. A ticklish problem then arose because it was the Coal Board's firm rule that no one was to commence negotiations with men on strike. Usually, however, I compromised by meeting the strikers and urging them to return to work so that proper negotiations with the union could start and try to resolve the cause of the dispute.

Eventually, I became resentful of the constant weekly altercations and finally, after some thought, decided to change completely the system of calculating piecework wages. I had come to realise that I was not managing the pit in any satisfactory sense of the word. It was then that I began consciously to change my managerial approach to the human problems affecting the colliery, a difficult and far-reaching subject of which I shall give an account of my efforts in the next chapter. But first, the wages problem had to be tackled.

In principle, the road ahead was fairly well mapped out in my mind. In practice, however, there were several obstacles to be overcome, some involving the union and workmen, others the senior staff in the area. To bypass those associated with the staff, I read a paper to the National Association of Colliery Managers, which was published in the Association's journal. In it I set out my proposals in detail and had the satisfaction of receiving congratulations on the paper from the Area General Manager. I took his praise, provocatively and presumptuously perhaps, as a green light to go ahead with my plans.

The obstacles presented by the union and the workmen would have been much more difficult, if not impossible, to overcome had it not been for the support of the lodge secretary. Jimmy Williams, or Jimmy Ianto as he was known to everyone, was a young man who had been elected to his office on the day that I took up my post as manager. We had come to know each other well and through our common experiences, had come to trust each other. I spent an afternoon with Jimmy outlining my plans, which in the context of the coal industry's conservatism were revolutionary. Two major tasks required to be done, firstly to define and set a price upon what could be called a unit of work and secondly to choose a formula using that price to arrive at a wage reflecting the work done, while at the same time ensuring that any variation arising in a wage from week to week should not be too great.

To fulfil the first task it would be necessary accurately to measure a man's work in terms of the physical effort needed to produce a given quantifiable result. Work-study technique had long been established in a number of industries but was alien to underground work in the coal mining industry. The Coal Board, however, had set up a small department in order to improve methods of work on the surface and a branch of that department existed in the north Wales area. To have any hope of successfully applying the technique underground, two conditions had to be met. Firstly and crucially, pieceworkers had to accept the good faith of the management and the professionalism and complete independence of the work-study engineers and secondly, management had to abandon its traditional authority for the setting of tasks.

I had already made a number of changes in the style of management practised at Bersham. The underlying intention was to eradicate, or at least ease, the confrontational relationship between management and men traditional to the mining industry. For example, one of the first reforms I introduced was the abandonment of the requirement that deputies should 'clock on', an inappropriate requirement for staff presumably committed to their colliery. The interesting and unintended result, by the way, was their tendency to work longer hours! I had also enlarged the agenda of the colliery consultative committee, a committee established at every colliery after nationalisation, but which alas, normally paid lip-service to the concept of meaningful consultation. At Bersham, the agenda now included all facets of the work of the pit, including future plans (the Plas Power quarrel had created an impression on everyone), finance, costs, safety, in addition to that well known satirical topic, the price of a cup of canteen tea. The only item not on the agenda was wages, a subject reserved for formal negotiation with the union lodge committee. My brushes with my superiors at Llay had had a welcome side effect too, in the sense that the feeling of independence, 'Bersham against the world', had itself fostered a team spirit among the workmen. And to crown everything, as a unique symbol of that independence we had started to hold an annual 'Bersham Colliery Labour Rally' on a Saturday in the summer. I was vice-chairman of the Wrexham Constituency Labour Party and together we felt that it was appropriate to celebrate the nationalisation of the mines each year by holding a rally at the colliery supported by the party — a party having the overwhelming support of mineworkers. We had well known speakers such as Jim Griffiths and Dai Francis of the south Wales Miners' Federation to address the rally from a platform erected alongside the pithead on my contentious lawn. I could not resist picturing Mr Glossop becoming apoplectic had he been present. Curiously enough, especially in the light of Mr Attlee's injunction on vesting day forbidding the flying of any flag over a pithead other than that of the Coal Board, none of the other political parties protested at what they could have seen as a tendentious use of state assets.

The commitment of Bersham's manager to the idealism of the 1947 slogan 'This colliery is managed by the National Coal Board on behalf of the people' was obvious and sincere. Thus with the support of the lodge committee guided by Jimmy Ianto, I dared to call in the specialist team of work-study engineers to make a study of a selected set of colliers on a coal face in good condition. We knew, Jimmy and I, that we were taking a chance, but things turned out better than we had expected. The work-study team was accepted with good grace, they made their study and in due course I reached an agreement with the union on a price for a standard unit of work. It was a remarkable leap of faith on the union's part for none of the committee members had expertise in or experience of the system; they accepted the venture only on condition that if it were not successful, we would revert to the old way. We were now ready for the next step, the algebra.

In one sense this was a simple matter. There are a number of well-known formulae (to the specialist in the field) to keep fluctuations in piecework earnings within acceptable limits, even if the work performance itself exceeds or falls below such limits. The formula that was chosen and accepted after what, in the opinion of the participants, was a learned exposition and discussion, was an adaptation of that known as the Low Task Rowan formula. The biggest difficulty was explaining to the workmen, how the dampening coefficient of the complex formula worked and convincing them that it was fair in the sense that their wages would be independent of allowances, would vary with their efforts and with the vicissitudes of face work, but not vary too much.

The system worked well and within a few months every set of pieceworkers was being paid by it. It was necessary to keep the work-study team more or less permanently engaged reviewing work assessments as conditions altered in various districts, but the advantages of the system far outweighed the cost of employing two or sometimes four men continuously. They were providing a substantial element of objectivity in a field that for far too long had been a hotbed of prejudiced disputation. The weekly disputes and strikes ceased as the prickly bargaining with the deputy became a thing of the past and as men began to appreciate the objectivity of the system and being able to rely on receiving their anticipated wages on payday. The lodge committee and I were generous in our self-congratulation as we felt that we had completed a significant, if not historic, achievement.

There are three postscripts to the story, however. Some years later but before the Aberfan conference farce, my bete noire Mr Glossop, discovered that the system of calculating piecework earnings at Bersham had changed. I was obliged to listen to the usual sermon except that this time it was fire, brimstone and perdition all round for the feckless bunch at Bersham and the sermon ended with his telling me that I was sacked. I went home that afternoon to tell my wife that

I had had the sack and I went to my office on the following and subsequent mornings to await a formal notice of dismissal. None arrived, so I carried on with my work, ignoring his instruction to reinstate the old system because the advantages of the new one were manifest to any fair-minded person. I heard no more from Mr Glossop about our wages system, not at my monthly meeting with the Divisional Board at which he was present, nor at our next meeting on his annual visitation at which I was anticipating a final dressing down and possibly demotion.

That the dressing down and demotion did not happen is the second postscript to the story. No less a person than Alf Robens, chairman of the Coal Board, realised in due course that the system common to the whole industry of calculating piecework earnings was a mess and that it was having a disastrous effect on the industry's performance. He decided to reform the system, but unfortunately he chose an inappropriate, because too simplistic, alternative. He decided that pieceworkers would be pieceworkers no longer. From an idealistic point of view I sympathised with his intention of paying face workers a fixed weekly wage, but anyone with the least experience of the coalface would have known that the idea was completely impractical. Despite the extensive mechanisation programme, face work still demanded considerable physical effort; it was far from being process work like, say, pressing buttons in a power station and the physical effort required to perform it satisfactorily meant that there had to be a direct monetary inducement for its fulfilment. A fixed weekly wage would not provide that inducement because it did not take account of the frailties of human nature. Despite this, Lord Robens went ahead to institute a fixed wage for face workers at every colliery, including Bersham. Our achievement, of which we had been so proud, went into oblivion after working successfully for some years, or at least that is what we all thought at the time.

I was bitterly disappointed, but there was nothing I could do; I was also about to leave the coal industry for the greener background of the benches of the House of Commons. I had been adopted as the Labour Party's prospective parliamentary candidate for Wrexham, a seat normally having a Labour majority of some 15,000. I therefore watched the consequences of the change in the payment of wages, firstly with a little detachment from my office at Bersham and later with a greater detachment from those comfortable green benches at Westminster, while regretting the whole time that our successful attempt at reforming on a local level one of the major weaknesses of the industry was followed by another attempt which turned out, not unexpectedly, to be a complete failure.

The coal industry's output per manshift (OMS), a key economic indicator, which had been rising steadily since 1947, fell substantially. One had to distinguish between two long-term influences on OMS. The first was the mechanisation programme implemented increasingly over the years, although its effect of steadily improving the industry's performance had diminished after 1970 and the 'true' overall OMS of the industry had reached a plateau. The second influence was the effect of the closures of badly performing collieries. From the end of the 1950s onwards the demand for coal fell in the face of competition from oil, gas and nuclear power. Pits had to be abandoned and naturally the least efficient ones were those to go. Each time an inefficient pit closed, the overall performance of the industry improved, but of course, the *reductio ad absurdum* of the process would have been a highly efficient coal industry comprising the one best colliery. It was important, therefore, to concentrate on the first influence to halt the decline of the industry. Lord Robens' system of paying wages had a disastrous impact on this.

And thus we come to the third postscript to the story. I was in my Westminster office early in 1971 when Pryce Williams, my former clerk at Bersham, phoned me. He wanted to know whether I had been speaking to someone in the Coal Board's headquarters, because that morning he had received an instruction to send to London those documents relating to our preparatory work for the introduction of the piecework payments system operating at Bersham a few years earlier. I learned that afternoon, with a little smug satisfaction, that the Board's intention was to introduce the Bersham system, or an adaptation of it, into every pit in Britain.

What Robens had not appreciated sufficiently, however, was the crucial importance of preparing the culture at each pit to accept such a revolutionary change. Almost a quarter of a century after nationalisation, the industry was still clinging to the old reactionary tradition of suspicion and confrontation between manager and worker. It would have needed a decade or more of hard work and inspired leadership on the part of management and union to change that tradition. Alas, there was neither the time nor a sufficient number of men of vision at hand to do the job and to make matters worse Arthur Scargill had by now become a powerful influence in the union and a thorn in the side of Joe Gormley, its President.

Robens' efforts were a complete failure. Within a few months it had become necessary to reinstate the hopeless old system of allowance payments and Scargill, who in due course faced a worthy opponent in Ian McGregor, was busily preparing to sound the knell of the coal industry with the bells of his two clashes, firstly with Heath and terminally with Thatcher. I remember saying at a meeting of the Wrexham Labour Party that while I could easily understand why my father during the 1926 strike had shouted "Down with the owners" from his soap-box, I found it difficult to see how Arthur Scargill could in effect trumpet the same slogan when he himself was one of the owners. Such are the tears of things.

9. Management Theory

One of the most important functions of a manager is to make decisions. It is routine for every manager to do so at whatever level he acts, whether as managing director of a company employing thousands of people, as a manager on the staff of a company at one of a number of levels, or simply as a farm hand pleaching a hedge under his own direction. It is important, however, that managers dealing with people should distinguish between different types of decisions and appreciate that in a particular environment, one type of decision can be more appropriate and beneficial than another for a company's prospects. It is important also to recognise that the management culture of a company determines overwhelmingly the kind of decision making commonly practised at all levels throughout the company, whether to its long term advantage or not.

Decisions can conveniently be divided into two classes, programmed and non-programmed. Programmed decisions are those to which the manager is inescapably bound by rules pertinent to the circumstances of the decision. An income tax inspector, for example, deciding on a tax problem, makes a decision to which he is bound by tax law, which he applies punctiliously. However complex the problem may be, the decision is programmed. Similarly the driver of a motorcar deciding to change gear is committed to the decision by the steepness of the hill and the strength of the engine. A manager making a programmed decision does not exercise his judgement except insofar as he has to decide how closely he is following his guiding rule.

Programmed decision making was the foundation on which the military and ecclesiastical hierarchies were built, both early examples of a management system for large organisations. Their rules, designed to cater for every situation calling for a decision by a junior manager, officers and clerics alike, were framed by the small group at the head of the hierarchy. The philosophical basis of this system of management is induction, being expectant on the basis of past events. The system is thus most appropriate in a stable environment, or one that changes only slowly. Those at the head of the hierarchy can then anticipate recurring situations and frame rules applicable to them. The manager at a particular level simply applies the rules, or if a problem exceeds the formally acknowledged competence of that level, refers it upwards.

As industrial undertakings grew slowly in size towards the end of the eighteenth and throughout the nineteenth century, management modelled itself on the proven military and ecclesiastical hierarchies, the only available example of large-scale management. Gradually the industrial environment coloured the whole of Victorian society, a society that still reflected at a local level the authoritarian, deferential and conformist inheritance of feudalism. Those social attitudes and prejudices prevailed until the end of the Second World War. The whole of society was programmed, so to speak, by authority and wisdom applied from above. Tennyson captured the temper in his celebrated couplet "Theirs not to reason why, Theirs but to do and die". The couplet was a hymn of praise for the gallant six hundred and the public greeted its sentiments with enthusiasm, whatever it thought of the quality of the poetry. There was a worm in the wood however, which led ultimately to a cultural revolution, whereby the

Light Brigade's obedience would be regarded as more stupid than praiseworthy.

Industry began to use science deliberately and positively for innovative purposes. The trend, which had been a trickle during the 19th century, became a torrential flood after 1945. Rapid technical and commercial change became a common feature of industry, especially new industries such as electronics. Consequently, the inductive method as a principle of management was outmoded. New and unexpected situations arose daily at all levels of management within a company, each one calling for a technical or commercial decision and none having guidelines which a junior manager could follow. It was necessary, therefore, for that junior manager to judge for himself what best to do. He made a non-programmed decision. By the end of the 1950s the evidence was clear that, in a rapidly changing environment, those companies prospered which had adapted the old style of management to the new circumstances, or had adopted from the start what became known as organic management and that those industries failed which retained the old 'mechanistic' style of management.

I began fully to appreciate the analysis outlined above when I attended a two months' course at the Coal Board's staff college in 1963. I had expected an enlightened exposition of those modern man-management characteristics which I instinctively felt appropriate to the times and which, in my view, the coal industry urgently needed to adopt. Alas, the staff college course was a disappointment and had little relevance to the management problems besetting the pits, in particular that of abandoning the atavistic glorification of the 'down-to-earth-no-nonsense-practical-man' school of management in favour of more contemporary social attitudes. I had in fact protested on a number of occasions when this management style had goaded me beyond endurance. Perhaps the most notable occasion was when Mr Mitchelhill, the new Area Production Director, made his first underground visit in north Wales. He was a plain- spoken Yorkshire man and on his visit to Llay Main colliery where I was deputy manager, he rounded intemperately on an overman who I knew was a thoroughly competent and conscientious official. I lost my temper and said, "We don't want Yorkshire-style management here".

"What do you mean by Yorkshire-style?" he asked.

"All wind and piss," I responded. Mr Mitchelhill and I, after a few difficult early months, eventually had a friendly relationship.

I felt, as a somewhat sceptical child of the times possessing that feeling of dissent engrained in the Welsh, that the ageing overtones of Britain's former industrial greatness did not meet modern requirements. I did not have the intellectual justification, however, for publicly exposing the inadequacies of the coal industry's management in the face of the conformist attitudes of my more senior managerial colleagues. I hoped, therefore, that I would find the justification on the course. In fact, had it not been for a lucky chance, the staff college would have been a complete let down. Fortunately, I came across a newly published book in the college library that fired my imagination and inspired me to embark on a thoroughgoing programme of reform at Bersham.

The Management of Innovation by Tom Burns and George Stalker, two sociologists at Edinburgh University, has become a classic of management theory and marks a turning point in the art and practice of man-management. Over a period of fifteen years they studied sixteen post-war electronics companies, all operating, of course, in a new environment where innovation was of the essence. Nine of the companies prospered and seven failed. Burns and Stalker's striking discovery was that the main determinant of the success or failure of the companies was the nature of their management. These fell into one or other of two broad types and in particular whether they practised programmed or non-programmed decision-making. Each type of management was characterised by a number of structural and social features, differing according to type. The great value of the book is that it describes the various features in detail and demonstrates their significance for the fortunes of the companies. The authors gave the names 'Mechanistic Management' and 'Organic Management' to the two broad styles, the former being typical of the bankrupt companies and the latter of those which prospered.

Common features of mechanistic management are: hierarchical structure; obedience and loyalty to immediate superiors; comprehensive rules existing in large numbers and minute detail; strict application at each level of management of the rules appropriate to that level; formal relations between managers on different levels; managers being responsible only to their immediate superiors; formal communication, much of it in written form; deference to ideas from above; the top of the hierarchy seen as the source of all wisdom and authority; and so on. The Aberfan Tribunal's report corroborated the general tone. Its appropriateness as a management system can be readily accepted in circumstances where change is rare or is initiated only at the top of the hierarchy. The civil service is an obvious example. The system was also the right one for the 'thin red line' of the British Empire where the disciplined soldiers fired their rifles as one man on the bark of the sergeant.

Common features of organic management are: horizontal rather than vertical company structures; loyalty to the overall purpose of the company rather than to a superior; readiness of staff at all levels to exercise their own judgement; informal relationships, socially and structurally; paucity and generality of rules; ideas often originating and being developed at junior levels; and so on. To continue in a military key, it is clear that the style is more appropriate to the SAS than to the 'thin red line'.

Organic management may appear idealistic and impractical if not anarchic to many people reading this book, but that would be due to the brevity and inadequacies of my outline. Burns and Stalker gave a convincing account based on a wealth of hard practical evidence from the companies they had studied. Decisions of the most far-reaching and fateful kind were often taken at astonishingly junior levels, sometimes by persons with little apparent expertise in the overall business of the company but having an intimate knowledge of a narrow set of circumstances. There are, however, two key requirements for successful organic management. Firstly that it should operate in an environment of change and secondly that the culture of the company be prepared so as to respond positively to the management style.

The paradox of the coal industry was that the nature of the work called out for organic management whereas it was managed mechanistically. Like the farm hand pleaching his hedge, the miner worked very largely under his own direction and depended on his own resourcefulness to meet each new problem as it occurred at the whim of nature. In addition there was the post-nationalisation trend towards mechanised mining, for many years largely experimental and involving considerable change. A striking example of the failure of mechanistic management was its inability to cope with changes in the methods of supporting the roof at a coalface where a system of mechanised mining had been introduced. Under the prevailing mechanistic management culture there existed countrywide rules giving precise instructions for the setting of props, bars, chocks and other roof supports. Plans showing in detail the system of support conforming to the rules laid down nationally in regulations made under the Mines and Quarries Act had to be posted at each mine. A breach of the plan was a breach of those regulations and was thus a breach of law. For the majority of the new systems of mechanised mining, however, it was impossible to comply with the nationally imposed support rules. The law could not be changed quickly enough and possibly often enough, to legalise the new and untried methods, even though they were potentially safer than the old system of coal getting. The dilemma thus arose of either breaking the law or of abandoning attempts at introducing new methods. It was resolved by making local agreements. The colliery manager concerned had to draw up suitable support rules for the particular face and type of mining and have them authorised by the local Inspector of Mines. The precise legality of the arrangement was unclear.

Bersham, like other collieries, was steeped in the old mechanistic management tradition. Thus, when I began instinctively, almost from my first day, to depart in small ways from the accepted pattern and doing so without an intellectual argument that I could present to justify the departure, I succeeded only in creating doubt among the firemen and workmen about my intentions. The general response of the firemen was their implied accusation that I was a weak manager, insufficiently firm in my dealings with the men and lacking the will to penalise miscreants as they, the firemen, thought fit. Nor were they happy with the personal insecurity they felt as a result of organic management, even at its most elementary. Indeed Burns and Stalker showed that personal insecurity was the common reaction when the change took place from the one management style to the other. Staff who had been apprenticed to mechanistic management yearned for the certainty of knowing their place to the inch. The accusation of weakness was ironic. Often, for example, when I visited a district and drew attention to some work or other that had not been done, the fireman would excuse himself by saying that he was waiting for instructions from the under-manager. On most occasions, I replied that it was a matter for the fireman, not for the under-manager. At times I felt as if I were required to decide into which hole every nut and bolt in the colliery should be fitted. Another weakness of the management style was that everything was seen in terms of black and white so that the concept of the two sides of industry 'Them' and 'Us' persisted strongly in the pits despite the fact of 'common ownership'. The weekly triangular confrontation between men, firemen and under-manager was a constant irritant buttressing the concept.

At first, my problem in attempting to change the management system was my lack of a clear idea of what I instinctively wanted to do. I could neither explain nor justify to my officials the changes to the style of management that I wanted to see implemented. As a consequence, for a period of four or five years, a managerial feature at Bersham was confusion, although it was gradually allayed as people began to respond to what they saw as my quirkish idiosyncrasies. Matters improved more positively after 1963, however, when I was able to preach the virtues of organic management with a conviction based on understanding, especially when I turned from abstract theory to an emphasis on the concrete fact that industries in a changing and competitive environment succeeded or failed according to the type of management being practised. The coal industry by this time was in crisis with pits closing because of failure to compete. I read a paper to the Association of Colliery Managers which received a less than warm welcome from my colleagues, 'practical' to a man as they were, who saw the concept of organic management as the light-headedness of a manager dwelling in the clouds. In Bersham, however, the message was reaching home, partly on the principle of many a knock breaks the stone and partly with the help of a few enlightened union leaders, including those of the firemen's union. I gained some satisfaction some years later, albeit tinged with sadness, from the fact that Bersham, which on technical grounds should have been one of the first pits in the Wrexham area to have been closed, was in fact the last to do so. There was no doubt that the team spirit built up over several years had contributed greatly towards keeping the pit on its feet, so to speak, far beyond reasonable expectation. The situation at Hafod, as I came later to see for myself, was very different and the pit closed ahead of its time. By the mid-1960s, however, I was reasonably happy with the situation at Bersham from a managerial point of view and I began busily to prepare for the future.

10. Development

Bersham's overriding weakness at the end of the 1950s was the dearth of its coal reserves. The pit was almost 100 years old and there were no extensive and readily accessible areas of unworked coal remaining. The shafts had been sunk originally to the Main Coal, which had been immediately exploited. Extraction from other seams higher in the strata followed, so that by 1960 the pit was scratching for coal from faces in five seams scattered across the colliery take in the few small remaining areas of reserves. It was thus a tantalising fact that two seams — the Ruabon Yard and the Wall and Bench — existed in their virgin state, 100 yards and 130 yards respectively below the Main Coal and even more tantalising that a scheme had been prepared in 1957 to sink a brand new shaft to reach the two.

In the meantime we were driving a tunnel as a stopgap — the one where the inrush of water occurred which I described in a previous chapter — towards a piece of Quaker coal under Erddig Park on the outskirts of Wrexham. The Main Coal had been worked in that area during the 1930s by means of a method called the Pillar and Stall system. Small pillars of coal left to support Erddig Hall, a large mansion house narrowly rectangular in plan, showed on the plan as the black squares of a draughts board, except that they were much smaller than the white squares denoting the areas from which the coal had been extracted. It was obvious that the pillars were of the smallest possible size short of causing damage to the Hall. I suspected that the reason for this rather risky policy was the character of the landowner and owner of the Hall, Simon Yorke or 'Squire Yorke' as he was known to everyone in Wrexham, a man with whom I was to have a great deal to do in due course.

I first met Simon Yorke in a corner shop, or rather not so much that I met him as that I saw and heard him, because we did not speak to each other that first time; I simply listened with some astonishment to the conversation he was having. I had been married for two years and I occasionally undertook minor chores for my wife. I had thus called at the shop a few yards down the road to buy groceries. At the counter ahead of me stood a stranger in conversation with Mrs. Randles, the shopkeeper, about the price of the sweets she had on display in a row of bottles on a shelf.

"How much are those red ones?" he asked, pointing at a bottle.

"Three-pence-halfpenny a quarter," replied Mrs. Randles.

"And how much are those?," moving to the next bottle.

"Three pence a quarter," came the reply.

And so on along the row of about a dozen bottles. At the end of the row, the man pondered a while and then, pointing at a bottle said, "I'll have a halfpennyworth of those". It was a surprise to be told after he had left that the man was Squire Yorke and that he always bought his sweets by the halfpenny. Little did I think that within a few years I should be dealing with him on a much more costly matter than a bag of sweets.

It was when I was manager of Bersham colliery that the Quaker coal was worked under Erddig Hall, causing serious damage to the building. When the Main Coal had been worked under Erddig Park in the 1930s, the coal industry was privately owned and the seams under large estates were the property of the landowner, or in the case of the Bersham take, Simon Yorke. As the owner of the mineral rights he received royalties for allowing the seams to be worked under his land, being paid a sum of money for each ton of coal extracted. He had the choice of not allowing the colliery company to work the coal under the Hall. The royalty payment, however, must have been a greater attraction to him than the need to avoid any risk of damage to the Hall through subsidence. As things turned out, Mr Yorke was in luck, very little damage being done to the Hall, although the pillars of coal had been too small to guarantee that that was going to be the case, while at the same time he had been paid for the additional coal produced. He had wanted every halfpenny and through the workings of providence he had got them and had kept his Hall intact to boot.

The end of the war and the return of a Labour government brought a change, although not necessarily an end, to Simon Yorke's good fortune. Compensation was paid not only to the coal owners, but also to landowners, when the coal industry, together with the coal seams on which it depended, became the property of the state. Landowners, however, were able to forfeit the compensation in respect of the areas of coal underlying special buildings such as Erddig Hall on the outskirts of Wrexham and thus safeguard their property from risk of subsidence. Alas, the squire of Erddig chanced his luck a second time and accepted compensation for the loss of his royalties. He forfeited to the Coal Board the right to work the coal under the Hall.

This time, the consequences were inevitable and disastrous. No-one at the Coal Board's Manchester headquarters had any interest in Erddig Hall nor sympathy for its owner, although I did try, rather faint-heartedly it must be said, to have the coal worked by the Pillar and Stall method, a difficult proposition for modern mining methods, but my efforts, quite rightly, were of no avail. The coal was to be extracted in full from under Erddig Hall; Simon Yorke's luck had run out. When the damage to the Hall became evident, Mr Yorke, as one would expect, was furious. In effect, subsidence had broken the back of the long building, causing damage that was clearly visible. For example, there was a gap in the facade under the eaves of about six inches. Unfortunately, Mr Yorke saw me personally as the direct perpetrator of the deed. I became his greatest anathema, a difficult position indeed to be in, believe me. The more I tried to persuade him that he was being unfair, however disarmingly I tried to do so, the more he became enraged. Gradually, however, the quarrel between us subsided and the time came when we no longer met; his demand for compensation became a matter for the Coal Board's solicitors.

Simon Yorke was a crusty, cantankerous old bachelor, difficult to put up with and very different from his younger brother Phillip. I felt a heavy burden go off my shoulders when I no longer had to face his weekly, at first even daily wrath. And yet, I felt a mixture of admiration for his stubbornness, sadness at his foolishness and guilt for the Coal Board and myself. I was shocked when I heard that his dead body had been discovered under a tree on his estate. Memories came to mind, sad ones, delightful ones and rueful ones, such as his buying sweets from Mrs Randles, our sending a load of coal by tractor to Erddig Hall during the heavy snow of 1963 and, of course, the inevitable damage to the Hall from our mining activity. The most befitting memory, perhaps, that I can have of the lonely, sad old bachelor is that evoked by R. S. Thomas' lines marking the end of Twm, another old bachelor and a crofter, who was found dead on his lean acres, just as was Squire Yorke on his fat ones:

> ... and a fortnight gone
> Was the shy soul from the festering flesh and bone
> When they found him there, entombed in the lucid weather.

Phillip inherited the estate and in his wisdom and generosity, together with the demand for houses in Wrexham, he succeeded in restoring the Hall by selling much of the land to a building company and transferring the proceeds and the Hall to the National Trust. Erddig Hall stands today in its old glory as one of the celebrated tourist attractions of Powys Fadog.

Throughout the period that we were working the Quaker coal under the Erddig estate, I was preoccupied with Bersham's long term prospects. I was especially concerned at the long delay in reaching a decision about sinking a new shaft. The project, which had been prepared by the area planners at Llay in 1957, had to be authorised at the London headquarters as its cost was higher than that permitted at area level. Unfortunately, the market for coal had weakened considerably and it was no longer a matter of coal at any price. Opinion in London was that a decision on the Bersham shaft should be postponed indefinitely, presumably to wait until market conditions improved.

It was clear to me, however, that the new shaft would never be sunk. I therefore proposed that we should abandon the project and in its place drive two tunnels from the pit bottom to provide access to the two deeper seams. It was a much less ambitious plan and would be within the cost limits allowable at area. I expected that the idea would be accepted fairly readily to release us from the horns of the dilemma on which we were hooked. 'Two thirds of the job is its beginning' was the Welsh proverb I quoted as I attempted to proselytise the area management. Their decision, such as it was when I finally extracted it from them, was that we should wait patiently for a while on the grounds that authorisation for the shaft would be bound to come in due course, or to put it in another Welsh proverb 'Every desire has wings'. It seemed to me, however that there was an aura of deviousness about their decision. My frustration was compounded by the constant difficulty we were experiencing because of the shortage of our coal reserves.

After two years of fruitless debate and with the pit's future becoming increasingly uncertain, I decided, without authorisation, to start on the tunnelling plan, keeping it a secret for the time being until it was irrevocably under way, or better still, as one hoped, until the new seams were reached. Looking back once again over a period of forty years I marvel at my audacity; I suppose one can put it down to the rashness of youth. When finally we began the project, after much soul searching on my part on account of its boldness, everyone at the pit welcomed the break from the prevarication that for so long had clouded the promise of the two new seams. It was a wry pleasure to sense the conspiratorial glee enjoyed by everyone at the colliery. This would surely be the secret kept by the largest number of persons ever in the history of the coal industry — as long, that is, as it remained a secret! To keep it so, involved much subterfuge, in particular making sure that anyone from Llay going underground was conducted along roadways in the pit bottom area away from the mouths of the tunnels. Fortunately, the number of visits I received from my superiors had for some unexplained reason become much fewer and had thus eased the cloak and dagger requirements. One can now see with hindsight that this was the period when Bersham made a decisive claim to have its own identity within the Coal Board's dominion, having interests and ambitions that did not necessarily coincide with those of the Board.

The tunnels had advanced 100 yards when someone from Llay discovered what had happened. I had an acrimonious telephone conversation with the area production director who ordered me to stop the work until he and the area general manager could come in a couple of days time to see the scandalous undertaking and put me in my place. It was precisely what I had hoped would happen. I knew that the relationship between the two men was a difficult one and I had taken advantage of it in the past. On a number of occasions when the three of us had discussed a contentious issue calling for a decision, I had noticed that the two disagreed almost instinctively. That meant, of course, that I was always in a majority of two to one and therefore able to have my own way more often than not. That is what happened this time. The general manager was in favour of my carrying on with the tunnels and the production director was against. After a long discussion a compromise was reached with an agreement that the area-planning department should draw up and cost a plan for working the seams over the next decade and that area should authorise it before I could proceed with the driving the tunnels. Faces were saved all round, in more senses than one, but the paper work swallowed three valuable weeks. Afterwards, however, the tunnels were driven much more quickly because I was able to deploy more men to the job. The psychological effect on the pit was considerable; one could almost feel the unity and team spirit of the miners.

The tunnels were being driven to the dip at the steep gradient of 1 in 6 and it took several months to drive the 600 yards to the Ruabon Yard, the first of the two seams. Throughout that time the pit's financial position was so hapless that I dreaded my monthly confrontation with the divisional board, when I seemed to do nothing but trot out excuse after excuse. Much now rested on the success of the first face in the new seam, which we designated number one at the risk of tempting providence for the subsequent faces two, three and so on. They were all to make positive contributions to the pit's performance. The coal itself was high quality coking coal and we knew that it had been successfully worked at Hafod, our next-door neighbour. Hopes were high, but it was not to be.

Unlike the geology at Hafod, barely a mile away, that at Bersham turned out to be unfavourable. The roof of the seam consisted of a friable mudstone, overlain as in the Quaker seam by a sandstone bed. The thickness of the mudstone, however, was just four feet and therefore it broke more easily and was more difficult to support than the 12-feet thick mudstone of the Quaker. In practice, supporting the stone proved impossible as it fell in lumps immediately after the shearer had ripped out the coal from under it. The result was that for every ton of coal produced, there were two or three tons of stone mixed with it. After three months of effort, failure had to be conceded. The blow seemed a fatal one in the light of the colliery's desperate financial position. At best, it meant that the potential reserves had been halved and there was no guarantee that the Wall and Bench seam could be worked successfully. Even if in fact we were allowed to drive the extra 200 yards to that seam, it would be at least six months before a face could be opened, six months of crippling losses that the divisional board would surely not put up with. The workings of the Coal Board were mysterious, however. For some unexpected and totally inexplicable reason, we were given 'a last chance', We received permission to drive the tunnels to the Wall and Bench.

The tunnels advanced at about 15 yards a week, until one fateful morning I arrived at my office to read in the night deputy's report that the Wall and Bench could be seen at the base of one tunnel. I could not restrain myself from going underground immediately, but when I reached the face of the tunnel, it had just been fired. I had to wait while the rubble was cleared and then at last, the whole seam and the strata above it were revealed. I thought that the prospects were promising, but 'jam tomorrow' had been the refrain for so long that I felt it better to express mild doubts. The seam was a little over a yard thick and had a strong roof, but it would be some months before we had a face ready to tell us definitively whether we had struck black gold. I kept on warning myself not to be too celebratory and contented myself with sending a sample of the coal to the laboratory for analysis. Two days later came the good news that it was extremely high quality coking coal. Up to that time Bersham had been in the steam coal market but it was now clear that if we were to stay in production at all, the whole of our production would, within a year or two, have to go to the coking coal market. That would be an advantage since we would no longer be competing against oil, gas and nuclear power and would instead be selling in a much more stable and foreseeable market. Little did I see the impending failure of the British steel industry!

With the prospect of a dependable customer in mind I decided to try and repeat my Wrexham Gas Undertaking exploits. I wrote to the manager of the coke ovens at John Summers' steel works on Deeside, some twenty miles away. Selling coal was, of course, a matter for the marketing department, but I was anxious to explain to the manager the background to Bersham's position and our prospects for the future. Lionel Leach listened carefully as I explained that I did not know how easy it would be to work the new seam, but if it proved to be as I expected, then we would be producing about 4,000 tons weekly within a couple of years. I presented a copy of our laboratory report and left a sample of the coal, knowing that he would be doubly impressed when he did his own analysis.

Within three months the first face was in production. All our hopes were realised to a degree greater than we were entitled to expect and within a year Bersham was selling coking coal to the steel works. Lionel Leach and I became close friends, a relationship that directly influenced Bersham's fortune two years later when the marketing department at its London headquarters tried to replace Bersham coal with coking coal from a Stoke on Trent colliery. Lionel Leach insisted on having Bersham coal, mainly because of its quality, but also, I like to think, because of the close relationship that had developed between us. Each year the colliery consultative committee received an invitation to visit the steel works and have lunch with the senior management. It was during one of these lunches that the lodge treasurer endeared himself to everyone. An excellent lunch had been provided in the sumptuous dining room, quite different from the canteen facilities at the colliery. The *hors d'oeuvre* was a succulently dressed slice of melon, but when the young waitress placed his plate before the treasurer, he turned towards her with a disarming and excusing smile to say, "No thank you, I don't like cucumber". Maldwyn Williams, the lodge treasurer, was a delightful character who had a weakness similar to that of Madame Fuzzy's of habitually using the wrong word, except that his gaffes took the form of what can be called 'vowel-substitution spoonerisms', For example, there was the occasion when the consultative committee was discussing a complaint from the workmen on the screens whose job it was to separate coarse rubble from run-of-mine coal. Occasionally a stone would be so large that it had to be broken with a sledgehammer. The 'occasionally' had become 'frequently', hence the complaint. Maldwyn's contribution to the discussion was "We must illuminate these stones".

The colliery's performance gradually improved until it was almost at break-even point. I was, if not euphoric, at least well satisfied, so that an instruction from the production director to incur expenditure on a unique project left me unperturbed. We were to drive a tunnel at Bersham's expense for the benefit of Hafod. There were ventilation problems at the latter colliery and the purpose of the tunnel was to reduce the airflow resistance of its wind roads by, in effect, providing an additional return airway through connecting one of Bersham's return airways to an airway at Hafod. The opportunity of using this somewhat extraordinary method of solving Hafod's ventilation problem was a totally unexpected spin-off from Bersham's methane drainage programme that had significantly reduced the methane content of its own air. There was nothing unusual in itself, of course, in driving a tunnel, but two features made this particular exercise an interesting operation. The first was that it would be driven through the Tŷ Gwyn fault, a large fault with a throw of about 100 feet that acted as a natural barrier between the two collieries. The second feature was much more significant from the point of view of the colliery surveyors in that it called for surveying accuracy of an unusual kind in order to link together the underground layouts of the two pits. The shafts of the two collieries were about a mile and a half apart and there were over two miles of roadway in each pit leading respectively to the starting and finishing points of the new tunnel, itself about a quarter of a mile long. There were thus nearly six miles

I shake hands with Jim Hyslop, manager of the Hafod Colliery (left) after breaking through to the Bersham pit. On my left are Jack Berry (under-manager at Bersham) and Nicolai Savochenko.

of roadway to be surveyed, underground and on the surface. That part of the job was routine and did not present a problem. Aligning a particular direction, say true north, at each pit bottom, however, was a much more difficult task and one which had to be done very precisely since a slight error of alignment between the initial bearings at each pit bottom would have a cumulative effect leading to much greater error at the proposed connecting point of the two collieries. It was necessary to hang two weighted ropes down one of the shafts at each colliery at a distance apart of about 10 feet, stopping the colliery fan for several hours in the meantime to arrest the flow of air so that the ropes became absolutely stationary. The direction of the imaginary line connecting the two ropes could then be measured at the surface relative to true north. The corresponding direction at the pit bottom was thus established and the alignment of the underground workings of the one colliery relative to the other was determined. The need for such accurate measurements at the pit bottom would not have been necessary when the shafts were originally sunk because if, for example, pillars had to be left under important buildings, the acceptable margin of error could have been a dozen or so yards in the horizontal plane, while the vertical plane was irrelevant. The surveying work for the present purpose was carried out on two successive weekends, but it was impossible to say, until the connecting tunnel broke through, whether or not it had been done sufficiently accurately. It was only then that we would know whether the Bersham colliery surveyor, who was responsible for the work, deserved a medal or not. In the event he deserved a gold one, but instead of presenting him with one, we laid on a celebration party after the connection with Hafod was made to within an inch, both in plan and in section, a few months later.

The celebration was barely over, however, when the news came that Llay Main was to close in three months time. Everyone knew, of course, that pits had been closing in other parts of the country, but even so, that one should be closed so close to home was a shock. The announcement had an immediate effect on morale at Bersham. Men adopted a fatalistic attitude, saying that our time was not far off and that it was pointless trying to avoid an inevitable end. In fact, Bersham survived another twenty years, a period long enough, it seems to me, to have justified the effort involved to keep the colliery alive. I felt at the time, however, that the best response to the announcement of Llay Main's closure was to put the facts of Bersham's position, together with my honest opinion of our prospects, to the workforce. I therefore called a meeting of all who were employed at the colliery. The meeting was held at the Wrexham Miners' Institute one Saturday morning that summer of 1966. A large crowd of about 500 men attended and we discussed Bersham's future for nearly three hours. The meeting became a penetrating inquiry into the colliery's future, conducted by ordinary miners with a seriousness and a pertinence worthy of a forensic examination by experienced barristers. I was delighted by the responsible understanding shown throughout the morning and the acceptance without a trace of scepticism, let alone cynicism, of my honest opinion that we had a fair chance of continuing in business, especially as we had broken into the coking coal market. I said that I was prepared to forecast that we would at least outlive the other collieries in the Wrexham coalfield. Collieries had obviously become expendable and the only people who could safeguard Bersham's future were the people employed there. I emphasised openly the notion that it was a case of Bersham against the rest and I was thrilled to feel the response that followed.

I went home from the meeting full of enthusiasm for the future, but I had not anticipated the workings of providence. About a month after the meeting, the Area General Manager called at my office and released a thunderbolt. Hafod colliery was in serious difficulty, losing money heavily and the relationship between workmen and management was desperately bad. If the situation continued for much longer, the pit was sure to close. Would I be prepared to go there as manager? I was dumbfounded. After getting my breath back, I gave the area manager an account of the meeting that I had called a month earlier. I said that it would be difficult to reconcile my call to arms of 'Bersham against the rest', with my deserting the colliery just a month later. What would everyone think? And in any case, I said to myself, I had made many friends at Bersham who knew my ways and with whom I had a very constructive working relationship. On the other hand, I thought, was not manager of Hafod the ambition I had cherished for many years until I had been seduced by the environment, which had grown around me at Bersham? There was also the flattering thought that Hafod was in trouble and I was being given the opportunity of riding in as the white knight to rescue the damsel in distress. All these thoughts were jumbled in my mind while

I was talking to the area manager. If I had been given twenty-four hours to brood over the matter, I might have declined the offer, but the area manager was insistent that he wanted an answer that afternoon. I suppose that what finally tilted the balance was the fact that no-one had actually said officially that the pit's days were numbered and my congenital optimism expressed itself by thinking that where there is life there is hope. I agreed to go to Hafod and I began to prepare myself for what was bound to be a difficult task there and for the even more difficult task of explaining to my friends at Bersham why I was saying farewell.

11. Death of a Colliery

There was a world of difference between Hafod and Bersham collieries, both technically and, in recent years, in human terms. Hafod had always been the easier enterprise in matters of geology; its take was divided conveniently by a few major faults into large undisturbed areas of coal, roofs were stronger and more easily supported, the pit was dry and not especially gassy. Furthermore, it had enjoyed substantial capital investment after nationalisation so that its production facilities were better than those of its neighbour. Its big weakness, which it shared with Bersham, was lack of reserves, a hardly unexpected inadequacy for a pit sunk in 1864.

Hafod also shared with Bersham a loss-making record reaching back over several years. Morale was low and even more worrying was the deep antipathy between the workforce and the management, an antipathy expressing itself in endless curmudgeonly bickering. It was quite obvious that the will-to-win was non-existent, a weakness that did not take one long to realise was the result of deplorable management practices extending over a number of years. The immediate technical problem facing the pit appeared to be an extremely simple one, however; so much so that its solution almost blinded one by its conspicuousness. For several days I could not bring myself to believe that it could be so obvious and I fretted over

Manager of Bersham Colliery.

whether I was failing to see some hidden difficulty or other.

There were four principal coalfaces at the pit, each in a different seam. Not only was this an inadequate number but, to make matters worse, two of the faces were being worked as hopelessly unprofitable concerns. A quarter of the underground workforce was employed in the Smith seam, or Top Yard as the Coal Board called it, a seam two feet four inches thick. Unfortunately, firstly because a 'bind coal' roof six inches thick had to be left to support the mudstone roof and secondly because the shearing machine was itself 42 inches high, as much fireclay was sheared from the floor as coal was sheared from the seam. To make matters worse, the 'run-of-mine' mixture of coal and fireclay was ground by the machine to a small size so that in order to wash the product to an acceptable quality, a large proportion of the coal was washed away with the fireclay. The result was that only about 100 tons of saleable coal was finally produced for every 400 tons run-of-mine brought to the surface. The economic viability of the face was hopeless.

A second face was being worked on the far side of the Tŷ Gwyn fault that in the past had been recognised as the boundary between Hafod and Bersham collieries. This face was the result of an attempt by Hafod to exploit an extremely disturbed and difficult area of Quaker coal that had been abandoned by Bersham some years previously on the very grounds of its difficulty and unprofitability. Another quarter of the Hafod workforce had been employed here for two years, during which the face workers had performed miracles to work the face at all. The output during that time, however, had been less than one twentieth of the output normally expected from that seam. To persist with the district was not only very foolish but deserving of censure in the light of the dangerous face conditions, the like of which I had seen only on the excessively long Quaker face at Bersham which I had been forced some years earlier to shorten. There were two other districts, one in the Powell seam and the other in the Main Coal, the latter seam being easily the most productive and profitable. Unfortunately, the Main Coal reserves were sufficient for little more than three years at the current rate of extraction.

My first action as manager was immediately to abandon the Quaker face and re-deploy the men to prepare a second face in the Main Coal. The effect of this decision on the profit-and-loss account was marginal. Within four months the new face came into production and made a significant improvement to the colliery results although they still showed a loss. Of course, there was now a life of barely 18 months remaining in the Main Coal and there was a desperate need for a really substantial rescue package. That package stood out like a lighthouse on a headland.

I recalled as a boy hearing my father boasting about the Four Foot seam and how he had earned good money 'filling' for my grandfather in it. His wages then, he used to say, were good enough for him to get a mortgage and build a new house in Pant in 1936. The seam was in fact 54 inches thick and according to my father was easily worked. Now in 1966, there were reserves of coal in the seam sufficient for 25 years' exploitation. But if the seam were so good, I asked myself, how was it that it was worked for a mere four years up to 1939, only to be abandoned? This was the question over which I had fretted for several days. At last I had a brainwave. I paid a visit to the former colliery agent who had been responsible to the board of directors during the 1930s. An old man, he still lived in Wrexham and he greeted me warmly, anticipating a welcome gossip about matters mining. He provided an immediate and convincing answer to the Four Foot conundrum, which with my socialist upbringing I should have rumbled earlier. When war broke out in 1939, commercial pressures on the coal industry lightened considerably and thus, management took advantage of the opportunity to work some of the more difficult and less viable seams. The Four Foot was kept, in the old agent's words, 'for a rainy day'. It was the perfect answer to my questioning and, to crown everything I had the pleasure of hearing the roadway leading to the seam called 'Bob Ellis's road' after my grandfather who had driven it initially.

I immediately began the preparatory work for developing the seam, making use of the workmen from the abandoned Quaker face for the purpose. The work entailed a considerable amount of reorganisation making new roadway junctions, driving additional roadways to the seam, rearranging haulage facilities and so on, which meant that the seam would not begin producing coal for some nine months, or in other words about four or five months after the new Main Coal district had commenced production. I anticipated that there would then be a substantial improvement in the colliery's performance. Then too, we would abandon the Smith seam and develop second and third faces in the Four Foot. Overall, the colliery's prospects would have been transformed 'just like that' as Tommy

Cooper might have said. It was an inexplicable mystery to me and remains so to this day that the management at the colliery early in the 1960s had not grasped the lifeline presented to them by the Four Foot. My guess is that their lack of initiative stemmed from a stifling relationship with the central bureaucracy, a relationship that a major objective of mine at Bersham, almost from the start, had been to loosen.

The bureaucracy in fact demonstrated its appalling managerial incompetence almost immediately on my arrival at Hafod. On my second day at the colliery I found that a requisition had been prepared at Manchester for the purchase of a replacement for the main colliery fan. The old Waddle centrifugal fan was to be replaced by a new axial flow fan at a cost of about a quarter of a million pounds (at 2004 prices). The pit could clearly not afford a new fan unless there were compelling reasons of safety justifying the expenditure of such a large sum. I had a ventilation survey carried out which showed that the existing arrangements were satisfactory. The connecting tunnel driven from Bersham colliery a short time previously had fulfilled more than was expected of it and there was now no difficulty in providing adequate ventilation for the whole of the underground workings. I thus tried to have the requisition cancelled, but the vested interests of the engineering department at headquarters succeeded in having my vehement protests disregarded. The fan was installed a few months before the colliery closed.

I attended the meeting of the colliery consultative committee for the first time a fortnight after arriving as manager and did so in a decidedly up-beat mood. I felt that outlining the highly positive strategy that had providentially fallen into my lap would be a good start towards improving morale. The committee's response was grievously disappointing. I had expected my message to bring some cheer in an all-pervading gloom, but the members took what I had to say as nothing more than propaganda having no relationship with the facts. Furthermore, they wished to make it clear that they would not allow me to deceive them with empty words. Nor would they be prepared to facilitate the considerable upheaval in the employment of their members that my plans required. The atmosphere of unbridled nihilism was heart breaking, but I consoled myself by hoping and indeed expecting, that their attitude was not something congenital, but a response to the appalling relationship that had developed in recent years between men and management.

I had already heard the gossip about the former manager and the under-manager who, in Rhos, had acquired the reputation of bogeymen. I was aware of the allegations of uncontrollable temper against the manager and, in particular, of the now notorious, if possibly apocryphal, incident when in a meeting with a union delegation he threw his telephone through the window, breaking the glass in the process, while shouting deafeningly in response to an appeal for calm, "I'm not losing my temper".

The under-manager was more implacable in his narrow self-righteousness, more insidious and more destructive. He was a Lancastrian and had been employed for most of his working life at collieries in the Wigan area until coming to Hafod in 1962 as my father's successor. He was unhappy at Hafod for two reasons in particular. The first was the language. Welsh was spoken habitually by the large majority of the workmen and the under-manager had come to hate hearing it spoken, so much so that he appeared paranoid about it and accused people of abusing him behind his back, so to speak, by deliberately talking to each other in Welsh in his presence. I sympathised with him, but at the same time realised that to a considerable extent he had created his own misfortune by his unseemly arrogance from the day when he first arrived at Hafod. After all, I told him, there had been many managers and under-managers working happily there over the years who spoke no Welsh. My sympathy was misplaced for he seemed to regard the workmen as sub-human and, of course, little by little, his reputation spread. When I arrived at the colliery the workmen's attitude towards him had reached the stage when he was laughed at, with the men doing the very thing he hated, talking about him in Welsh in his presence and doing so more flippantly than scornfully. For example, someone would shout in Welsh as he approached a group of men "Look out Bill, here comes bogeyman". A wry and rather sad question that he once asked me involved a Welsh word for 'bogeyman'. He had obviously heard it many times as it had become part of a catch phrase. "What is this '*bolol*' I keep hearing?" he asked.

Apart from his troubles with the language, however, with which I sympathised in the sense that I knew that many people become irritated if they feel excluded from a conversation, there was a deeper reason for his misanthropy. The man was verging on being pathologically mentally ill. I realised with dismay that I had a serious problem, one to which I never succeeded in finding a solution. As under-manager he was highly competent in a technical engineering sense, industrious and meticulous in his work. His failure was in managing men and in his inability to lead a team. Quite to the contrary he created discord and strife as he made clear his perception of the workmen as a lower species to be driven as oxen before the plough. I had several long conversations with him to try to persuade him to modify his attitudes, saying that the men, if driven, would be as stubborn as mules, but that if led, they would follow to kingdom come. Our conversations, however, were those of the deaf. Indeed, from the certainties of his convictions he saw me as a weak manager, prepared to compromise at the drop of a hat. I had long been accustomed to such accusations, which were a reflection of the management culture traditional in the industry.

I explained the problem to the Area General Manager and told him that it would be extremely difficult to turn Hafod colliery around if the under-manager remained there. I suggested that the best solution would be to transfer him to Gresford where little Welsh was spoken and where the cosmopolitan workforce was more amenable to abrasive management. He rejected my suggestion and therefore, as a poor alternative, I began to develop a style of management whereby I by-passed the under-manager and worked directly through the overmen. I trusted them sufficiently, at least to half-explain my problem and to admit that I was deceiving the under-manager. Naturally, I found the tactic an extremely disagreeable one to implement; the overmen, no doubt, found it not only disagreeable but also highly demanding, as they had to serve two masters of very different persuasions. They responded extraordinarily well, not to say deviously, but it was an extremely unsatisfactory situation and a serious obstacle to my efforts at improving the pit's performance. Despite the difficulty, however, the work of preparing faces in the new seam went ahead quickly and I looked forward eagerly to the day when we would start producing coal from the Four Foot seam.

Unknown to me, however, our fate had already been decided. The first fateful step was taken when the North Wales Area was abolished as a semi-autonomous administrative unit within the Coal Board's managerial structure. There were originally three bureaucratic levels in being, the London, the divisional and the area offices. In the North Western Division, some 60 collieries were located within the five areas of Burnley, Manchester, North Wales, St Helens and Wigan, each area having a fair measure of independence in terms of policy-making. At vesting day in 1947, eight collieries — Llay Main, Llay Hall, Gresford, Point of Ayr, Bersham, Hafod, Black Park and Ifton — formed the North Wales Area and employed about 9,000 men.

Black Park and Llay Hall were closed peremptorily and without fuss early in 1947, but the closure of Llay Main in 1964 caused a great deal of concern. By this time pits were being closed in many areas and inevitably, the time came at the end of 1965 when the Board's administrative arrangements were reorganised. The five areas of the

North Western Division were abolished and replaced by a central headquarters at Manchester. The loss of the North Wales Area's independence and identity was fatal for Hafod, although I did not realise it at the time. The first sign that a cold wind was blowing in our direction came six months after we had started developing the Four Foot seam when I received a note from the marketing department — now based in Manchester — claiming that the quality of the Four Foot coal, which they said had an ash content of 16 per cent and a sulphur content of 3 per cent, was not good enough for the market. I was annoyed for two reasons — firstly I knew that the figures quoted by the marketing department were not correct and secondly it was clear that the department was being disingenuous. I knew that coal of worse quality than that quoted for the Four Foot was in fact being sold currently in the Coal Board's north-west region and that in any case Four Foot coal had been sold successfully in the 1930s when the market was even more discriminating than in 1967.

Individual departments in large enterprises often tend to regard their own interests as of overriding importance. It seemed natural, therefore, that the marketing department should demand the best quality coal possible and its response to our developing the Four Foot seam at Hafod was not necessarily grounds for abandoning the project. Instead, we gave an eminently practical reply to the criticism. About 150 tons of Four Foot coal was produced laboriously by hand from the short length of face that had already been opened and was put through the normal washing process even though the resultant saleable product would underrate the quality of the coal for two reasons. Firstly, the coal won by hand was larger than the slack and fine coal produced by a disc shearer. As a consequence, the sulphur disseminated throughout the hand-got coal in the form of pyrites would not be so well ground up to be washed out in the colliery washery. Secondly, not enough coal was available for the test to provide a washing time long enough for the various settings of the washery machinery to be at their most precise for the new type of coal.

The test was supervised by the Board's scientific department who produced an estimated analysis of Hafod 'washed smalls' on the assumption that half the colliery output came from the Four Foot seam. The department's figures of 10.9 per cent ash and 2.5 per cent sulphur content compared favourably with the 20 per cent ash and 3.0 per cent sulphur of coal being sold in Lancashire at the time. At Hafod, therefore, we continued to prepare for the Four Foot with some confidence.

A second gust of cold air blew a little later, however and this time much more strongly. I received a note from the production director asking me to arrange a formal meeting between him and the union leaders at the colliery. The note included a formal statement that the prospects for the pit's future were poor and that, in the Coal Board's jargon, it was to be placed 'in jeopardy', At the meeting the director read a lengthy statement containing a large number of statistics, which, he claimed, showed that it would be impossible for the pit to improve its performance significantly even when the Four Foot was in full production and that the continued existence of Hafod in the long term was doubtful. He made the mistake of overstating his case and gradually his figures, piling one upon the other, became ever more tendentious and suspect. Typically, he had no copies of his statement to distribute, but under pressure from the union he promised to provide them in due course. When they finally came to hand, it was clear that his assessment was so prejudiced as to be grossly misleading. Thus began a debate, never to be resolved, about the contribution of the virtually virgin Four Foot seam to the colliery's performance.

Collieries are closed usually for one or other of two reasons; either because their reserves of coal are exhausted, or because their exploitation cannot be continued at a commercial level acceptable at the time. The two factors are, of course, interdependent because the more the coal is worked, the more difficult and costly and therefore the less commercially viable, the remaining coal becomes to work. A reciprocal relationship exists between extensiveness of extraction and commercial viability and it was arguable in the case of Hafod as to where on the scale of that relationship lay the decision to close the colliery. It is clear with hindsight, however, that a third factor was in fact the ultimate determinant. It was an extraneous one and quite arbitrary in terms of its immediacy. From about 1958 onwards, as difficult post-war circumstances eased, normal commercial judgements began to play an increasingly important role in the management of the nationalised industries, not least the coal industry. An indication of the new mood was the government's White Paper *The Economic and Financial Obligations of the Nationalised Industries,* published in 1961, which set out to clarify, if only partly, the criteria by which the performance of the industries was to be judged. In 1967, the government acted even more directly in the case of coal by instructing the Coal Board to cut its annual output to a figure of 155 million tons by 1970. A large number of collieries had to close and thus Hafod's fate was decided, although at the time we at the colliery were not aware of the fact.

One of the more human consequences of that first meeting with the director was the sending of samples of Four Foot coal to the wives of members of the Coal Board, including Lady Robens, asking for their opinion on its suitability as a household fuel. We received replies from several of the wives, all of whom expressed satisfaction with the coal, although of course, they could have done so for reasons of what might be called 'old style' political correctness. The replies were certainly diplomatic in the sense that no one said that her home was centrally heated by oil or gas. Alas, the housewifely opinions, most welcome though they were, had no effect on Hafod's future.

The next development, however, was far from welcome and it was cruelly sudden. Three weeks after the meeting with the director, the colliery closed on the Friday afternoon for the annual fortnight holiday. On the Saturday morning, when the majority of the union leaders could not be contacted, I received a message from the director instructing me to call a special meeting on the Monday a fortnight hence when, on the colliery's resumption of work, he would meet the union representatives. He and some of his senior colleagues would attend 'to discuss the pit's position'. The meeting took place on the stipulated day when the director read another long statement full of statistics 'proving' that it was necessary to produce a daily output of 1927 tons for the colliery to 'break even'. "That is not possible," he said, "and therefore it is my solemn duty to tell you that Hafod colliery will close on 18 November 1967".

The union representatives were stunned, not simply by the statement itself but by the manner in which it had been announced. Their response was bitter, angry and sarcastic. One man commented that he disputed the figure of 1927 tons: "It was clearly at least a hundredweight too high". After two hours of quarrelling and barren argument, I terminated the meeting, the union officials having said that they would appeal against the decision. For my part, the policy now became one of commencing production from the Four Foot as soon as possible. I estimated that the face would be ready by mid-September and that, therefore, there would be two months within which we could prove its potential. I had not, however, foreseen the perverse mood in Manchester.

Two days after the meeting, I received an instruction that the work of preparing the face in the Four Foot was to cease forthwith. I protested vigorously on the grounds of the decision's perverseness: there was nothing to lose, I said and at least we would have a definitive answer to the question of the seam's commercial viability. The response was curt and categoric: under no circumstances was I to allow the work to continue. I took that to mean that the director was determined that our argument was not to be put to the test and that the pit was to close on the 18 November, come what may. Those last words were shortly to be proved wrong by a wholly unexpected intervention.

The National Union of Mineworkers supported our efforts to keep the pit open as a going concern. Their chief mining engineer came to Hafod a few days after the closure announcement to prepare a report on the pit's prospects if it were allowed to continue in production. The report, which was presented to the National Coal Board a fortnight later, supported the validity of our arguments and urged the Board to accept them and allow the pit at least to demonstrate the new seam's potential. During the previous week, however, the unexpected intervention occurred which rendered the proposed closing date academic. Providence, in the unlikely guise of Harold Wilson, intervened to provide us with a breathing space.

Controversy had arisen nationally when it became apparent that the Board's closure programme involved closing sixteen collieries in various parts of the country. The prime minister intervened personally to delay the programme, presumably for populist reasons and each of the pits was given a four months' extension of life over the winter. The financial burden would be carried by the taxpayer. I noticed with some cynicism, incidentally, that the monthly profit and loss accounts of both Hafod and another north-west colliery, which was one of the sixteen, appeared suddenly to have worsened greatly, while those of one or two other collieries improved inexplicably. The effect of the prime minister's intervention on life at Hafod was not especially dramatic. Indeed, one of the more intriguing aspects of the uncertainty and waiting during this period, was the seeming indifference of the miners to the prospect of losing their employment. While the colliery management and the union leaders worked up great heads of steam, the miners themselves, once the first shock was over, seemed as if they were spectators enjoying the humour of a comedy of errors. I recall one young haulage hand telling me that he had been offered a job in another pit with a terraced house thrown into the bargain. The drawback was, he said, that there were two Chinese families residing on each side of the house. "I see no problem with that," I said, "where's the pit?"

"In China," he replied dryly. It was only towards the end when the detailed administrative arrangements were being applied that the bitterness and anger became manifest.

The next significant development was the Coal Board's refusal to accept the report of the NUM engineer; worse still, the Board confirmed the divisional director's decision not to allow the colliery to work the Four Foot seam during the four months extension of life it had been granted. It was an astonishing decision, because if the seam were worked, it would indubitably improve the colliery's performance and Hafod would not make as great a loss as it would otherwise do (I personally believed that it would make a small profit), thus saving the taxpayer money. Such a consideration, however, was apparently too trivial to matter and in any case it would be embarrassing if the arguments advanced from colliery sources were confirmed. The NUM report was based on a much more plausible assessment of statistics than that of the Board; it had also been presented cogently by the general secretary of the union. When, therefore, it became clear that the Board was adamant in face of all the evidence, even to the point of not allowing the pit the cost-free opportunity of justifying its case, I decided that the battle was lost and that there was nothing further we could do to save the colliery. We had to direct our energies at 'abandoning ship in an orderly manner' as I told the union officials in that rather worn cliché.

Their response, however, was uncompromising. They were not prepared to accept that the pit was to close and they would do all in their power to reverse the Board's decision. Their first move was to the political arena where they met the minister of state at the Welsh

Office and later the Economic Council for Wales. Their efforts were fruitless and although they continued to hold a number of large protest rallies at the Rhos Miners' Institute and refused to meet the colliery management to discuss closure arrangements, the fate of the pit was by now beyond doubt.

Winter was passing and March was approaching. The need arose to make arrangements for sending dismissal notices to the majority of the workmen. The intention was that some 200 men would be retained for a few months at Hafod salvaging the most valuable underground machinery, 300 would be transferred to Bersham and Gresford collieries, a handful to Point of Ayr or other distant collieries if they were prepared to make a long daily journey or to move home and the remainder would be dismissed. My plan was to set up four teams to interview every man in the presence of a union official and attempt to place as many men as possible according to their wishes. Unfortunately, the union advised its members not to attend for interview. Consequently, men were allocated to the various categories by management alone, taking into account factors such as age, length of service, work experience and so on. Appropriate letters were prepared, addressed to every man, ready for posting at a moment's notice. Nothing then remained to be done other than to wait for the day of posting.

In the meantime, however, a little diversion took place, which warmed my heart with its pleasing expression of human nature. An elderly back-ripper came to see me: he wanted to purchase his oil Davy lamp when the pit finally closed, a lamp, which he had carried for many years. He felt a sentimental attachment to it and was anxious to have it as a memento of a lifetime in the pit. I explained that the Coal Board did not in fact own the 250 oil lamps at the pit, but hired them on a monthly rental basis from a private company. I did, however, promise to make inquiries about the possibility of purchasing them; and so began a small business venture of mine when I found that the company was prepared to sell all the lamps at a price of two pounds fifty pence each. I took a deep breath and bought the lot. The news that the lamps were on sale spread like a fire in a haystack and within a few days I had sold them all except three. For the more business-minded of my readers I hasten to say that I sold them at the same price as that at which I bought them. The three remaining lamps — my own, that of my father when he was under-manager and that of my uncle Edward who had been an overman at the pit — stand today on the mantelpiece of our drawing room for the same reasons of sentiment as those of the back-ripper.

A spark of hope flashed at the end of January. The personnel director at Manchester had directed that the dismissal notices should not be posted until he authorised the action. The last day of posting according to the director if the notices were to have legal effect was, surprisingly, five weeks before the closure date of 9th March. At three o'clock on the Friday five weeks before the day, I had not received authority. Could there have been a change of policy at the last moment? I phoned Manchester and received the reply I half-expected; there had been an administrative error and I should have been authorised. I posted the notices and waited for the reaction.

Many workmen felt that they had been affronted and were furious; some who wished to be transferred to another pit had been dismissed, others who wished to be made redundant and to collect their redundancy payment had been transferred elsewhere. I spent the next few weeks trying to resolve as many of the problems as possible, ignoring the legal niceties in the process. The union still maintained its uncompromising stance and refused to cooperate in the heartbreaking exercise.

On the last Friday a special meeting of the consultative committee was held, a very special meeting. Its tenor was more bantering than sad, at least on the surface and everyone had something to say; indeed the meeting was more like a fellowship meeting in a Welsh chapel with my asking everyone in turn to 'give his experience'. On 9 March 1968, at 104 years of age, Hafod y Bwch colliery wound its last rope of coal and on the following Monday work began on closing the pit literally. I was shocked and rather disappointed to find myself deriving some satisfaction at being the last colliery manager at Hafod and I tried to put the childish thought out of my mind, but I knew that many of the miners had similar childishly sentimental feelings on that last day. The very last dram of coal was taken to the Hafod Miners' Club to be, if hardly a monument, at least a memento of the effort and enterprise undertaken beneath the fields of the Maelor for a hundred years.

I remained at Hafod for the following three months supervising the work of dismantling the machinery underground and transporting it to the surface for despatch to other collieries. It was a leisurely task after the hurly-burly of running a pit in production and I became accustomed to start the day by reading a newspaper for half an hour and to taking an hour for lunch at a country pub on the bank of the river Dee nearby. I kept pondering pointlessly what would have happened had I gone to Hafod as manager three years earlier than I did. The great mistake of my predecessors was their failure to develop the Four Foot and thus be in a position to provide jam today rather than promise it for tomorrow. The reasons for their failure remain a mystery.

Towards the end of the three months of leisure, when I was beginning to tire of it, the production director called at my office to say that I would be returning to Bersham the following week. Thus, eighteen months after leaving the place, I walked once again at 8 o'clock one morning up the familiar stairs to my office. I was happy to be back, although I knew that almost certainly I would not be there for long. I had been adopted as its prospective parliamentary candidate by the Wrexham Constituency Labour Party to contest the Wrexham constituency, a safe Labour seat.

12. Change of Tack

I was born the son of a coalminer who was an ardent member of the Labour Party, the party of unquestioned local hegemony in the Wrexham area. It was hardly unexpected, therefore, that I should have embraced the politics of the Left. My mother, however, saw things differently. She was sceptical of the nirvana in which my father expected to find himself when a Labour government was elected with a good majority in the House of Commons. Their attitudes reflected their temperaments, my father positive and optimistic, anticipating daylight at the end of the darkest night, my mother negative and full of foreboding, drawing a peevish pleasure, as the dusk grew gloomier. I inherited my father's temperament and followed him with the same confidently held illusions into the fold of the Labour Party. I became a member in 1943 at the age of nineteen.

Looking back with the hindsight of sixty years, I see that it was not so much filial piety, important though that was, as the idealism and naivety of youth that drew me to the Labour cause, characteristics that should not be scorned out of hand in a political party, although at times they have been stumbling blocks in the way of good democratic government. I add the qualifying clause because these were the hallmarks of the pre-war Labour Party and they did it great harm years later. They were enabled to do so mainly because Labour was, above all, a doctrinal party, a characteristic the dangers of which became manifest at the end of the 1970s, when the naivety and narrowness to which its doctrine had succumbed, undermined its appeal and rendered the party unelectable.

The intrinsic weakness of Labour doctrine from the beginning was its emphasis on economism, a preoccupation blinding the party both to the potential and to the problems of a developing mass-democracy. Not only did the words 'production, distribution and exchange' form the core of the Labour Party's constitution, but also they were activities for which only the state was to be responsible. The more the party focussed on them and yoked them to the state, the more it lost sight of crucially important, subjective human needs, needs which after the war were becoming ever more obvious and ever more pressing. In short, the immediate post-war Labour Party was slave to an epistemology of which Marx had been the foremost victim; as a consequence economic technique dominated its thinking and blurred its political vision. During the period of the Attlee government, however, that strategic weakness was masked by the memory of the great depression of the 1930s and the immediate need for post-war economic recovery. Aneurin Bevan's goal of capturing the commanding heights of the economy carried enough resonance, not only for party activists, but also to a lesser degree for the public, to justify the election of a Labour government.

The idea of promoting 'subjects of the crown' to the status of citizens of a democracy, in so far as it was thought about at all, was

Facing page: Wrexham Labour Party Committee, 1922, at the time of the election of Wrexham's first Labour MP. Back row (L–R): W. Evans; Cyril O. Jones; James Idwal Jones; Sam Green; Arthur Davies; Colenso Fletcher; Naden Povah; E. Williams. Middle row: E. J. Williams; Dai Mitchell, Dan Thomas; Rev Wyre Lewis; Rev E. K. Jones; Rev D. Morris; Tomi Rogers; Francis Lettsome; S. T. Jones. Front row: Miss Dolly Punchard; Mrs E. M. Edwards; J. W. WIlliams (Jac Wil); Hugh Hughes; J. T. Edwards; Harry Edwards; Mrs E. Barnett; Mrs B. Povah. Inset: Robert Richards, M.P.

seen not just as a diversion, but as a positive hindrance to the state's task of economic management: after all 'the man in Whitehall knew best'. Labour positivism deemed the concept of an empowered and responsible citizenry incompatible with the need for a body-politic as an aggregation of docile, identical and interchangeable subjects living regulated lives under centrally imposed conditions. Whatever other 'warring antinomies' might have afflicted Labour doctrine, social change and the erosion of deference by the spread of technical knowledge, rendered an enthusiasm for social engineering infeasible. The long-standing failure to appreciate this profound social change remains a weakness at the higher levels of New Labour and Britain remains a stunted democracy in which the public, perhaps more than ever in the sense of not knowing their place, lead politically irresponsible lives. David Marquand has summed up the situation as follows: 'In the prevailing view of politics, the public are not only passive, they are also irresponsible. The politicians answer to them, but they answer to nobody. All they have to do is to express their privately determined preferences in the secrecy of the polling booth. Responsibility for translating those preferences into action lies conveniently with someone else and there is always someone else to blame if things go wrong.'

In a concluding chapter to the book *Democracy: The Unfinished Journey*, John Dunn distinguishes two components of that state of affairs which has made democracy the dominant ideology of the modern world. The first is simply democracy's great human appeal as an idea, the second is the combination of circumstances — economic, social and political — which have given it validity. 'If we look back to the second half of the eighteenth century and ask why it is that a political conception that seemed so comprehensively crushed by historical experience could revive so dramatically and begin to turn the tables so thoroughly on its adversaries, the contrast between appeal and viability gives a decisive clue to the answers.' Dunn links the viability with the growth of the market state and finds the linkage definitively confirmed by the demise of communism, democracy's ideological rival. He is referring, of course, to the representative democracy of the modern state and suggests that it provides citizens with three main benefits — moderate government, responsibility of governments to the governed and a less obviously consequential economic benefit from the interaction between democracy, the state and capitalism.

The first two benefits are fairly self-evident although the democratic processes leading to them can be complex and difficult to trace in detail — the moderation of democratic governments, for example, is all the more remarkable in the light of the revelation during the twentieth century of the populist nature of totalitarianism. The two benefits result from modifying both the state and Athenian-style democracy, or as Dunn memorably puts it, representative democracy 'draws the sting of two extreme and potentially perilous ideas'. The totalitarian tendencies of the unconstrained state are a matter of historical experience; the potential hazards of random power-to-the-people are often advanced as an argument against full participatory democracy, the experience of post-revolutionary France, for example, being one of the most striking instances.

More complex factors surround the third benefit of economic well-being. The complexity conceals a parallel progression between the economic and the democratic processes in at least one important respect. The initial premise of Dunn's economic argument is that 'extravagantly complicated and deeply unobvious causal judgements' are involved in the efficient working of a modern economy. The inherent difficulties are compounded by the fact that in such an economy a multitude of free individual choices are made in two wholly different fields, the economic and the political and 'there is no reason whatever why the choices made in either field should ever dovetail neatly with those made in the other'. Sound choice from the point of view of society as a whole implies an 'understanding [of] what is really going on', that is to say an understanding of the limitless range of factors which go to make modern societies and modern economies what they are. Conventional practice delegates the shouldering of 'these awesome cognitive responsibilities' to the state. Dunn argues persuasively, however, that the state alone as an institution is inadequate to the task. His argument is buttressed by the economic success of constitutional democracies in comparison with undemocratic states, a comparison providing powerful evidence for the political legitimacy of representative democracy as a modifier of the state.

The legitimacy has been deepened by a phenomenon appearing on a comprehensive scale during the latter half of the last century, a phenomenon which in one sense links the two parts of this autobiography. The influence of scientific innovation on the norms of successful industrial management was discussed earlier in the chapter on management theory. Its effects extend beyond industrial management, however. More perhaps than any other single influence scientific innovation has finally weighted the scales against communism and other dirigiste systems in favour of democracy. That is because the social and political consequences of management attitudes, structures and requirements are reflected in society generally, just as they were in Victorian times and are ever more influential as society adapts to the new climate, although more successfully in some countries than in others. Advanced industrial societies routinely demand knowledge, initiative and responsibility of millions of citizens. Political structures and culture have to reflect this social reality if they are to be effective. Dunn's 'awesome cognitive responsibilities' have become even heavier as innovative capability has become indispensable. In short, democracy has progressed from a merely viable to an essential condition.

Dunn ends his chapter with 'three great questions still

[confronting] representative democracy as a state form with unique claims to legitimate political authority'. Britain's misfortune at the beginning of the twenty first century is that her democracy has yet to reach the stage at which these questions pose themselves with any degree of refinement. The first question concerns economic causality and the role of government: how should economic determinism be mediated by political and social considerations? In other words, what degree and what quality of interventionism is appropriate to the government of a representative democracy and what governmental structure would best provide it? The second question is related directly to knowledge, especially scientific and technological knowledge — the new fourth 'factor of production' — and its relationship with the claims of politicians to rule, or of citizens to decide between the merits of different possible rulers. And the third question is how far representative democracy can travel advantageously along the road to participatory democracy? We are unable to answer these questions with any authority. A measure of the wretchedness of the British predicament, however, is that we are not yet asking them publicly in serious political debate.

The foregoing speculative analysis did not bother me in 1945, of course, nor for that matter did it bother anyone else in the Labour Party. The aim was simpler and more immediate, that of dispatching Mr Churchill and his party to political oblivion. I played a small but enthusiastic part in the general election campaign. The Labour Party organisation in the Merioneth constituency was weak and consequently I shouldered responsibilities that were unusually heavy for a twenty one year old callow youth. I came to know and become friends with some notable party members such as the philosopher Rupert Crawshay-Williams and his wife, a couple who together tragically committed suicide a few years later. They lived on the Portmeirion estate and I retain happy memories of suppers at their home following evenings canvassing together. I recall one occasion when we set out to raise funds for the party by canvassing the hotel and estate with a collecting box and asking for donations. We had had permission to do so from Clough Williams-Ellis, whose brother-in-law, John Strachey, was a well-known member of the Labour Party. The collection was disappointing: if I remember correctly the harvest from two hours work was less than half a crown.

A few months after the general election I accomplished two feats for the first time. I stood as a candidate for public office, namely for a seat on the Deudraeth Rural District Council and I wrote a document in Welsh for presentation to the public. My election address was written with a dictionary at my elbow and was full of grammatical errors and clumsy phraseology translated literally from an English version I had prepared full of English clichés — at the time my political thought processes were still carried out in English. Fortunately, a friend edited the address into a more idiomatic style, making it a little more presentable. I came bottom of the poll.

Three years later I was back permanently in Wrexham and attending meetings of the local party. A branch of the Fabian Society, of which I became a member, also existed in the town. The issues of the day were debated regularly at meetings of both institutions, the debates at the Fabian Society tending to be the more knowledgeable and those at the party meetings the more passionate. People spoke frankly at both sets of meetings, but at those of the party the debate sometimes tended to become rancorous. I disturbed a wasps' nest, so to speak, for the first time when I was implicitly critical of Harold Wilson shortly after he had succeeded Hugh Gaitskell as party leader. He had been asked during a radio interview about the direction he intended to lead the party and had responded by saying that he would fly the plane by the seat of his pants. As it happened, his remark turned out to be a fair summary of his premiership, the opportunism and lack of principle of which prepared the ground for the seeds of irresponsibility that grew to possess the party by the end of the 1970s. By that time the party's high-minded, if mistaken, idealism of 1945 had degenerated into obdurate dogmatism and its naivety into vicious cynicism. I did not foresee that development in 1963, of course, but instinctively I felt sufficiently worried to take Wilson's rather slick remark at its face value and cap it with an equally slick, if immature, comment of my own to the effect that no great prime minister flew the plane by the seat of his pants. The wasps buzzed around my head mercilessly in the party meeting that night, the first of many occasions for them to do so.

My first attempt to enter parliament was at the 1966 General Election when I stood as the Labour candidate in the West Flintshire constituency. The seat, held by Nigel Birch, a well-known right wing Tory, was a safe Conservative one. Some months before the election which was expected to take place fairly soon, the prospective Labour candidate resigned in order to contest the Merioneth constituency, which in due course he won, thus succeeding his Labour predecessor who had been made a life peer. The West Flintshire Labour Party, now without a candidate for the imminent election, was in some difficulty. I was asked to fill the vacancy a few weeks before Harold Wilson called the election and I accepted the invitation unhesitatingly. I spent the whole of my annual holiday on the four weeks of the election campaign to the strong disapproval of my children who covered the windows of our house with posters proclaiming 'Vote Tory'. Serious politics played no part in our campaign, which was mostly a matter of circus razzmatazz, driving up and down the streets of Rhyl and Prestatyn with a jazz band on a lorry to the slogan 'Let's knock Birch off his perch!' In the event we gave him a shock, cutting his majority from 13,000 to 3,000. The election of June 1966 was, of course, an extremely good one for Labour across the whole country.

I returned to Bersham colliery never expecting to contest another general election. Two years later, however, the sitting member for Wrexham announced that he would retire at the election expected in a year or two. I decided to seek the nomination to fill the vacancy and in due course I was chosen from a short list of five people. The election was held in June 1970 and I was elected Member of Parliament for Wrexham with a majority of 15,000.

I had not thought deeply about the politics of the Labour Party for some years — my preoccupation with the pit had prevented my doing so. I was therefore in something of a fog and had no clear vision of Labour's doctrinal weakness or even an intimate understanding of the Wilson government's record. Indeed, the only issue on which I had spoken passionately at a constituency party meeting was Ian Smith's unilateral declaration of Rhodesian independence. I feel embarrassed now when I recall the strong views I expressed without fully understanding the finer details of the situation. I argued that Wilson was making a great mistake in announcing publicly that in no circumstance would he use force against Smith and his colleagues. I was accused of all manner of iniquity, in particular that I was prepared to accept the slaughter of innocent people. Despite my embarrassment today, which has to do with the superficiality of my knowledge at the time, I believe that I was correct in my view and that the constituency party was wrong.

To come back to the aftermath of the 1970 General Election, a much more important matter developed that was to split the party and cause considerable acrimony between Wrexham party members and me. For many years I had been a supporter of British entry into what was called the Common Market. I can still recall the interest with which, in 1947, I read reports of Robert Schuman's speech outlining Jean Monnet's plan to create an European Coal and Steel Community and my growing enthusiasm as that Community led to the creation of an Economic Community. I was vociferous in my support of the latter and cherished in particular the first clause in the preamble to the Rome Treaty which read: 'Determined to lay the foundations of an ever closer union among the peoples of Europe ...'. It may have been that the word 'peoples' rather than 'states' was chosen simply for presentational purposes, but nevertheless it registered with me who rather enjoyed feeling 'the slight dissociation of the Welshman' from the all-pervading Anglo-Britishness of the state.

Britain's second attempt at membership of the Community, made by Harold Wilson, had been vetoed by President de Gaulle and by the time of the general election our proposed entry into the Community had become a highly controversial matter. That controversy, more than anything, caused me, now a full-time politician, to start thinking more deeply than previously about the Left in British politics and its doctrinal shortcomings. I began to realise how the Labour Party was prisoner, not only of its old economic rigmarole, but of British nationalism. A pleasing family development at the time was that my father, too, was becoming sceptical about the Labour Party's ideals. After the party had lost the election and become the opposition at Westminster, many members felt free to criticise what had been the party's European policy and a number of factors surfaced to reverse that policy to one of opposition to British entry. So called Euro-sceptics — Europhobes would have been a more accurate description — presented what they claimed were powerful reasons supporting their stance. In fact, many of these were misguided, others were trivial. For example, the narrow old economism surfaced: was not the Community a capitalist conspiracy, a 'rich man's club' that no right-minded socialist would submit to being a member of? At a more trivial level, 'candle-ends' arguments were advanced that Mr Gladstone would have appreciated. No one, it seemed, saw the development of the Community as a historically momentous happening; on the contrary, opponents of entry lowered the debate to the level of balancing the accounts. Would Britain be paying into the Community budget more than she would be getting out of it? A decade later at the Dublin summit, Mrs Thatcher was still arguing at that level and 'demanding her money back'. Roy Jenkins, who was then president of the Commission, commented acidly that Mr FitzGerald (Irish prime minister) had made Dublin a great international centre while Mrs Thatcher had turned London into a seedy provincial backwater. The budgetary arguments took place during a period when the total Community budget was one per cent of its gross domestic product. Another criticism trumpeted rather pathetically as a note of derision was that the European Assembly (as it was then called) was a mere talking-shop, not a 'proper parliament'. At the same time, the critics perversely complained about the Community's lack of democratic accountability. Other 'arguments' accused the European Commission of all kinds of nonsense: door-to-door milkmen were to be made illegal, bananas would have to be grown straight, not curved and so on.

The arguments were sophistical ones aimed at concealing the true reason for the antipathy towards the Community, namely British, or more precisely English nationalism. One understands how, in relation to the European Community, this particular nationalism is more virulent than nationalisms based on other ethnic, cultural, regional or linguistic characteristics and why it transformed itself into an irrational abhorrence of the political institution on the continent. The British generation into which I was born was reared in the glow of an empire 'on which the sun never set', when platitudes like 'the thin red line' denoted a handful of gallant heroes repelling hordes of barbarians, when the King Emperor could review the world's largest navy at Spithead, when we sang (although not all of us) "God who made thee mighty, make thee mightier yet," and when London was the hub around which the world revolved and so on. The inheritance, already eroding in principle before the war, was ruined in practice by the time the conflict was over, although many people refused to acknowledge the fact. Indeed, the Conservative Party under the leadership of Sir Alec Douglas-Home contested the 1964 General Election with the slogan 'a seat at the top table' as the main plank in its platform, that is to say, the United States, the Soviet Union and Great Britain if you please, jointly were to determine the destiny of the world and all its peoples. Garbage of course, but many people swallowed it. Acceptance of the loss of supremacy and of reconciling the country to a more modest role in world affairs was a more difficult pill to swallow.

13. A People's Representative

I was a 46-year-old man with some experience of the world when I was elected to Parliament at the 1970 General Election. Politically, however, I was still starry-eyed, not so much as a political theorist as in terms of down-to-earth politics. A trivial but highly significant incident in my first month as MP began for me a process of education and disillusion.

At that same general election, Sir Anthony Meyer, Bt., who years later stood against Margaret Thatcher for the leadership of the Conservative Party, succeeded Nigel Birch as member for West Flintshire. He had been defeated in his Slough constituency at the previous election and now was elected for the first time as member for a Welsh constituency. Sir Anthony, who lived within 'division-bell' distance of the House of Commons, was a generous man. He decided to hold a reception at his home for all the 36 members from Welsh constituencies, seven or eight of whom had been newly elected. I received my invitation within a month of arriving at St Stephen's and I immediately sent a note of acceptance. A few days later Leo Abse, Labour MP for Pontypool, told me in a conversation I was having with him, that I had acted deplorably in accepting an invitation from a Tory and that under no circumstance should I attend the reception. I ignored his advice and was the only Labour member present at it.

The winning candidate outside the count at the William Aston Hall, Wrexham. On the right is Nona and on the left my agent Silas Davies.

During the following week I was reproached by several members of the Welsh Labour Group and reprimanded by the Welsh whip for my solecism. I had sinned against the party.

It was a moot point, who was the more offended at my colleague's attitude: Sir Anthony who had received an unpardonable personal snub, or myself whose idea of enlightened politics had been affronted. One did not have to be a profound political theorist to realise that such a reactionary political response to a gesture made in good faith, was based on a reversion to a derelict culture that should have been decently buried at least a generation previously. They were more the politics of the 'Tonypandy Riots' of 1910 than of the words at the head of this chapter.

A less trivial but equally significant experience soon followed. I had decided to make my maiden speech at the start of the parliament during the debate on the 'Queen's Speech' in order speedily to dispose of a daunting ordeal, but also to give me a wide choice of topic on which to pontificate. A central proposal of the Heath government's first term was the introduction of new trade union legislation. I therefore devoted my speech to the subject of industrial relations, setting out some of my experiences in the coal industry. The speech must have registered with someone because, to my surprise, I was chosen as one of the Labour team under the chairmanship of Barbara Castle 'to oppose [sic] the legislation'. I was intrigued at the thought of Mrs Castle leading the Labour team. The policy she had set out a few months previously as Secretary of State for Employment in the white paper *In Place of Strife*, had ended in a debacle with her and Harold Wilson being isolated in the cabinet. A number of powerful trade union leaders had been not merely a thorn in the flesh of the Wilson government, but were posing a serious challenge to the parliamentary democratic process. Their assaults had led Harold Wilson famously to tell Hugh Scanlon to "get your tanks off my lawn". Mrs Castle's legislation was meant to remedy matters but it failed to get the backing of the Labour cabinet, not least because of Jim Callaghan's support for unfettered trade union rights. In his autobiography Roy Jenkins sums up the saga: "It was a sad story from which [Harold Wilson] and Barbara Castle emerged with more credit than the rest of us".

I now looked forward eagerly to the first meeting of Mrs Castle's team and the prospect of proposing amendments to the government's Bill to curb its most reactionary proposals and to establish, one hoped, a framework for developing more sophisticated industrial relations over time. Alas, the attitude of the leader and her team was, in essence, that of my Welsh Labour colleagues towards Anthony Meyer's invitation: the Bill was to be rejected out of hand and fought clause by clause, line by line. No one was fiercer in his opposition to it than was Mrs Castle in hers. She was a different woman from what she had been as Secretary of State battling in cabinet to curb the irresponsibility of powerful unions. This time, however, it was not Barbara Castle who was isolated, but myself. After the first meeting of the team, I played little part in the subsequent debates and I was seen by the whips as a disappointment.

The experience resulted in my beginning to question the role of the political party. Mrs Castle, as I have said, seemed to have become a different woman, except in so far as her continuing fearsome vehemence in debate reflected what must surely have sprung from a great new conviction. I could not bring myself to believe that the conviction was insincere despite her complete reversal of policy in so short a time. It gradually dawned on me, however, that the dominant factor determining her attitude was loyalty to party, the blind loyalty of my party right or wrong. I was reassured as to the correctness of that revelation through thinking back twenty five years to my discussions with my father and our then unquestioning belief in the Labour Party. Now, however, during those first few months as a member of parliament, seeds of disillusion with Labour were being sown in my mind. More importantly, I was beginning to realise that party as such, however essential it was to the parliamentary process, was, at least in part, no more than an instrument and that it should be regarded as such. I did not imagine at the time though, that within ten years I would be leaving the Labour Party to help found the SDP, inevitable as the divorce had become, while at the same time feeling no sense of disloyalty or betrayal. In 1981 the Labour Party was just an instrument that was being abused and which therefore no longer had legitimate demands on me.

The new MP with his young family; a typically posed press photograph.
L–R: Mark, Susan, Charles, me, Nona and Graham.

Other developments in my early Westminster years strengthened my growing concern about the perverted role of party in the political process. One important development involved the steel industry. Steel had been a political football throughout the fifties and sixties, having been nationalised by Attlee in 1949, de-nationalised by

Macmillan, re-nationalised by Wilson and now seemed about to be re-de-nationalised by Heath. Each change, of course, meant major upheaval in the industry and a curb on long-term investment. The bare facts surrounding the British steel industry in the early seventies were ominous. Even if the industry were working at its full capacity, which it was not, it would produce about 28 million tons of steel annually at a productivity of some 140 tons per man per year. One or two other countries were producing at a rate of over 400 tons per man per year. One did not have to be an economist to appreciate the gravity of the position, although I admit that I had been blithely unaware of the facts when I was at Bersham producing coking coal a few years previously.

Fortunately, wiser counsels finally prevailed within Conservative ranks, at least until the advent of Mrs Thatcher who washed her hands of the steel industry by denationalising it for a last time. Under Heath, proposals involving substantial public investment for restructuring the industry were introduced. They involved the closure of some works and the expansion of others, as steel making was concentrated at a few large, mainly maritime, sites. One works at which steel making was to cease, although its rolling mills were to be retained, was that at Shotton, to which Bersham colliery sold its coal and at which a hundred or so of my constituents were employed. Before this programme could be implemented, however, providence intervened in the form of a miners' strike, a three-day week and a general election that resulted in the return of a Labour government.

The immediate consequence for the steel industry was the appointment of Lord Beswick to review the restructuring programme, presumably for political reasons. The review led to the mass lobby of the House of Commons by steel workers from Shotton during which a packed meeting of 200 men was held in a large committee room off Westminster Hall. Half a dozen Labour MPs, of whom I was one, addressed the meeting. The MPs all made the same speech: 'good lads, you are performing wonders at Shotton, fight on, backs to the wall, we shall overcome' and so on. I was the only dissenting voice as I stressed that the Deeside economy was dependent on just three main industries — steel, textiles and aircraft manufacture — each of which at the time was facing an uncertain future (textiles and steel soon disappeared, aircraft has prospered). I suggested that advantage could be taken of the steel closure to put pressure on the government to attract new industries to the region. I was booed from the floor. One of my colleagues, whose constituency had even closer connections with Shotton than mine, had made outrageously optimistic remarks at the meeting. Afterwards, when I asked him why he had said such things, he replied: "That's what they wanted to hear, so I told it them!". He had not been alone among the platform MPs in his false optimism.

The foregoing examples of my growing unease with the Labour Party were in fact marginal ones. The decisive issue that forced me truly to reappraise my early views of the party and to continue with that reappraisal over time, was the European Community and our tortured relationship with it. During the 1970 General Election, the Labour Party was strongly in favour of re-applying for membership after President de Gaulle had vetoed Britain's application some years previously. That certainly was the message I had enthusiastically trumpeted in Wrexham during the election campaign and in my innocence I had not the slightest doubt that it would be Labour's policy, come what may, after the election. After all, had not Harold Wilson and George Brown together traipsed up and down the capitals of Europe a little while earlier preaching to the text "We will not take 'No' for an answer"? And indeed had not George Brown himself preached the sermon at a public meeting in Wrexham a week before polling day?

In 1971, Edward Heath's Conservative government put the most momentous piece of legislation since the war before the House of

Commons, legislation on which there should have been no party division as both main parties advocated membership of the European Community, even though individual MPs of both parties might have had sincere differences of opinion on the question of membership. Parliament's decision on the issue would decide Britain's future over a very long time; it was thus hardly the stuff of knock-about politics. President de Gaulle had died, Britain's application for membership had at last been accepted and the necessary legislation for ratifying the government's action was now to be debated. Astonishingly however, the shadow cabinet decided to oppose the Bill despite its own determined efforts when in government to achieve the same objective. Labour had regressed beyond the Tonypandy Riots to Disraeli's axiom that it was the opposition's job to oppose. One was hard put to decide whether this axiom or Harold Wilson's 'a week is a long time in politics' deserved the booby prize for cynicism. The unprincipled change of policy on so important and long term a matter shocked many Labour MPs. We were shaken by the brazen cynicism of our leaders as well as frustrated with the change of policy, so that when the vote on the second reading of the Bill took place, 69 of us voted with the Conservative government despite the three-line whip imposed on us to vote against. I was one of the 69 and I feel proud of my action to this day. Had we not voted as we did, it is possible that the Bill would not have become law as there were rebels in the Conservative ranks who, sincerely following their consciences, also defied their whip to vote against it. Britain's membership of the present day European Union would have been delayed even more than it already had been.

My constituency party at Wrexham did not share my pride and a special meeting of the 25-strong executive committee was called to discuss my vote. The only item on the agenda was a motion of no confidence in the MP. This was the first of five such motions between 1971 and 1981 when I resigned from the Labour Party, having by then become totally disillusioned with many aspects of its performance. Among other actions of mine that led to votes of no confidence were my attitude to the restructuring of the steel industry and my becoming chairman of the Labour Campaign for Electoral Reform, but more of this later. I survived each one of the votes, but with a steadily diminishing majority. It is interesting on looking back to see how the composition of the executive committee changed over time, gradually at first but rapidly during the 1970s. I have a photograph of the Wrexham Constituency Labour Party executive committee taken in 1922, the year when for the first time a Labour MP was returned from Wrexham. At least 18 of the 26 members were Welsh speakers, three were ministers of religion, at least two were lay preachers and at least three were chapel elders. The chapel influence was less evident in 1970, but the same high-mindedness was readily discernible. During the 1970s new faces began to appear and late one night in 1978 at the end of a long meeting when some members had departed, it was decided to hold future meetings at the Wrexham Labour Club. At the first meeting at the club several new committee members appeared, bringing glasses of beer with them to the meeting. The conduct of meetings deteriorated, intemperate language became common, older members stopped attending and Liverpool accents became common. It was clear by 1979 that the Militant Tendency had arrived.

The controversy about the European Community in 1971 and during the following years was a revelation to me. I began for the first time seriously to question not only the ideology and doctrine of the Labour Party, but also the role of party as a political institution, in particular as an institution to which the public had remarkably little access. It was this latter concern which led me to take an increasing interest in the topic of electoral reform and come to regard it as being a matter of profound importance for the British political system. First, however, I tried to define for myself a radical doctrine of the Left that would be valid in the light of the far-reaching developments taking place on the continent, or the mainland as I mischievously called it in the hearing of some of my Euro-sceptic colleagues. There was more than a little justification for the mischief in the face of their self-deception regarding Britain's role in the world. Indeed. I upset the apple cart at one meeting of the parliamentary Labour Party as I tried to ram the message home. I said that debates on the floor of the House, especially on foreign affairs or defence, came across to me like Denbighshire County Council settling its policy on Vietnam. I made few friends that night.

It became increasingly evident that the Labour Party, on the one hand, was possessed by adulation of Britishness and on the other, that it had succumbed totally to the materialist ethic of capitalism and the positivism nurtured by that ethic. The political institution that had supported more than any other the growth of capitalism was the nation-state. The views of Yves Person, a distinguished French anthropologist, on this topic, made a profound impression on me. I came to know him and to have a number of discussions with him during his visits to London. Through these discussions I came to believe that the antinomy at the heart of Labour Party socialism was deepened by English chauvinism, but that the basic problem was the party's total seduction by 'the politics of production', seen in the nineteenth century as valid and self-evident. Its great claim was that it was better fitted than anyone else for the managing of 'production, distribution and exchange'. The doctrine, even after the party had split in 1981, continued to exercise its spell, with its primitivism being propounded fluently, perhaps over-fluently, by Neil Kinnock when he was a candidate for the leadership of the party. I quote from an article by Mr Kinnock in *The Times* (18 July 1983).

> Labour has a claim to present itself as the party of efficiency with far more justification than a Tory Party committed obsessively to the *Sozialmarktwirtschaft* which is rapacious in its use of finite resources,

requires the mass unemployment of labour and cannot make up its mind whether it wants expensive money for the rentier or cheap money for the producer.

The Labour Party's ideological confusion became increasingly evident as the effects of technology permeated the free market to undermine the role of the classical European nation-state as capitalism's guardian. Global capitalism demanded a wider territory than that of the nation-state. What would have been a rational development if capitalist positivism had been given its head in Europe in the twentieth century, would have been the establishment of an all-encompassing European nation-state, with all its inhabitants — its mega-ethnie to use Yves Person's scornful term — speaking the one official state language under the hegemonic rule of the dominant 'organic' nation. It did not happen although millions of lives were lost in the attempt. That experience, incidentally, is one justification for Jean-Paul Sartre's claim that to speak an oppressed minority language is to attack capitalism at its softest spot. A similar claim, aimed at the consumerist materialism of global capitalism, is made in a poem by R. S. Thomas referring specifically to the Welsh language:

> ... In a world
> oscillating between dollar
> and yen our liquidities
> are immaterial. We
> continue our relationship
> with the young David, flooring
> the cheque-book giant
> with one word taken,
> smooth as a pebble, out
> of the brook of our language.

What in fact did happen after the Second World War was the establishment of a variety of international institutions on a 'voluntary' basis, such as the Bretton Woods monetary system, the General Agreement on Tariffs and Trade, the International Monetary Fund and so on.

The Labour Party, faced with the dilemma of how to practise a British state capitalism in a global economy, attempted to resolve it in two ways, the one impractical and the other less than honest. The first was to 'defend' the country's economy by imposing tariffs and restricting the importing of goods — 'pulling up the drawbridge' as the policy was described. The second response was to fall back on the platitudes of the class war by setting up the EEC as an Aunt Sally and arguing that since the battle was world-wide, the European Community was futile and was in any case the tool of a few rich capitalist countries. To join the Community, the argument ran, was to betray the international working class and therefore betray socialism.

My own support for the Community was not ultimately based on economics, although I was of course aware of the validity of the economic arguments and I supported them. I regarded the political argument as by far the more significant. There were, it seemed to me, at least two incontrovertible arguments, with one of them possessing considerable socialist potential. The first and most obvious, was Monnet's original idea of a steady advance, using economic measures one step at a time, to reach the political goal of making war in Europe impossible. Three times in seventy years, 1871, 1914 and 1939, Germany and France, Teuton and Gaul as Lloyd George put it in 1916, had waged war on each other, the conflict developing on two occasions into a world-wide conflagration. That ambition of Monnet's was in itself sufficient justification for the European Union of today: his inspired concept of reaching a political goal by taking economic steps was a flash of genius.

My second argument, stemming possibly from Welsh dissent and an instinctive repudiation of oligarchy, is to do with hegemony. One could persuasively argue that an appropriate definition of modern socialism is encapsulated in the claim that a socialist society is a non-oligarchic one, or in the case of nations, is a non-hegemonic federation. In such societies, democratic politics are perforce a great deal less subservient to economics than they are in oligarchies. This is so in the European Union. There has been little discussion of the Union's non-hegemonic structure, although much has been said about Britain's 'loss of sovereignty'. It is clear that countries, by sharing each other's sovereignties, are in effect taking decisive steps towards non-hegemonic government. In the European Union, it is necessary to have majority agreement at the Council of Ministers, the Union's main decision-making body, for governmental decisions. This is not just a point of political theory. It has an important significance and not merely in terms of practical policy. There exists, in the Union, a governmental structure strong enough when necessary to resist the determinism of the capitalist process. We are back with one of John Dunn's questions posed in the previous chapter: what degree and what quality of interventionism is appropriate to the government of a representative democracy and what governmental structure would best provide it, or in other words, what should be the relationship between economic causality and the role of government; how should economic determinism be mediated by political and social considerations? The poets had long since seen the dangers of unbridled positivism in fields larger even than the economic. For example, R. S. Thomas has accused David Hume, possibly the first of the empiricists, of doubting human nature, of doubting even human love, thus leaving us at the mercy of:

> ... the beast that rages through history; that presides smiling at the councils of the positivists.

The problem with the Labour Party's devotion to the British nation-state as I suggested earlier is that it is consequentially at the mercy of impersonal economic development, often at cross purposes with the deepest human needs. The result is an increasingly common political reaction by, for example, minorities whose quality of life is impaired by economic development, or by people who most readily appreciate damage done in non-economic fields such as the environment. R. S. Thomas justified his espousal of Welsh nationalism mainly on the grounds that it was "a counteraction to the impersonal process of uniformity which is today everywhere at work". One suspects that his primary concern was the tide of 'Anglo-American mass mono-culture pitched to the level of the least discriminating' sweeping across the western world and causing, amongst other effects, a Welsh language crisis. That crisis is a direct example of economic determinism and its assaults on a minority language stemming from a lack of indigenous employment in Welsh-speaking areas, the increased numbers of non-economically active immigrants to those areas, the failure of the planning system to intervene and the shortcomings of the native higher education system. Governmental subservience to such developments at a British level happens for two reasons: firstly because the state is in any case not powerful enough to resist the determinist thrust and secondly because the London-based hegemony of the state ensures that such non-economic considerations are seen as unwarranted.

One sees politics prevailing more readily over economics in the European Union. The most obvious example is the Common Agricultural Policy. It is not, of course, necessarily the best available policy, either from a social or an economic standpoint, indeed demands for reform of the policy have become increasingly strident. That, however, is not the point. The policy was framed in the first instance according to political rather than economic considerations to do with balancing the interests of predominantly agricultural countries like France with countries such as Germany more oriented towards manufacturing. The sharing of sovereignty necessitated political compromise rather than a slavish bowing to global market demands. It will be interesting over the next few years to see how great an effect the entry of a number of eastern European countries has on the CAP.

There are many examples of economics overriding politics in the nation-state. Regional policy is one example of a political intention being subverted by economics, even though the ultimate aim is itself economic. The political intention when regional policies were introduced was supposedly to redress the balance of economic well being between what were called the depressed areas and the more affluent areas of the country. That intention, implied by the adoption of the euphemism 'development areas', was to reach broad economic equality across the country as a whole, a highly desirable state of affairs, not least from the point of view of national economic management. The goal has eluded all governments because none has been prepared to jeopardise the economic performance of the country. The argument goes that national economic growth is a prerequisite of growth in the development areas and that national economic growth is impossible without growth in the affluent areas. A Labour government presented the argument quite starkly in a 1975 white paper.

> Although regional policy is a factor in the decisions made by industry about the creation or maintenance of employment and the location of investment, it is not the only one or the most important. Industrialists are concerned above all with the prospects for the national economy and the government measures directed at demand management in the economy as a whole. To apply an effective regional policy based solely on incentives would be costly to the Exchequer; and to base it solely on direct controls by government would be costly for the firms concerned.
> [*Regional Development Incentives*. Cmnd. 6058, May 1975]

Not the least baleful effect for the minority nations of the UK of this governmental weakness in the face of economic determinism, not to say collusion with it, were the qualitative and demographic consequences. A Welsh example of the qualitative aspect of regional deprivation was made evident in a report published by *Y Gymdeithas Wyddonol Genedlaethol* [National Scientific Society] in 1973. The

Society examined the opportunities in Wales for employment in scientific research. It showed that in the physical and biological sciences the proportion of Welsh students graduating in Britain in 1972 was slightly greater at 5.15 per cent than the Welsh proportion of Britain's population. Of 99 government research establishments, however, employing a total graduate staff of 13,825, only two small ones employing a total of 50 graduates were located in Wales. Similarly, not one of 38 industrial research associations and only two out of 26 nationalised industry research establishments were based in Wales, the two between them employing 20 graduates. Another example of Welsh disproportionality was the fact that, of 458 UK graduate posts advertised in the journals *Nature* and *New Scientist* during 1972, only three were in Wales. A Welsh graduate who wished to pursue a career in scientific research was unable to do so in his own country. To make matters worse, the mass migration from Wales during the 1920s and 1930s, still happening, but on a lesser scale, was compounded by the substantial inward migration of retired people. The result, especially in the Welsh-speaking areas, was a growing social catastrophe.

Economic determinism of this kind undermines the human sense of identity. It is not my purpose to attempt a social analysis of the subject, but it is worth pointing out that many distinguished writers have seen economic determinism as a kind of new barbarism turning the individual into a mere economic unit within a uniform, massified consumerist society — T. S. Eliot, Simone Weil, George Orwell, R. S. Thomas, are some who come to mind. Indeed, the English translation of Simone Weil's classic *L'Enracinement* is titled *The Need For Roots*. The response to one typical act of Welsh resistance against the trend is captured in one of Raymond Garlick's poems titled *Archetypes*. In it he scathingly refers to the clerk of a Welsh magistrates' court, where Welsh language activists accused of defacing English language road signs were being tried:

> Herod, called king, poor thing,
> but merely Pilate's clerk,
> rootless deracinate –
> become a dog to bark
> at his master's bidding;
> to snap from a manger
> no honest man covets.
> To justice, a stranger.

Speculations of this kind, together with my Welshness, led me to consider my country's place in the United Kingdom and, in particular, the question of devolution, a matter which from the last quarter of the nineteenth century had from time to time raised its head. I had discussed devolution on many occasions with my father, who in some respects was a better Welshman than I, but who was characteristic of his mining generation in his loyalty to the Labour Party and in the platitudes he trotted out about internationalism and the brotherhood of man, without seeing the irony of condemning Welsh nationalists while he himself was a member of what in fact was an even more nationalist British party. Happily, he gradually changed his attitude and by the end of the 70s had resigned from the Labour Party, mainly because the party had by then become asinine, but also because he had begun to see the futility of exalting the British nation-state. I had childish pleasure on one occasion responding to a member of that party with whom I had a chance encounter in Wrexham. He greeted me after the launch of the SDP by saying that my father would be turning in his grave if he knew that his son was a founder member of the new party. I replied with some satisfaction that my father was a tolerant man, that he had resigned from the Labour Party before me, that he had become a member of the new party and that in any case he was still alive.

Yves Person, whom I had adopted as a kind of distant mentor, summed up the situation persuasively when he wrote: 'It often happens in history that the moment of triumph comes just before the fall. It is a fact that the nation-state, after a career of two centuries, appears suddenly unable to respond to men's expectations. It is therefore under attack, from above and from below ... from below the nation-state comes face to face with the claims of minorities who are no longer prepared to see the subjective quality of their lives, of their existence as a minority even, being sacrificed for an abstract structure that offers them nothing in return.'

My doubts about the stifling Britishness of the Labour Party were growing, not just because of its attitude towards the European Community, but also its attitude towards Wales. When the devolution bills were introduced, largely as a result of the electoral success of the Scottish National Party during the 1970s, I like many enthusiastic devolutionists was disappointed with the feebleness of the proposals for Wales. Nevertheless I supported the measure while consoling myself with the thought that half a loaf was better than no bread at all. More to the point, I believed that any elected assembly, however weak its initial powers, would inevitably develop and acquire additional power over time.

The government suspended the House of Commons for a week prior to the referendum required by the Devolution Act, so that Labour MPs could have the opportunity of campaigning for the government's policy that had not been welcomed enthusiastically in Wales. It was hardly a wise move, or at least that was what those of us believed who were not cynics. An important reason for the lack of enthusiasm was the unscrupulous campaign, which had been carried out for several weeks by Welsh Labour MPs opposed to devolution. They now redoubled their efforts making the most of the old adage that the devil has the best tunes. I was outraged, not by their beliefs which they were entitled to hold, but by their lack of scruple in what they said. The debates in the House of Commons had been bitter, the bitterness coming not from the opposition benches but from within Labour's own ranks, Welsh Labour ranks in particular. I may be forgiven, perhaps, for quoting part of my speech during the second reading of the bill in the House of Commons: it gives a taste of the antagonism within the Labour Party to the concept of devolution.

HANSARD 15 NOVEMBER 1977

Mr Tom Ellis (Wrexham): I should like to take up the remarks of my Hon. Friend the Member for Pontypool (Mr Abse) who made an interesting speech. I want to follow the philosophical and theoretical points that he made as a socialist. I wish first of all to emphasise a fact that is of importance. It is the basic reason behind this and the Scotland Bill. It is the 'onlie begetter' and the raison d'etre of the Bill. The fact is that Wales is a nation.

The right hon. Member for Down South (Mr Powell) said that the people of Northern Ireland did not believe that they belonged to a separate nation. I assume that he meant that they regarded themselves as English. The right hon. Gentleman knows more about Northern Ireland than I do, but his statement surprised me. I believe that behind all the difficulties in Northern Ireland there is an ethnic issue. We have barely begun to scratch the surface of the psychology of the ethnic group. That is one of the great lacunas in Marxist philosophy. It is important that we appreciate that Wales is a nation.

When my hon. Friend the Member for Pontypool said at a meeting of the Parliamentary Labour Party that to him as a socialist, a coal miner in Senghenydd was exactly the same as a coal miner in St Helens or Timbuktu, I told him that if he had said that to me 30 years ago when I was down a coal mine in Wales working my guts out, I should have told him that he was talking through his hat. I am not the same. I am no better and no worse than an English coalminer, but I am different. My hon. Friend talks of the 'evil of ethnocentricity'. It is not an evil, nor is it a virtue. It is a fact. One cannot be human without a sense of nationhood. One has to have a sense of history, a sense of the past to support one, otherwise one would be merely a member of a species, like a tiger or an elephant.

Mr Abse: I believe that the race to which I belong is the human race. Gwent has the second largest population in Wales. The majority of its people are drawn from all corners of the British Isles and their inheritance comes from all corners. Will my hon. Friend explain their ethnic group to them?

Mr Ellis: This Bill does not deal with devolution for the county of Gwent. There are libraries full of books on nationhood. It is difficult to define, but it exists. That is the short answer to my hon. Friend's question.

Mr Ioan Evans: My hon. Friend referred to what my hon. Friend the Member for Pontypool (Mr Abse) said about the people in Wales having things in common with people outside Wales. He seemed to resent that. Does my hon. Friend not recognise that Welsh miners would say that they have more in common with Scottish, Yorkshire and other miners than they have with Welsh property speculators and asset strippers? They do not regard themselves in a narrow nationalist sense.

Mr Ellis: I am coming to that. I was a Welsh coalminer and I had a lot in common with an English coalminer. I once drew a horse in a raffle. I asked the fellow who sold me the ticket "Is it a good horse?" "Yes," he replied. "It's got four legs". It was a horse. Clearly a Welsh coalminer has a lot in common with an English coalminer.

I am obviously ruffling a few feathers. I was making the point that one cannot be human without having a sense of nationhood.......the socialist theory of my Hon. Friend is based on the concept of separate and disparate individuals contracting together to form an abstract state, the '*Grande Nation*' of Rouseau as compared with an organic nation with its own language, customs, traditions, history and so on. The '*Grande Nation*' concept, which some socialists swallowed hook line and sinker, is clearly outmoded and has been shown to be far short of coming anywhere near a socialist solution to the problems of the world. That kind of mechanistic philosophy is precisely the philosophy of capitalism that all that matters is production. Some who claim to be socialists have said 'To alleviate our consciences, we shall not talk so much about production but about distribution.' But today even socialists in this country who are 50 years behind the times in socialist thinking — I refer more particularly to the left wing of the Labour Party — say that distribution does not matter much more than production. It is in this sense that when my hon. Friend talked about the Bill's being anti-socialist he was up a gum tree.

The result of the referendum was a tragedy. I was angry with those

Welsh Labour MPs who had campaigned against devolution, not because of their views — I could excuse, though not easily, their misguided attitudes — but for the totally dishonest arguments they had advanced, arguments that influenced strongly an already doubtful public disinclined to accept change. I kept my scorn, however, for the junior minister who informed his local newspaper that pressure of work would prevent him taking part in the campaign. When I complained to his boss, the Secretary of State, that the minister was not making an effort to sell his own government's policy, I was told that that was not the case, no matter what the local paper said. He would in fact be addressing meetings in Tenby, Haverford West and Milford Haven, towns at the opposite end of Wales from his own constituency. The junior minister's constituency party was fiercely against devolution.

By this time the Labour Party, apart from the devolution issue, was in a hopeless condition. The so-called 'Loony Left' had come to dominate many constituency parties and had become a strong extremist influence in the party as a whole. After the party lost the 1979 election the extremists became seemingly unstoppable and insisted not only on adopting what many people regarded as absurd policies, but also on changing the party's constitution with the object of ridding the party of its more moderate MPs. It had been clear for some time, however, that the political party as such, a powerful but indispensable institution within the British polity, was in serious need of reform. There were and had been for some time, party members who were supporters of electoral reform, but their sole aim was to ensure proportionality between the parliamentary seats won by a party and the total number of its votes at an election: in essence their concern was one of 'fair play for parties'. This, if achieved, would, they believed, lead to an improved political system and a more effective parliamentary democracy. The idea of reforming party itself was not at the front of their minds. I thought proportional representation, welcome though it would be, was a limited aim and that electoral reform should aim beyond it at providing the public with greater access to the inner workings of party. Nevertheless, I welcomed the fact that there were people in the party who supported the idea of proportionality. Sometime in 1974, a few of them, including two or three MPs, began meeting in one of the committee rooms of the Palace of Westminster. We labelled ourselves 'The Labour Campaign for Electoral Reform' (LCER) and I was elected chairman, to the dismay of my constituency party. I had also become a member of the Electoral Reform Society some years previously and had been elected to its Council. The structural reform of the political party through the introduction of one particular electoral system became one of three major interests for me, the others being devolution and the development of the European Community.

14. Political Preoccupations

Gradually, the activities of the Labour Campaign for Electoral Reform (LCER) became one of my two main preoccupations. Support within the Labour Party was sparse, opposition plentiful and vehement, not least in my constituency party after I had taken part one year in a fringe meeting at the party's annual conference. The meeting took the form of a debate at which Tony Benn spoke against reform and I spoke in favour. I scored a cheap debating point when Tony claimed that the instability of French governance was a consequence of proportional representation. I replied that I found it difficult to debate meaningfully with him, as he clearly knew little about the subject. France, I pointed out, did not have a system of proportional representation. There were some delegates present from the Wrexham constituency who were less than enamoured with my performance, partly no doubt because Tony Benn, then in his extremist phase, had become something of an icon for them. Shortly after the conference I faced a motion of no confidence at a specially convened meeting of my constituency party on the grounds that my support for proportional representation was against party policy. The motion was defeated, although many members who voted against it were also strongly against PR. David Owen made a similar faux pas during the first meeting of a commission established jointly by the SDP and the

Liberal Party to recommend an electoral system for the House of Commons. One or two participants had spoken approvingly of the Single Transferable Vote (STV) system. David then surprised me with what seemed to be his familiarity with the subject when he dismissed STV as an unsuitable system. His faux pas towards the end of his contribution completely undermined his argument, such as it was. He asked "Anyway, who decides the quota?," a question the answer to which the most cursory acquaintance with the system would have provided. My existing doubts about David's leadership potential were strengthened.

The cause of electoral reform slowly began to make headway, however, not a little helped by the work of an all-party committee under the chairmanship of David Ormsby-Gore (Lord Harlech) which provided a semi-professional public relations service. Public interest in the subject, although never high, was mildly stimulated. I had several pamphlets published by LCER and more significantly, I contributed one half of a Fabian Society tract in which the case for and against electoral reform was argued respectively by me and Phillip Whitehead, MP. I tried to make the case for reform against the background of Britain's broad political and social circumstances, keeping the algebra so to speak, to a minimum. Despite its having been written 25 years ago, I believe that the case then set out remains valid and that, unchanged it can usefully be set out once more. I have therefore included it as an appendix to this book.

My second main preoccupation, the European Community, was consummated on my becoming a member of the European Parliament. At the time of Britain's accession in 1973, that parliament was composed of delegates from the national parliaments, the membership of each national delegation being in proportion to the strengths of the various parties nationally. The British Labour Party, however, was seized with a fit of petulance to which it gave vent by boycotting the parliament. Hence, for some twelve months Britain's

Speaking on the floor of the European Parliament, Strasbourg.

delegation was under-represented and made up of Conservative and Liberal MPs and peers only. A year passed before the Labour Party stopped sulking and at last agreed to send its proportion of delegates. I leapt at the opportunity when I was asked to become a member of the Labour delegation, despite the fact that the Strasbourg parliament was derided as an impotent institution of little or no political authority. It seemed to me, ardent European that I was, that it would and should gain in stature and that in any case, I could play a more positive role as an MEP than I would be ever likely to do at Westminster. This was because of personal as well as systematic reasons. My four years service amply confirmed both these views.

The difference in atmosphere between the Westminster and Strasbourg parliaments was tangible. At Strasbourg, derided and impotent though the parliament might have been, one felt that its sights were on the future and that it was on the attack, no matter how weak the base from which its sorties were launched. At Westminster on the other hand, one sensed that the parliament, from however strong a bastion it saw itself facing the world, was on the defensive, hankering after past glories rather than advancing to meet new challenges. My personal disenchantment with the pretensions of uncompromising, two-party, Westminster politics became more pronounced as I responded to the excitement of serving in an institution whose radicalism I embraced enthusiastically. The excitement was heightened by the opportunities available, even to the most obscure member, for making a positive contribution. It was indeed ironic that whereas the principal role of the backbench MP at Westminster was that of lobby fodder, ordinary members at Strasbourg, because of the mechanics of that parliament's method of working, could routinely make significant contributions to its work.

From its inception the European Parliament was entitled to be consulted on legislative proposals by the Council of Ministers, within whose remit the final decision lay. (The Parliament, originally called the Assembly, became known in legislation from 1962 onwards as the Parliament, a change formalised by the Single European Act of 1986. The difference between 'Assembly' and 'Parliament' acquired a spurious significance during the debates on UK entry into the Community; one assumes that the term 'Assembly' appeared in the first instance as a mis-translation after the French *'Assemblee Nationale'*). However, the Council was not obliged to respond to the views of the Parliament. That discretion, as was to be expected, has been materially reduced by the Parliament's gradual assertion of its democratic authority. Today it has a much greater influence on European Union policy and legislation than it possessed initially.

Soon after becoming a member at Strasbourg, I was able to take advantage of one of the opportunities open to members by virtue of the Parliament's working arrangements. For some years the Community's atomic energy division had been receiving processed uranium from the United States. I had been an MEP for only a few months when it transpired that the Community legislation controlling the supply and movement of radioactive material was belatedly deemed unsatisfactory by the U.S. authorities, who threatened to withhold supplies unless the Community introduced a more stringent legislative control. The Commission thus began to prepare a draft bill. In Britain, such a draft, when finally agreed by ministers, would be published as a Bill for presenting to Parliament. During its passage through the enactment process the Bill would possibly be amended, in particular during the committee stage of the process. The amendments, however, would be of marginal consequence: the government, having nailed its colours to the mast by publishing the Bill, would be loth to lose face by having to accept any substantive changes to it. Members of the government majority serving on the committee, led by the appropriate minister, would accept only minor changes that would leave the Bill substantively intact, even if a substantive change were shown to be desirable. An obvious consequence of the process was the partisan approach to legislation, even in the case of comparatively non-ideological or technical bills. Party amour-propre counted more than ratiocination.

The legislative role of the Strasbourg Parliament, however, apart from the inherent consultative weakness, was different from that at Westminster in at least two significant respects, both reflecting the over-riding circumstance that the Parliament did not serve an hegemonic government bent on enacting its own partisan legislation. Firstly, the committee responsible for scrutinising a piece of legislation initiated and drafted by the Commission, appointed from its own ranks a raporteur, supported by specialist parliamentary staff, who was answerable only to the committee and Parliament. His responsibility was to make himself familiar with the proposed legislation and its background and to lead the committee in its scrutiny of a so far confidential Bill. At the conclusion of the committee's deliberations, the raporteur presented its report to Parliament. The Bill at that moment, amended or not by the committee, was made public for the first time. This was the other significant difference between the Westminster and Strasbourg procedures.

I was appointed *raporteur* by the Scientific Committee to monitor the new legislation on Community controls for radioactive materials, a topic of which I was totally ignorant. My immediate priority, therefore, was to educate myself in the complexities of an arcane subject having implications for international security under the Non-Proliferation Treaty. These implications became more apparent as my education in the subject developed. Together with a specialist member of the parliamentary staff, I had lengthy discussions at the Vienna headquarters of the Atomic Energy Agency, the body set up to monitor the application of the Non-Proliferation Treaty. One began to appreciate, for example, the dilemma facing an inspector visiting a nuclear installation who found that there were a few kilograms of

'MUF' (material unaccounted for) at the installation, sufficient in fact to manufacture a bomb. The dilemma was that of assessing correctly the circumstances surrounding the accounting discrepancy and of deciding what to do about it.

The first meeting of the committee took place a few weeks after my appointment as raporteur. Dr Guido Brunner, the responsible commissioner and members of his staff, attended all its meetings. I had, of course, become conversant with the terms of the draft legislation and had found them less than adequate. The committee met several times and during the cut and thrust of debate the shortcomings of the draft became ever more apparent. So much so that the Commission finally agreed to withdraw its original proposals and prepare a completely new draft in the light of the committee's criticisms. This second draft was in due course presented to Parliament, accepted by it and was later 'enacted' by the Council of Ministers. A comparable experience in enacting legislation at Westminster is almost inconceivable.

The European Parliament is, of course, a multi-lingual assembly, an agreeable characteristic to my taste, possibly because I happen to be bilingual. Even so, I marvelled at the quality of the simultaneous translation provided routinely by the interpreters. Theirs was a rare skill, as I know from the few occasions when, on behalf of a colleague, I have tried to translate simultaneously from Welsh to English. I recall asking a French interpreter over coffee one morning how he would translate the words 'deft poise', He replied instantaneously '*aplomb agile*', It may not have been literally correct but it conveyed the precise meaning of R. S. Thomas's poem *Chapel Deacon*:

> Tell me, Davies, for the faint breeze
> From heaven freshens and I roll in it,
> Who taught you your deft poise?

I dare say that with the help of a dictionary I could have found a literal translation, but it would hardly have been reflex. During the course of that coffee break with the Frenchman I laid down a challenge that on the following day, when there was to be a parliamentary debate on metrication, I would make a speech in normal English which he would find untranslatable. I prepared the speech carefully, peppering it with arcane idioms, archaisms like rod, pole or perch and cryptic epigrams such as 'Cricketers of the world, unite, you have nothing to lose but your chains'. A couple of minutes into my short speech and the interpreters' booths fell silent. It was an interesting demonstration of the profundity of the link between a language and its social background. A friend of mine, who was the chief officer of Gwynedd County Council during the 1970s, remarked upon that link. The council of 67 members, all but four of whom habitually spoke Welsh, decided to introduce a simultaneous interpretation service for its meetings which hitherto had been held in English. The quality of the council's debates improved noticeably.

The presiding officer scotched a serious attempt on my part to symbolise the legitimacy of minority languages and argue their value for society generally, during a debate on what seemed to be the appropriate topic of 'European Culture'. I decided to speak in the debate and to make my speech in Welsh. I intended to set out some of the arguments advanced by people like T. S. Eliot, Simone Weil, Jean-Paul Sartre, Saunders Lewis, R. S. Thomas and others for the long term benefits accruing to a pluralist polity from minority languages. I made special arrangements, of course, to have the speech interpreted into the parliament's 'working languages' by preparing an English translation of what I would say and handing copies to the various interpreters who were all happy with the arrangement. I had also checked Parliament's standing orders and had consulted the parliamentary clerks who saw no reason to prevent my speaking in Welsh. A precedent in fact existed in that various political dignitaries had from time to time addressed the parliament in languages such as Spanish, Portugese and Japanese. Out of courtesy I informed a vice-president of the parliament of my intention prior to the debate. It was a mistake. The vice-president, who happened to be W. B. Yeats's son, responded immediately by saying that I would be out of order if I spoke in Welsh. I disagreed with him and decided to go ahead with my plan. During the debate on the following morning, however, almost immediately after beginning my speech, I was interrupted by the presiding officer who had obviously been made alert of my intention as he himself was listening through headphones to a French translation. He told me that I had to speak in one of the official languages. A number of speakers intervened on points of order and a mini debate developed on the propriety or otherwise of my being allowed to speak in Welsh. It became clear from the applause that followed objections that, if the matter had been put to the vote, a Welsh speech would have been ruled inadmissible. However, a compromise was agreed that the question should be referred to the Committee on Procedure. I therefore agreed to speak in English and this is what I said as recorded in the official bulletin. I reprint it because in its spontaneity it conveys something of my depth of feeling on the issue.

Mr President, I will try and make a speech possibly less banal than my prepared speech, I think, would have been. At least I can say one thing. I have established one point, that is to say, the importance of culture. What you have said — and I do not mean you personally, but you as President — and indeed what the rules say if you have interpreted them correctly, makes a mockery of all the fine words that have been spoken in this debate so far.

Culture is not just international concert going, a kind of wandering minstrelsy. Culture is something fundamental and I would like just in the few brief moments that I have to try to point out how fundamental it is from the point of view of a socialist. And I make no bones about it: I think as socialists we have made a big mistake in the past by an overwhelming preoccupation with economism — a mistake going back as far as Karl Marx. I think only fairly recently Sartre, for example, makes a point, speaking in relation to what then was admittedly a despotic Castillian-Basque relationship, on the situation of the Basque language in Castillian Spain. Sartre said that to speak an oppressed language is itself a revolutionary act. It is to attack capitalism at its softest spot. That is quite a major assertion and of course Sartre gives his reasons and his arguments why this should be so.

And I would like just to sketch out why it should be so, because you see the issue fundamentally is one of hegemony — the control by a small group of a large number of peoples. Now my nation are not Johnny-come-latelies in Britain. We have been there for 2000 years. We lived there as a nation under the Roman occupation, under the Roman emperor. We have been there a long time. I might even mention a story about my illustrious compatriot David Lloyd George, if I may bring a little bit of humour into this. When he was a young man in the House of Commons and somebody attacked the Welsh language, he made the point and he did it with typical brilliance, that Welsh was the language of princes when the English were swinging by their tails in the Balkans.

The point I am making is that we are not a recent immigrant group; we are a well-established native indigenous nation living in Britain. And when I came here today I thought I was going to be able to speak in the only parliament I have that permits me to speak in my mother tongue. And if we are talking as socialists about something, I think there is something terribly profound about that, that in the only parliament I possessed up to five years ago, which was the House of Commons, I was not allowed constitutionally to speak my mother tongue. Bear in mind that I do not mind — I am perfectly fluent in English — but there are many of my compatriots who could be elected to parliament who are not so fluent in the English language. I make this point quite seriously, because I sometimes feel that some of my English compatriots think it is just some sort of little whimsy on my part.

Just to give another practical illustration, one of the county councils in my country five years ago decided to adopt a bilingual system, with the headphones and so on just as we have here and there are 67 members of that council and 63 habitually speak Welsh and four habitually speak English. The point I wish to make is this: the chief officer of the council, who is a friend of mine, told me some years afterwards that the remarkable thing about it was that the standard of debate had rocketed upwards when they established the bilingual system. So it is not just a whimsy — it is something real and profound; it is just the same as if one goes to a court of law if one is charged with something serious. The ability to be entitled to speak in one's own language is a very precious heritage.

So when we are talking about culture we are talking about something very, very profound and very, very real. I might add that the great advantage that Europe — the European Community — has for me is that it offers an opportunity, not to acquire hegemony for my party or my people but to replace hegemony. We have the opportunity here, if we are skilful enough, actually to go ahead and do this and this is one of the profoundly socialist reasons why I am a European. Equally why I am a staunch advocate of devolution in my own country — and it is coming. It is not just in Wales. It is in Scotland and Britanny and Alsace and Galicia and Asturias and the Basque Provinces and Catalonia and Corsica and Schleswig-Holstein and the Friesians. It is not just some little whimsy. It is so general that there is something very profound happening and what the profundity stems from basically is that ordinary people are beginning to sense that economics are not enough — that mechanistic materialism is not enough.

Therefore I must say, and I am going to finish on this Mr President, that I am a little disappointed, having heard all these fine words about monuments, concerts and so on, — all important things, I am not decrying it. For me, it really comes down, fundamentally, to a cultural issue which might challenge 'the state', which is what I am talking about — challenging 'the state', you recall Marx — the revolutionary overthrow of the state. That is highly impractical. I do not want a revolution; I want to do it by civilised, proper, political means. That is what I am dealing with and that is what the people of my country and all those other countries I have named are, increasingly, dealing with. That is why I place my hope in starting from small beginnings. Mr Amadei's report is dealing with marginalia, but it is starting from small beginnings. I wish him well and I wish the Commission well, because they are on a major undertaking. All the scorn and fun that is poured out by people who do not understand will come to no avail because, I almost feel like singing, 'We shall overcome'.

15. Parliamentary Life

In previous chapters I have outlined some of the attitudes and beliefs I held about various aspects of the social and political environment. I had held them sufficiently strongly over a number of years to have wanted to participate actively in British politics and was therefore thrilled on election night in 1970 to become the member of parliament for Wrexham. It was an ambition fulfilled, but of course, significant though it was for me personally, becoming an MP was in itself the fulfilment only of a limited ambition. I now looked forward to participating much more directly and as I thought, much more positively, in the affairs of the United Kingdom. I should have known that I was riding for a fall.

Looking back over three and a half decades, I now realise that within the conventions of the British political system I was temperamentally unsuited to being a successful MP. I knew that 'politics is the art of the possible' and that prudence is a sound democratic attribute. A necessary ingredient of political prudence is pragmatism and I was prepared to be a pragmatist. I had not anticipated, however, that to be a 'successful' politician —successful in the sense of 'climbing the greasy pole' — it was necessary to go way beyond pragmatism. I was shocked at the depth of cynicism plumbed by the leadership of my party. I hasten here to disabuse readers who might suspect me of pompous self-righteousness. I am not claiming to be a knight on a white charger, ever ready to ride to the rescue of a fallen damsel. Like most members of the human race I possess many of its frailties. I am aware, moreover, that there were successful politicians in the Labour Party who were so gifted that they were able to impose acceptable limits to their pragmatism and yet achieve ministerial rank. Unfortunately, I lacked the talent necessary for this.

My first year at St Stephen's was a muted one for two reasons. Firstly, there was the stance adopted by Labour as it responded to the government's Industrial Relations Bill, a stance I deplored as I have already indicated. I simply could not bring myself to participate in the debates during the committee stage of the Bill in the manner that my colleagues expected, partly because the views I would have been expected to express were arbitrary, dogmatic and negative, but also because the amendments I had suggested at private meetings of our team (under Barbara Castle's chairmanship), which I believed were enlightened ones, were regarded almost as treachery, tantamount to conniving with the enemy. The unanimous view of the rest of the team was that an all-out-attack should be mounted on the Bill, not a line of which was to be accepted *or* amended. The result was that the Bill, which might have been improved at least marginally, eventually became an Act in precisely the reactionary form which government had intended.

A striking example of the obduracy of our side was displayed at the third reading of the Bill, when we spent five or six hours in the early hours of the morning simply trooping through the lobbies to vote 'No' on clause after clause. Each vote through the lobbies of the House of Commons takes about twenty minutes to complete and, after some three hours of this process, I complained to Jim Callaghan about the fatuousness of such an empty gesture, only to be told that it was a good thing to keep ministers out of their beds. My political education had begun in earnest.

An interesting human aspect of the frequent all-night sittings was the almost instinctive reaction of our small group of Welsh-speaking Labour MPs to while away the time together in the smoking-room. The group consisted of its patriarch — Cledwyn Hughes — Denzil Davies, Wil Edwards, Gwynoro Jones, Elystan Morgan, Caerwyn Roderick and myself. There were, of course, other Welsh-speaking MPs of all parties, but they did not habitually join us in what might be called our impromptu '*seiadau*' [fellowship meetings]. The star turn was Cledwyn. He was a gifted mimic and raconteur whose *piece de resistance* was John Elias o Fôn's 'auctioneer' sermon. We savoured it many times — by popular request so to speak. Cledwyn would gradually work up steam as he recounted the sinner's being put up for auction — "Who will have him? He is going cheap! What! No bid from the Methodists, what about the Baptists? No bid from them either. Surely there'll be a bid from the Congregationalists. No! No bid even from that quarter. The Church of England then, they'll accept anybody". By this time Cledwyn was in the *hwyl* and the rest of us were doing our bit '*porthi*-ing' as we responded to the sermon. The nonplussed other occupants of the smoking room regarded us as a bunch of mad Welshmen.

I recall one occasion when I had gone to the bar to buy a round of drinks at the conclusion of the sermon and Quentin Hogg at my side insisted upon reciting a limerick which concluded with the words 'Blaenau Ffestiniog'. Regrettably, I do not remember the limerick. Quentin Hogg, with characteristic flamboyance, had accused members of the Welsh Language Society of being "baboons," and I was tempted to recite him a verse from a poem by Raymond Garlick. I did not do so because I could not remember the verse accurately. The poem, one of whose verses I quoted in a previous chapter, was written during the period of language protests when several members of the Society were prosecuted in the courts. It is titled *Archetypes* and consists of four verses, each of which describes a character involved in the legal process: the Lord Chancellor (at the time Quentin Hogg), the judge, the clerk of the court and the defendant. The first verse relates to the Lord Chancellor:

> Holy, histrionic,
> Lord Caiaphas,
> high priest of this mumbo jumbo,
> flunkey surrounded, policed:
> rip your black robe, gold laced,
> tear your periwigged hair,
> and stamp your lord high foot
> on justice prostrate there.

The second reason for my muteness during my first parliamentary year was my membership of the Russell Committee. This was a committee, chaired by Sir Lionel Russell, set up in 1969 by Ted Short, the Secretary of State for Education, to "Assess the need for and to review the provision of non-vocational adult education in England and Wales". I was the only Welshman on the committee of fourteen, although one of the six HMI assessors was also Welsh. It became clear during meetings that the committee members had little understanding of, or sympathy with, the distinctive Welsh educational tradition and its needs. I therefore decided to write a minority report dealing with Welsh circumstances. To do justice to the subject the report would have to be a fairly lengthy one. I began work on it in the autumn of 1970, a month or so after the new parliament began work. In due course it grew into the 15,000 word essay which was my major preoccupation during my first eighteen months or so at St Stephen's.

There are two main differences between the Welsh and English educational traditions, the one clear-cut and the other more elusive. The first, of course, is that Wales is a bilingual country with one of the languages in a much more powerful position than the other. The second difference springs from the different historical experiences of the two peoples. I tried to define the difference in a historical introduction to my report. This is not the place to repeat the exercise, although it might be worth giving an example of the complete lack of understanding within the committee, not merely of the cultural differences, but even of the respective positions of the two languages. One of the committee members asked me what the Welsh word was for ambulance. I replied that I did not know and then asked him what the English word was for it. He looked at me as if I had asked a silly question. My readers will, I hope, forgive me for quoting the following typical paragraph to give something of the flavour of the report:

The second of the two interdependent historical phenomena is the language. It is not the purpose of this analysis to expound on the treasures of Welsh literature or on the flourishing contemporary writing in Welsh, but there can be no doubt that modern Welsh is a rich and flexible language. The language is more than a literary medium: it is a contemporary instrument adapted to present-day conditions which has undergone a remarkable renaissance during this century. There has been a surge of interest and feeling for the language in professional and academic circles, especially since the war and this has resulted in a general improvement in the standard of Welsh written and spoken by educated Welshmen in the Welsh-speaking areas. The language has become adapted to the demands of technology and the mass-media to an extent that would have been regarded only forty years ago as highly ambitious, not to say improbable. Paradoxically, while this development has been taking place, the number of people in the factories, shops and offices of urban Wales who speak the language at all has declined. Tremendous inroads have been made by a huge output of American-oriented pseudo-culture using all the sophisticated techniques of its trade so that one of the two historical roles of Welsh, its insulating role — oftimes its strength, increasingly a weakness — has been completely shattered. As the numbers who speak the language decline, so too does the blight of a uniformly imposed mass mono-culture which impinges all the more sharply on Wales as it erodes away the native product. One has remarked elsewhere that not for nothing is it a Welsh poet who writes:
… Among the forests

Of metal the one human
Sound was the lament of
The poets for decidous language.

To return to life at Westminster, there is more than a little legitimacy to the label 'The Westminster Village'. The Palace of Westminster, or more colloquially the Houses of Parliament, is a self-contained establishment under whose roof several thousand people work, of whom a fair number live their lives there. My first impression of the place was of being met in the central lobby by Arthur Probert, member for one of the Rhondda constituencies. "I'll give you the advice Aneurin Bevan gave me on my first day," he said, "Don't be overawed by the grandeur of the place." My immediate reaction, which I recall vividly, was one of surprise that Bevan, whom I then hero-worshipped, should have thought so trivially. I had heard him speak twice at public meetings and had been mesmerised by him on each occasion. He was one of only two truly great orators I have heard and been thrilled by. The other was J. T. Jones, the headmaster of my old grammar school at Ruabon, who as a pulpit orator must surely have matched the Welsh giants of the past. I have also heard Lloyd George, but at one remove. I have ten minutes of him on tape, which probably does not do him justice. I find his style too florid for contemporary taste and his voice, at least on tape, seems too highly pitched.

I was allocated a small room to be shared as an office with two other MPs who were as unlike each other as one could possibly imagine; one an intellectual, the other a very raw Yorkshire miner. We each had a telephone, thereby markedly consolidating that distaste for the instrument which I had acquired during my coalmining days. It was impossible to concentrate when one, sometimes two, of my room-mates were talking loudly a few feet from my ear. Our conversations were sometimes bizarre. The intellectual would be speaking in French, the miner in equally incomprehensible Yorkshire and I in Welsh, all at the same time in a room about ten feet square.

On the other hand there was humour too. I recall a delightful half of a conversation when the miner had the floor, so to speak, to himself. His wife acted from home as his secretary and on this occasion she was clearly telling him that a constituent had phoned her about some problem. "How many times do I have to tell you?," he shouted, "Tell him to write — r – i – t – e — write!"

When the telephoning became insufferable I would retreat to the 'Welsh table' in the members' tea room. There was always someone there to spread the latest gossip or to reminisce about the past. S. O. Davies, the elderly member for Merthyr Tydfil who used 'S.O.' as his first person singular pronoun, even when talking informally to a friend, told me a nice tale about Aneurin Bevan. Apparently Roy Jenkins had made an impressive maiden speech and had been warmly praised. However Iori Thomas, a notoriously sardonic member, added an extra chill to the cold light of the following morning by claiming that Roy would not go far because he was too lazy. "Lazy!," expostulated Bevan with his little stutter, "Lazy! Anybody from Abersychan who speaks like that can't be lazy".

One of the, dare I say it, few saving graces of the House of Commons is the wit, sometimes barbed, sometimes humourous, to be heard there. Words are the stock-in-trade of the politician and their skilful use is often on display. I have become a kind of amateur connoisseur of parliamentary rhetoric. Examples go back a long way. Disraeli said of Gladstone: "He hasn't a single redeeming defect," and earlier still Daniel O'Connell said of Robert Peel: "He has a smile like a silver plate on a coffin". Bevan was a master of this kind of invective. Here he is attacking prime minister Neville Chamberlain who, older readers will recall, was a tall, thin, dry, stick of a man in a pin-striped pair of trousers, with a high-winged collar round his neck, a neatly clipped moustache under his nose, a black Homburg on his head and a furled umbrella on his arm. "Listening to the prime minister," said Bevan, "is like paying a visit to Woolworths: everything in its place and nothing over sixpence". That becomes almost affable, however, in comparison with Lloyd George's crucifying of John Simon — who had resigned from one party for another, not once, but twice, to be a member at different times of three different parties of strongly contrasting colours. There are many instances, of course, of MPs crossing the floor of the House of Commons. Indeed, I myself have been a member of three parties — Labour, SDP and Liberal Democrat. John Simon, however, crossed the floor for what on each occasion was thought to be a dishonourable reason. Lloyd George highlighted it brilliantly: "Many right honourable and honourable gentlemen have crossed the floor of this House, but none has left behind such a trail of slime". It is strong stuff which Lloyd George later compounded by famously saying of Simon that he had sat on the fence long enough for the iron to enter his soul. Again, in a public speech at the time of his 'People's Budget', when he threatened to nobble the House of Lords, we have him declaring: "Mr Balfour says the House of Lords is the watchdog of the Constitution. It is not, it is Mr Balfour's poodle". The secret of this kind of invective, of course, is imagery. Lloyd George was witty too, saying of Neville Chamberlain, for example: "He would probably make an average Lord Mayor of Birmingham," a pause and then, almost as an aside, "in a lean year".

More recently wit has become the principal weapon of some politicians. Harold Wilson said of Harold Macmillan that he had had an expensive education — Eton and Suez. An opposition backbencher said of a junior minister that he was the only man in Britain who could spend all day reading the *Daily Mail*. Wit is best when it is kind. Wilson was witty but his wit was more barbed than humorous. Self-deprecating humour is best of all. A good example is George Thomas, when he was Speaker of the House of Commons, poking fun at himself to contain a backbencher who was out to make trouble. A member, with a strong Glaswegian accent, was speaking when the troublemaker rose on a point of order. "Surely, Mr Speaker," he said, "the honourable gentleman is out of order. His accent is so strong that no-one can understand what he's saying. How can members reply meaningfully to him?" George Thomas rose to his feet and said: "There are many accents in this House. I sometimes wish I had one!" The House burst into laughter, of course and the troublemaker was squashed. George gave another example of his wit when a member was making an unparliamentary attack on another member. George admonished the man and ordered him to withdraw his accusations. "But they're true, Mr Speaker," said the offending member, offering convincing proof, "they're in all the papers". "So is my horoscope," said the Speaker.

George Thomas was not my favourite MP. Our relationship had been soured almost from the start because of my objection to the weekly column he wrote for the *Liverpool Daily Post*, a newspaper circulating extensively in north Wales. Each week George poured vitriol on champions of the Welsh language. The effect was to tar with the same brush the five or six Labour MPs in those constituencies where the paper circulated, doing them most harm where a majority of the population was Welsh-speaking. Appeals to George to desist were of no avail, so together with Brynmor John (to his great credit since, as the MP for Pontypridd, he was not affected), I complained to Harold Wilson. I cannot recall whether our action had any effect on the weekly column, but it certainly affected our relationship with George. He voiced his displeasure with me at some length. From then onwards he frequently vented his spleen against me, although it was only after he became Speaker of the House that he was able to do so in practical ways.

One example was the occasion when members of the Wrexham Chamber of Commerce visited the House of Commons. They had asked me to host a St David's Day lunch in one of the public dining rooms and to invite Mr Speaker Thomas to be the guest speaker and propose the toast to St David. Rather sheepishly I put the request to

George who accepted. On the day, I sat next to him and at the appropriate moment expressed our thanks to Mr Speaker and invited him to propose a toast to St David. George rose, raised his glass, said "To St David" and sat down. He then turned to me, asked me "Did you enjoy my speech?" got up and went. It was an exhibition of almost pathologically spiteful childishness.

More serious from my point of view, serious in the sense that 'sticks and stones may break my bones, words will never hurt me', was George's vendetta as Speaker. It was unfortunately the custom that backbenchers wishing to speak in a debate wrote to the Speaker beforehand to tell him so. He would prepare a list of speakers to be called, which he gave to the Deputy Speaker who chaired the debates, except at their commencement and end when the front bench speeches were made. I say unfortunately, partly because prepared set-piece speeches lack the spontaneity that makes for a genuine debate. If a member, truly authoritative on a subject, were moved to speak on it during a debate solely because of the erroneous argument of another member, there was no possibility of his 'catching the Speaker's eye' to refute the argument. More importantly, however, it was unfortunate for me personally because my speeches, set-piece or spontaneous, wise or foolish, were hardly ever made. George ensured that my name was never on the list. I had to wait and hope that there were not enough names to fill the time until the closing frontbench speeches.

The most flagrant example of his spite was during a debate on the coal industry. I was the only Welsh member and one of no more than four or five in the whole House with direct experience of the industry. Furthermore, I was the only member with managerial experience in it. My name was not included on the list of members chosen to speak. I considered raising the matter as a point of order on the floor of the House, but did not do so, partly because there were members of parliament who in any case never spoke in the chamber and also because the only result would have been my appearing pompous, as if I thought that the world was waiting expectantly to hear my words of wisdom.

George Thomas in my view, apart from my personal difficulties with him, was not a good Speaker. He was a bully and like many bullies he toadied to people in authority. As a consequence he failed completely in his duty of safeguarding the rights of the House of Commons by allowing the prime minister, Mrs Thatcher, to have virtually complete freedom to ignore its rules, a freedom she exploited mercilessly. I was not surprised at the number of scathing obituaries which appeared after his death, least of all at the particularly execrable one by a senior civil servant who had worked under him when he was a junior minister.

I was relieved and happy to be chosen in 1975 as a member of the U.K. Labour delegation to the European Parliament, relieved to get away from the claustrophobia of Westminster and my frustration there and happy to play a more direct rôle, however small, in furthering the ambitious European venture. The style of the parliament was very different and much more refreshing, even at a superficial level, than that at Westminster. It was, so to speak, much more 'free-wheeling'. There was an almost complete freedom from the pettifogging restrictions separating the sheep from the goats at Westminster, even separating the different breeds of the same species. For example, there were separate bars, canteens and dining rooms for MPs, lords, press, palace staff and 'strangers', the latter, by the way, an odd title for citizens of a democracy, or even for subjects of the crown. No MP would visit the press bar without an invitation, nor would he sit at a table reserved for another party in the members' dining room, even if that table were unoccupied. Conversely, no member of the parliamentary press lobby was allowed to enter the members' dining room or smoking room, even by invitation. At

Strasbourg on the other hand, facilities were communal and one rubbed shoulders with all manner of people in all manner of places except for the chamber itself.

Politics are politics, however and they could be as fierce at Strasbourg as at Westminster, even though the authority of the European Parliament had yet to reach its present-day level. I became involved in a bitter dispute with French members over the case of an individual Breton nationalist — or *autonomiste* — named Yann Fouere, a man not unknown in Wales. My interest in the case arose out of a request by his son, Erwin, a member of the staff of the European Commission at Brussels, to speak on his father's behalf. I had met Erwin at an estaminet called *Le Tambour* (The Drum) which also bore the Welsh title *Y Tabwrdd*. It was a place frequented by many Celts and one was often able to hear Welsh spoken there.

Yann Fouere was in prison, gaoled on what I was persuaded were political, not criminal, grounds. He had been awaiting trial for nearly two years and was undoubtedly suffering an intolerable injustice because of his Breton nationalist activities. I therefore raised the matter at a plenary session of the parliament, setting out the facts as I understood them in a lengthy speech. The French members were outraged that a non-Frenchman should attempt to intervene in their so-called judicial process. They raised the red herring that Fouere had collaborated with the Germans during the war, seemingly without realising that such a charge would lose them whatever support from the German members they might otherwise have had. I say 'so-called' judicial process because the purport of my speech was to demand that the French government should either bring Yann Fouere to trial or release him without charge.

Nothing happened for a couple of weeks, so I raised the matter again, saying that I intended to take the case to the European Court of Human Rights, a body set up under the auspices of the Council of Europe of which France was a signatory. The French Minister of the

Interior, a M. Poniatowski, had a reputation as a hard-line reactionary, a trait that made me even more confident that Fouere was indeed suffering an injustice. A week later the French government released Yann Fouere without charge. It was one of the more satisfying moments of my parliamentary career.

One happy consequence of the existence of *Y Tabwrdd*, was a highly successful St David's Day dinner we held at one of the city's hotels. A Welsh news-letter (in English) circulated at the time across north-eastern Europe from Brussels as far as Rotterdam. We advertised the dinner in it and received the astonishing number of over 100 replies reserving places at the dinner. I wrote to the renowned rugby coach Carwyn James, then at the height of his fame, inviting him to attend as guest speaker, an invitation which he accepted. I was privileged to act as chairman for the evening. To pay for that privilege, I purchased several boxes of leeks and a large box of safety-pins. If the conclusion of the Yann Fouere affair was one of the more satisfying moments, the night of the dinner was one of the happier and more memorable ones.

In 1979, the European Parliament for the first time was directly elected. I was pleased that it was, because it represented another step towards a federal Europe, a goal that I supported for reasons of political theory leading ineluctably in due course to political practice. At the same time, I was sad to be ending what had proved to be an enjoyable and satisfying time playing a small part in the creation of the new Europe. With, initially, some reluctance I returned to the Westminster hot house for what was to be a turbulent final two years as an MP.

16. A New Beginning

During the autumn months of 1980, a dozen or so of us like-minded Labour MPs of moderate persuasion had been meeting regularly to discuss the crisis developing within the Labour Party from the seemingly inexorable rise of the 'Loony Left'. We were anxious to counteract the trend, but by the end of November the meetings had yet to reach a decision likely to lead to a convincing future strategy. There was a great deal of huffing and puffing which led to the formation of the 'Manifesto Group' (the title chosen to emphasise the manifesto on which Labour had fought the previous General Election): this was to be yet another Labour Party pressure group like many which had existed previously in the party. The intention was to mount some kind of propaganda effort that would weaken the dominance of the Left. As far as I could see, however, we were playing gesture politics that would have no effect. The party's leaders in the shadow cabinet seemed incapable of preventing the national executive committee of the party from adopting ever more extreme policies, while at the party conference left-wing party activists displayed a rampant triumphalism. Our group at first had no intention of founding a new political party and when John Horam and I independently suggested such a move, we were derided. At the time Roy Jenkins was still President of the European Commission and would not relinquish the post until the end of the year. He therefore played no part in our early discussions although in his BBC Dimbleby Lecture, he had, of course, expressed his desire to see a new party taking up the centre ground of British politics.

I had come to a personal decision early in November that I would not stand as a Labour candidate at the next election. I had discussed the matter with my wife who agreed wholeheartedly with me. The Labour Party had reversed its position on several significant policies that a few months earlier it had been advocating strongly before the electorate. I like to think that I was not sufficiently cynical to conform to the new party line on so many important issues and to go before the Wrexham voters preaching what was in fact an entirely different ideology from the one I had preached a short while before. Not surprisingly, I felt a considerable release after making the decision. I was more content with myself and, although I told no-one of my decision, I felt much greater self-assurance at meetings of the group; my contributions were more confident, more pointed and at times perhaps, a little scornful of its prevarications. Towards the end of November I wrote a short paper setting out my views on the need to form a new party, partly to clear my own mind and more importantly to try and convince the group of the validity of that course of action. I sent copies of the paper in December to twelve people, including Roy Jenkins and Shirley Williams (she had lost her seat at the previous election) and I also sent a copy to David Steel, leader of the Liberal Party. The paper is reproduced below.

STRICTLY PRIVATE AND CONFIDENTIAL

December 1980
Position paper on the formation of a Social Democratic Party.

Reasons justifying a social democratic break-away from the Labour Party originate in at least three areas, each of which is important and should be considered in conjunction with the others before deciding upon a course of action.

Firstly, there are matters of immediate policy. These are obvious. Labour Party policy conflicts with that of a Social Democratic Party on many issues, e.g. Europe, defence, import controls, incomes policy, mixed economy, pluralistic society, second chamber, representative role of MPs, dominance of Party (and associated sectional interests) over Parliament etc. Compromise could be reached, possibly, on some of these issues, but it would be impossible to compromise on a majority of them. The argument that the policy differences don't really matter because Labour in power (nudge and wink) would be more responsible, is itself a cause of the deep cynicism which is now part of the British malaise.

Secondly, continuing British decline has roots in a parliamentary system in need of radical reform. The unique 300 year continuum of the English ruling class sustained by historical circumstances now clearly discernible, has provided a rare degree of consensus and political stability which England would not have enjoyed if the composition of that ruling class had suffered from the discontinuities common to many other countries. The idiosyncratic forms of our parliamentary and constitutional machinery — an unwritten constitution with its overtones of gentlemanly agreement, an electoral system designed for a severely limited suffrage now malfunctioning grossly, an omnipotent parliament yet unable to bind its successor — have faithfully reflected a political and social consensus the remaining vestiges of which existed until after the last war when, for example, leaders of the Conservative Party 'emerged' into being.

This consensus has ended and the machinery, no longer reflecting social reality, is proving to be inherently divisive. The House of Commons today is a caricature of a confrontational debating chamber with angels who can do no wrong on one side and devils who can do no right on the other side intervening capriciously and in depth in the life of the country. Radical reform is essential and the first step towards it is to smash the stylised two-party system, which is at present sustained by a seemingly inevitable swing of the electoral pendulum.

Thirdly the intellectual barrenness of the Labour Party is reflected by its concern with outdated and irrelevant dogma and by the increasing dominance of party apparachiks. Karl Marx accepted the epistemology of his age without question. The positivism permeating his work resulted in socialists becoming almost exclusively preoccupied with economism. Today the Labour Party is still obsessed with the politics of productivity at their most mechanistic. Yves Person has put it scornfully that some socialists want to make men not only equal but identical and interchangeable. Conformity and centralism have become so great an impetus to party collectivism, that the Labour Party is now only a small step away from joining more thoroughgoing socialist parties in the totalitarian politics of the ant-heap. A major task facing a Social Democratic party in Britain, is thus to join forces with radical thinkers on the continent, who have already begun to look for a new philosophic base on which to build a credible contemporary democratic socialism.

Each of these areas — policy differences, national decline and the parliamentary system, socialist (social democratic?) ideology — justifies a new party and a new start. Taken together the case becomes overwhelming. No high-minded social democrat can therefore refuse to take up the challenge. Small groups of people in fact exist inside and outside parliament who have decided in principle to do so and the questions that now arise should simply be those of how best in practice to set about the task, not of whether it should be attempted. It is important clearly to recognise this distinction.

The most fruitful start unquestionably would be made by a few dissident Labour MPs refusing the party whip and announcing their aim of establishing a new party. This group of MPs would be greatly strengthened if a number of like-minded former MPs were to join forces with them. Many practical and policy problems arise, outline solutions to which need to be agreed before an initial announcement. The most important of these involve the Liberal Party and do so at many facets.

The great strength of the Liberal Party is that it exists. The party ordinarily would field 600 or so candidates at the next general election. It is useful to recall that in the spring election of 1974 the Liberal Party polled over 6 million votes. Had it gained a mere one or two additional percentage points in its share of the poll, it would, as a consequence of the peculiar arithmetic of our electoral system, have won upwards of

100 parliamentary seats. The partial vacuum at the centre of British politics in 1974 will almost certainly be repeated or exceeded in 1983/84 and, therefore, the Liberal Party in a three-party electoral situation might well manage to gain 7 million votes and over 100 seats. A reasonable guess might be that it would fail to gain a blocking third of seats and that the two-party system would remain intact, but that a hung parliament could be formed.

A new Social Democratic Party has to ask itself how many candidates it proposes to nominate in 1983/84 and for that matter whether to contest by-elections meanwhile. It would seem improbable, when one is assured on the highest authority, that there is a time to every purpose under the heaven, that a fully-formed party armed with its own philosophy could spring up overnight and contest 600 parliamentary seats in direct challenge, not only to the existing two main parties, but also to the Liberal Party. This is the difficulty facing any new party, not that it has to have a great bloc of sectional support upon which to build.

One concludes that a social democratic ideology is a medium-term objective, for the achievement of which it is more relevant in the first instance to establish a relatively limited parliamentary presence than, disingenuously, to aim for substantial parliamentary representation. The practicalities of contesting hundreds of seats in three years time also present major problems, which it would be foolish to dismiss. Finally, if a Social Democratic Party were to contest a substantial number of seats, no electoral understanding, tacit or explicit, which might in certain circumstances be of mutual benefit, could be reached with the Liberal Party.

The foregoing does not imply that the formation of a Social Democratic Party limited to contesting a small number of seats in 1983/84 is therefore of marginal importance. On the contrary, it underlines the importance firstly of accepting that the Liberal Party exists and secondly of exploring mutually beneficial collaborative arrangements. It would not be too fanciful to argue that this is the key to the success of the whole operation.

The theology of a possible collaboration with the Liberal Party presents no insuperable difficulty in the short term. At the next election, Social Democrats and Liberals will be in close agreement on the policy issues referred to at the beginning of this paper. Indeed, important though separate manifestos would be in order to underline the separate identities and longer-term aims of the parties, the difficulty most likely to arise would be that of distinguishing one manifesto from the other. Both parties similarly would agree that the divisiveness inherent in the British system will increase unless the two-party grip on it is smashed. Neither of the two major parties when in opposition seem to appreciate that parliamentary democracy simply cannot work without a degree of consensus. Thus, in the two areas referred to earlier involving short-term considerations, the identity of interest between a Social Democratic Party and the Liberal Party would be sufficient for both parties honourably to aim for a modus vivendi. The tactical advantages of such a modus vivendi are considerable for both. They spring from the catalytic role that a Social Democratic Party ideally can initially perform. A group of, say, 40 Social Democratic candidates for the most part (?), with ministerial or parliamentary experience standing in electoral agreement with the Liberal Party, would have its own credibility enhanced as a natural grouping representing a particular point of view in tactical alliance with an existing party machine. Similarly, the Liberal Party would gain in credibility from its endorsement by experienced parliamentarians including some eminent names who would add a note of realism into an election campaign. The joint appeal to disaffected Labour voters as well as to conventional Liberals cannot be dismissed lightly. The longer-term aim of each party would of course be un-compromised.

In addition, there are practical consequences of an alliance, which are of importance, not least being the extra availability of broadcasting time, which could substantially strengthen joint credibility.

I believe that it is in this way that the immediate objective of at least gaining a blocking third of seats in the Commons can best be achieved. There are influential members of the Liberal Party who would be prepared meaningfully to discuss what form of alliance could best be shaped and who would strive to get it accepted by their party.

Finally, a conclusion from the foregoing reasoning is that there is little time to spare. If the leaders of the Liberal Party are to persuade their fellow members, then a Social Democratic break must be made during the next two or three months. In my view January 25th would be an ideal date for an initial statement.

A corollary to the above is that there is no need to persuade more MPs to break away than there are sitting Liberal members. I believe five Labour dissidents is an adequate number for making an announcement although of course the more there are, the better it will be. If we recruit enough so that our numbers naturally become more than the number of sitting Liberals, all well and good, but no artificial significance should be attached to this figure.

My main concern was the reaction of the Liberal Party in the country to the entry of a newcomer into the parliamentary ring. It seemed obvious that Liberals in the constituencies, having soldiered on for years putting forward candidates with little hope of success, would now be welcoming the change in the political climate and the promise it held for their party. There were two clear portents staring at them. Firstly, they had achieved a remarkable feat at the two previous 1974 elections when they trebled their 1970 vote and increased their 1955 vote by a factor of seven. Secondly, the Labour Party's share of the vote of 36.9 per cent at the 1979 election was its lowest since before the war, having fallen by 12 per cent of the total vote from what it had been in 1951. It seemed that at last the inexorable two-party pendulum swing was faltering. Furthermore, Labour's post-election disarray now seemed to be pathological. Liberal Party members in the constituencies were hardly likely to take kindly to an upstart party, which appeared to be stealing their clothes. Their loyalty, blind loyalty as often the case with party activists, would not easily be overcome with arguments such as I had outlined in my position paper. Indeed, Cyril Smith, a popular Liberal MP, expressed the mood with some colour when he said after the launch of the SDP, that it should have been strangled at birth. It was precisely because of the danger of public disagreement and dissension between the Liberal Party and the new SDP that I had suggested a figure of about 40 Social Democrat candidates, a number that we could reasonably expect to negotiate amicably with the Liberals, especially as there would be some sitting MPs as Social Democrat candidates as well as one or two highly respected names. Public disagreement between the two parties would be very harmful and possibly fatal, to our objective of 'breaking the mould of British politics'. In the event my fears proved well founded. More than any other factor, I believe that the difficulties in agreeing the allocation of English constituencies between the parties was the cause of the failure, at least for the time being, of the whole enterprise.

I received only one response from my colleagues after posting my paper, but it was a heartening and important one. Roy Jenkins phoned one Sunday night to say that he broadly agreed with the burden of my paper and that he was looking forward to joining our discussions after he had completed his term with the European Commission in a fortnight's time. From the rest of the paper's recipients, however, there was silence, even at our next meeting. I had not fully appreciated either the depth of David Owen's hostility towards the Liberal Party, or the dominance he exercised over the other members of the group. It was obvious that I had sinned against his prejudice and that discussion of my paper was taboo. Regrettably, I had to conclude that the other members of the group were too diffident to question his views, which seemed to be accepted as ex cathedra injunctions. Surely, I thought, my colleagues must have been aware of some of the arguments I had set out, arguments that needed to be debated before we could adopt a firm strategy. For the first time I began to have doubts about Owen's authoritarianism as leader of our group, let alone as leader of a political party. The doubts were to be confirmed comprehensively as time went by.

David Owen did agree in that meeting, however, without mentioning my paper, that the Liberal Party presented difficulties, which would have to be overcome. I was pleased to hear him say so because it implied a possible new party contesting the next general election. This was the first time in half a dozen meetings for anyone except John Horam and me to hint at the possibility of setting up a new party. Owen was now, it seemed, prepared to face that possibility, but he added, referring indirectly this time to my paper, that if any new party of which he was leader fought an election, he would insist that the number of its candidates would be at least equal to the number of Liberal candidates. I was alone in rejecting that condition, which could have meant, of course, although I was not sure that this is what Owen had in mind, that the new party would contest 600 or so seats in direct opposition to the Liberals. The meeting ended with an agreement that Owen and Bill Rogers (who was a member of the group) should consult with Shirley Williams and Roy Jenkins with a view to preparing a statement declaring our intention of forming a 'Council for Social Democracy' within the Labour Party. On that note, the meeting broke up for Christmas.

The result of their consultation was the publication by the quartet on Sunday 25 January 1981 of the 'Limehouse Declaration'. The names of eleven MPs and two former MPs (Williams and Jenkins) who were behind the venture were given and the press coined the sobriquet 'The Gang of Four'. We had not yet decided to form a new political party, but I consoled myself that we were well on the way to doing so.

Before the next meeting of the group scheduled for a few days later, we received a note from David Owen saying that the meeting would be held in Shirley Williams' house and that she and Jenkins would be present for the first time. It was a memorable meeting lasting for over four hours. Throughout that time, Roy Jenkins slowly led the group towards taking what was to be a fateful decision. I felt considerable pleasure and admiration as I observed a powerful mind at work in a committee, a memory that has remained with me to this day. Two or three of us would make a contribution to the discussion and then Jenkins would summarise what we had said, each time taking the logical step with persuasive reasoning towards the inevitable decision to form a new party. The difference between his and David Owen's style was striking, the one obviously a big man with imagination, feel and humour, if perhaps short of assertiveness, the other a lesser man over-loaded with self-assurance. The unanimous decision of the meeting was to launch a 'Social Democratic Party' by the end of March at the latest. The last eight words were my small contribution to the debate.

A number of press conferences were arranged for 26 March — the first, a morning conference, was held in London. It was followed by afternoon conferences in Cardiff, Edinburgh, Manchester, Plymouth, Newcastle and Birmingham. Roy Jenkins and I held the one in Cardiff. I felt elated afterwards and went home determined, in Roy Jenkins' metaphor, to get the aeroplane off the runway and flying. The first problem was to build an administrative framework out of the human resources arriving in a flood in of letters of support from across the country. The establishment of a new party was an opportunity to provide a structure corresponding to the wishes of the new members, most of whom had become disenchanted with British politics and its political parties. David Owen's wish — and that of the majority of the former Labour MPs — was to have a centralised structure similar to the one in which they had been apprenticed, despite their claims that they intended "to bring politics nearer to people". The latter claim, one imagines, led to the somewhat bizarre superficiality of the press conferences spread across the country. Much more importantly, a small minority of MPs, including myself and the large majority of new members in Wales as we were to discover, wanted a federal structure for the party. The seeds of disagreement between Wales and London were sown from the start.

Two weeks later I placed press advertisements inviting supporters of the new party to meetings at Cardiff and Wrexham. About 150

On the platform alongside Roy Jenkins at an SDP press conference.

people attended the Cardiff meeting and 60 the one at Wrexham. Within a few weeks a skeleton administrative framework for Wales was in existence and at a meeting of our acting executive committee it was decided to hold a conference at Pontypridd. We were on the road to our objective of having a Welsh Party, at least de facto, as part of a federal British Party. A childish quarrel occurred between David

Owen and me as a consequence of that decision. I had previously suggested at a London meeting that we should hold a British conference in the autumn. Owen ridiculed the idea on the grounds that there was not sufficient time to appoint delegates with authority to vote, although of course, what I had in mind was a rally to maintain the party's momentum. It was as a result of Owen's dismissal of the idea that the Welsh committee decided to hold its own conference, except that later we called it a seminar to appease feelings in London. A day or two after the Welsh decision, I was chatting to John Roper in the member's lobby of the House of Commons. John was acting as our whip and I told him of our intention in Wales. He immediately went in search of David Owen to inform him. Within a few minutes both were back in the lobby and Owen instructed me that we were not to hold the conference. When I asked him why not? he replied "Because I'm telling you so". I wagged my finger in front of his nose and said: "David, don't you ever dare to speak to me like that again". He turned on his heels and left without saying a word. The conference was held on the 19 and 20 September, although as I said, we called it a seminar to try and mend bridges between Cardiff and London. It was a successful event attended by nearly 200 Welsh members, but this time I had sinned unforgiveably.

Our relationship was made worse when a little later Owen changed his mind and a British conference was planned after all. His demeanour in those early days was, I thought, verging on the dictatorial and his centralist management attitudes echoed those of the Labour Party, which had produced a reaction in that party leading eventually to an almost anarchic state of affairs. I became more and more concerned at our own centralised authoritarianism. Therefore when it was decided to hold an autumn conference, not at one venue but at three (Perth, Bradford and London), in order to demonstrate "our determination to bring politics nearer to people," the hypocrisy was more than I could stand. I wrote a letter to *The Times* pouring scorn on the arrangement and saying that what needed to be brought nearer to people was not administrative gimmicks but sincere political debate. I was grateful for the support of the Welsh Party when the storm broke over my head.

A week after the peripatetic conference we pushed the boat out further still. A formal meeting was held for the first time between the Welsh social democrats and the Welsh Liberal Party, to the annoyance of some people at the SDP's London headquarters. We had already written to the National Steering Committee asking for formal recognition as a 'Regional Party' with an office at Cardiff. Fortunately, the Liberal Party was a federal party and the Welsh Liberal Party was a constituent part of the federation. Its leaders were jealous of their considerable degree of autonomy. They agreed, unhesitatingly, to our request that they would refuse to enter into negotiation with the Social Democrats, unless it were with a delegation from the 'Welsh' Social Democratic Party. At that first 'Welsh' meeting three significant points were agreed:

i. An alliance of the two parties should contest every Welsh constituency at the general election;

ii. The allocation of constituencies should be broadly equal in number between the two parties, not only overall but also in respect of the more winnable seats;

iii. To facilitate the allocation of constituencies, Wales should be divided into three parts, north, midlands/south-west and southeast.

A small working party was set up to negotiate the seat allocations. None of us expected difficulties in meeting the second of the three conditions. Those seats, which might otherwise have been regarded as contentious, were clearly spoken for by the political circumstances. The SDP representatives on the working party had privately agreed that there were four seats, which the Liberals were obviously entitled to contest. They had a sitting MP in one Welsh constituency, they had held another seat for a very long time only to lose it narrowly at the previous election. In two other constituencies the same individuals had contested the seats four or five times and had nursed the constituencies for many years. I found it beguiling, therefore, when the leader of the Liberal team at the start of our first meeting, announced rather naively that no matter what was decided at the meeting, there were four particular seats, which would be contested by Liberals. I immediately said that this sounded more like an ultimatum than a negotiation. Nevertheless, we would accept his point, which meant that the SDP was entitled to choose the next four seats. Could he tell us which four seats he had in mind? They were, of course, the ones we had anticipated. The meeting and three subsequent ones then carried on amicably. The only real difficulty we experienced was at a third meeting when arrangements were finally agreed on the seat allocations. John Roper, MP arrived unexpectedly and without invitation. He said that he had come to represent the SDP's London headquarters, but he soon lost his credibility. He began to direct the meeting, issuing ex cathedra instructions, so to speak, on seat allocations, many of which had already been agreed. Unfortunately for him, he asked in a weak moment for a map to see where the Torfaen constituency was situated. The leader of the Liberal group intervened scathingly: he was not prepared to accept directives on seat allocations from a man who had to have a map to know where they were. From then on we were left in peace.

At a press conference in February 1982 Geraint Howells MP (leader of the Welsh Liberals) and I, publicly signed an agreement stating which of the two parties would contest each Welsh seat. The members of both parties had been consulted throughout the negotiations and the agreement was supported by a substantial majority in each case. Negotiations in England and Scotland were still proceeding, although apparently there were serious difficulties in England. By this time an understanding of sorts existed between the two parties. One could even argue that a de facto alliance had come

Welsh SDP Committee with Gwynoro Jones on my left and, on his left, Winston Roddick, later Counsel General to the National Assemby for Wales.

into being, the electoral prospects for which were highly promising. Opinion polls registered just over 50 per cent support for the two parties contesting the general election as a formal alliance. David Owen and David Steel who were meeting regularly had begun to talk of a 'partnership of principle' and of a new beginning for British politics. Roy Jenkins, not yet an MP, (he had been narrowly defeated in a by-election at Warrington, a normally safe Labour seat) was now at the Hillhead by-election emulating Gladstone's Mid-Lothian campaign and making superb speeches to capacity audiences night after night. The Labour Party was falling into ever-greater disarray. The future seemed bright.

Alas, there was a worm in the wood. Bang in the middle of the Hillhead campaign, the difficulty I had feared since the day David Owen claimed parity of numbers with the Liberals, suddenly became a calamity. The difficulty was that of overcoming the natural reluctance of constituency Liberals to concede large numbers of seats, which they had contested many times in the past. It was now proving insuperable. Bill Rodgers, who was leading the Social Democrats on the English joint working party, announced that he was breaking off all contact with the Liberals, who were impossible to deal with. That announcement was the fatal blow that killed off the Alliance's prospects, although the dying body continued to receive numerous other wounds inflicted by an insincere and politically inept SDP leadership.

Two memories of Bill's disastrous announcement remain clear in my mind. I was having supper at home with my wife one Sunday night when we heard the news on the radio. My wife turned to me and said, "Ho, you're just like the other parties, quarrelling amongst yourselves." I have always regarded my wife in her detachment from politics as typical of the great majority of the public and thus as my reliable political weather vane. I felt at once, therefore, that her comment was highly significant. My second memory is of a comment

Roy Jenkins made the following day in Hillhead. I had asked him what he thought of Bill's announcement. Like me he feared the worst: "We're in danger," he said, referring understandably to the Hillhead by-election, "of snatching defeat from the jaws of victory". The danger, I believed, would be even more widespread.

As it happened, Jenkins won the seat, but his victory was not sufficient to halt our slide in the opinion polls that began immediately after Rodgers's misguided declaration. Our support fell quickly to about 25 per cent, where it stayed until the election. There were other influences, however, also undermining our appeal. The first was our three-way split in a vote in the House of Commons on a trades union reform Bill introduced by Norman Tebbit, some of us voting in favour, others against and some abstaining. The press had a great time making fun of us, calling us a bunch of headless chickens with no sense of direction. I fumed at the lack of perspective of my fellow members — we were claiming that we were going to break the mould of British politics and yet we could not agree on a matter that was completely marginal to the establishment of the new political force with which to do the job. The second unfortunate influence was the election of a leader of the SDP, a matter that should have been a formality. Roy Jenkins was now an MP and the obvious man for the job. David Owen, however, quite presumptuously in my view, decided to stand for the post. Worse still, he was creating the impression of discord in the party, especially about our relationship with the Liberals and the 'partnership of principle', an impression that in truth was a reflection of the reality. This added impetus to our slide in the polls. A third unfortunate influence, possibly, was the Falklands War. One heartening incident, however, was the Gower by-election in September 1982. The Alliance candidate, a former Labour MP, achieved a swing of ten per cent in his favour as compared to the Liberal vote in 1979, a good performance although not as good as the 14 per cent swing achieved by Roy Jenkins.

By the Spring of 1983 the Alliance had succeeded at last in sharing the parliamentary seats between the two parties, 312 to the Democrats and 318 to the Liberals. David Owen's narrow objective had been realised, but the cost to the overall purpose of the endeavour was calamitous. We went into the election of June 1983 standing at about 22 per cent in the opinion polls, when not long previously we had been at 50 per cent. The Alliance gained 25.4 per cent of the vote and 23 seats, Labour had 27.6 per cent and 209 seats, the Conservatives had 42.4 per cent and 397 seats and I lost my seat.

17. Culmination

I was bitterly disappointed at the result of the 1983 election. The opportunity of 'breaking the mould' of British politics had been missed and, to make matters even worse, Thatcherism had been given its head. More pointedly, I had lost my own seat and I was now less well placed to make a contribution, however small, towards resuscitating the campaign for greater democracy. My immediate reaction on the morrow of election day was that of recrimination against the duplicity of a few leading members of the SDP whose covert scorn for the Liberals had eventually become manifest and had exposed the disingenuousness of their claim that the Alliance was a felicitous 'partnership of principle', Trust, that essential requirement for successful electioneering, had been grievously damaged. The recrimination was shared by the majority of SDP and Liberal activists in Wales, recrimination that subsequently and, rather paradoxically, made a positive contribution to the cause by stimulating yet closer collaboration between the two Welsh parties. As a consequence, the history of the Alliance after the election was influenced greatly by events in Wales where the trail was blazed that led to the formation of the Liberal Democrats. It was a story of increasing co-operation, one step at a time, with the initiative each time being taken in Wales, to be followed a few months later by the parties at a British level, sometimes reluctantly, at other times less so. The process finally reached its logical conclusion at a British level with the departure into political oblivion of a rump of SDP members led by David Owen and the formal merger of the two parties to become the Liberal Democrats.

Roy Jenkins resigned as leader of the SDP immediately after the election and David Owen was elected as his successor. Jenkins had been subjected to foolish, unfair and damaging criticism of his leadership voiced publicly from within the party during the election campaign. He was also not in good health. I was disappointed that he had resigned, not least because I foresaw a difficult period ahead for the relationship between the party in Wales and the new leadership in London. It turned out so, in spades.

One of the first difficulties concerned the Welsh party office at Cardiff. Its future was in jeopardy, partly because of the shortage of funds, but also because of pressure from London to centralise the administration and hence authority, for political reasons. Party offices were closed in Manchester, Birmingham and Bristol. The Welsh Council of the party, however, proposed that it should share an office with the Welsh Liberal Party, a constituent party of the federal British Liberal Party. The suggestion was anathema to the SDP leadership, but nevertheless, a joint office was in fact established at Cardiff in November 1983 to the accompaniment of a furious chorus of objection from London. During the same month the two Welsh parties agreed on the allocation of constituencies to be contested at the European Parliament elections in June 1984. More significantly, a small 'Joint Liaison Committee' was established having joint chairmen in the persons of Gwynoro Jones, a former Labour MP and parliamentary private secretary to Roy Jenkins and Winston Roddick, QC, a prominent Liberal who later became Counsel General to the National Assembly for Wales. A week later and more significantly still, the first formal meeting of the 'Alliance Committee for Wales' was held. The Welsh Councils of the SDP and the Liberal Party constituted this body and it was seen in Wales as the formal governing body for the Welsh Alliance. It was clearly an important step towards a union of the two parties, if only at a Welsh level. Its establishment was received less than warmly by the London leadership of the SDP and caused what seemed to be apoplexy on the part of some London-based politicians.

At that first meeting on 19 November 1983, a number of significant decisions were taken. They included first, the co-ordination of policy between the two parties in respect of Welsh matters, second, an agreement on the framing of a long term political and electoral strategy, third, the joint promotion of the Alliance in Wales and fourth, the establishment of a permanent joint administration in Wales.

Two months later the Welsh SDP convened a 'Consultative Assembly' at Cardiff to discuss two specially prepared papers, one setting out the case for a federal constitution for the British party and the other entitled *Wales and Europe*. The latter paper was the first to be prepared formally for discussion by the two parties. It was later debated and accepted at the annual Welsh conferences of both. The most significant consequence of the Consultative Assembly, however, was the unanimous acceptance of the first paper and the decision to submit a resolution based upon it for debate at the next meeting of the British Council of the SDP.

I had a brief respite from what had become a seemingly continuous round of committee meetings when, during the summer of 1984, I stood as an Alliance candidate in the North Wales constituency for election to the European Parliament. My agent and sub-agent were both prominent members of the Welsh Liberal Party. During that election campaign, undoubtedly the most pleasing incident occurred one fine morning, fine in more senses than one, when I canvassed the poet, R. S. Thomas, at his cottage in the Llŷn peninsula. He welcomed me warmly although I was a stranger to him. My excuse for calling on him, apart from the flimsy one of seeking his vote, was that I admired his work enormously and that I possessed every one of the books that he had published so far. He published several more afterwards, of course, bringing his total to 29 volumes of poetry (one published posthumously). I am the proud possessor of the complete collection. We chatted for over an hour, mainly about literary matters and, while it was not the most rewarding use of time from an electoral point of view, for me it was the most important and rewarding experience of the three weeks of campaigning, an occasion I continue to treasure and shall do so as long as I live. The one thing that would have been more important did not happen, I did not win the seat.

Another election during 1984 was the Cynon Valley parliamentary by-election for which the Alliance had chosen a 26-year-old candidate. At the time, David Owen insisted on interviewing prospective candidates at by-elections to satisfy himself of their suitability. Thus the day arrived when Felix Aubel was interviewed by the leader. "Don't you think that you're rather young to contest a parliamentary election?" asked Dr Owen. "Yes, I do," answered Felix, "but I'm reassured by the thought that I'm a year older than you were when you fought your first election."

Following the March meeting of the Welsh Consultative Assembly, a resolution calling on the British party to adopt a federal constitution was tabled by the Welsh SDP for debate at the next meeting of the party's Council in Edinburgh at the end of May. At that meeting the resolution was accepted by a substantial majority of the Council despite fierce opposition by the leadership. A federal structure for the SDP was now a serious proposition. An even more significant development in the long term took place during the summer, however, when the Welsh Joint Liaison Committee agreed the allocation between the Liberals and the SDP of parliamentary constituencies for the next general election in three or four years time. The significance lay in the method of choosing candidates. Two thirds of the Welsh constituencies were shared equally between the two parties and each party in those constituencies was to choose its candidate by its normal procedures. The remaining third of the seats, however, were to be chosen by one or other of two novel methods, each revolutionary in its impact on party autonomy, one even more so than the other. The methods were called 'Closed Joint Selection' and 'Open Joint Selection'. Under the first, one of the parties in a constituency would prepare a short list of candidates from members of that party and then the members of both parties in that constituency would vote to elect a candidate from the short list. Under the second method, or Open Joint Selection, the short list would include members of both parties. The constituencies where Joint Selection applied were not promising ones, to be sure, but the importance of the process lay in its establishing the principle under which the two parties moved still closer together.

By this time, poor old Gwynoro Jones had become a member of the SDP executive committee in London. At its meeting held after the electoral arrangements in Wales had been announced, he received an extremely hostile reception and was bitterly criticised when those arrangements were discussed. David Owen seemed to believe that it was Gwynoro and I who were the sole initiators of the agreement with the Liberals and that we were malign influences constantly leading astray the Welsh members of the SDP. As a result, it was decided to send a delegation to Cardiff to lay down the law to the Welsh Council for tamely accepting the misbegotten policies dreamed up by the two bogeys. The delegation, composed of Bill Rodgers, Mike Thomas and Alex McGowan (SDP general secretary), attended a specially convened meeting of the 30 strong Council. They were stunned by its response. They were obliged to listen for over three hours to speech after powerful speech supporting the Welsh leadership and bitterly criticising London for its lack of political vision and its apparent detestation of a Liberal Party, which twelve months previously it had been extolling as a fellow member in an honourable partnership. At the end of the meeting a resolution was carried unanimously which contained the following sentence: "In the light of the fact that this Council has not heard a convincing argument to the contrary, the Council sees no reason to withdraw its support for the Welsh electoral agreement and calls for an immediate decision by the London executive committee to support that agreement." A chastened delegation returned to London.

In the meantime, the Welsh Liberal Party at its Annual General Meeting had passed a resolution containing the somewhat sweeping sentence: "The meeting reaffirms its objection to discussing any matters relating to the Alliance in Wales with representatives from outside Wales." It was clear that the party members were aware of the attitude, at best ambivalent, of some SDP members towards the strengthening of the Alliance that was taking place in Wales.

The co-operation between the two Welsh parties grew ever closer over the following months, the momentum being given a further push by the Alliance candidate's victory in the Brecon and Radnor by-election in June 1985. A few months later, yet another significant development took place in Wales. It was decided to hold a conference of the Alliance as if it were a single party, the first such conference to be held in Britain. Preliminary discussions within both parties in Wales led to the decision to allow voting to take place on resolutions tabled for the conference. The conference, held in November 1985, was attended by over 300 members from both parties, of whom about 200 were voting delegates. David Steel and David Owen attended on the Saturday morning.

Two debates in particular aroused interest in the media. The first, on devolution, resulted in a vote of 139 to 55 in favour of a substantial measure to be introduced as soon as possible. It was generally acknowledged afterwards that the Alliance had put devolution back on the Welsh political agenda in line with the strong demand that continued to exist in Scotland. The second debate, on defence, was eagerly awaited by many observers who were anticipating a Liberal/SDP split on the issue, which was clearly defined in a prepared paper strongly supporting membership of NATO and the retention of a nuclear deterrent. The vote at the conclusion of the debate showed that an overwhelming majority of members agreed with its recommendations. The paper was adopted by a vote of 181 in favour to 5 against.

Following almost every such development in Wales and there were many, some bigger and some smaller, a similar development took place a few months later at a British level, until the day came when the question of merging the two parties to form a single party had become inescapable. Special conferences of both parties were held, at which decisions were taken to unite, albeit with a small number of dissentients voting against in each party. In the case of the SDP, a small group led by David Owen departed with the intention of forming their own new party, but in fact went into political oblivion as their rump party faded away. I retain cherished memories of the two conferences, especially that of the Liberal Party at which I was privileged to be allowed to speak. I recall one prominent Welsh Liberal telling the conference from the podium and with not a little conviction in his peroration: "We have reached a cross-roads; we shall never be at this cross-roads again and there are two ways we can go!" He earned deafening applause. I myself, I'm sorry to say, yielded to the slick glibness of the politician, by saying that I had never been a member of the Liberal Party, but that I had been a liberal all my life.

There was discussion after the merger on a name for the new party, some people, including Roy Jenkins, favouring the retention of the name 'The Alliance', Others felt the historical resonance of the name 'Liberal' so appealing as to merit its retention. In the end justice was done to the two founding parties by naming the new party 'The Liberal Democrats'. On looking back on my time in the pit and in two parliaments — British and European — I feel that the name of the new party combines two elements of my temperament and it is under that banner that I have continued to engage in political activities, although nowadays only at a local level.

18. Life After Death

When I left the Labour Party for the SDP early in 1981, I realised that at the following election I would cease to be an MP because Wrexham was a safe Labour seat. I was reconciled to the fact although I regretted it. Several months later, however, the Electoral Boundaries Commission decided to split the Wrexham constituency in two and combine each half with parts of other constituencies. In effect, one half of the old Wrexham became a radically transformed new Wrexham constituency and a brand new Clwyd South West constituency was formed out of the other half. Neither of the two new constituencies appeared to be a safe Labour one. My earlier fatalism had quite fortuitously received a salutary corrective. The Liberal/SDP Alliance decided to contest both new constituencies, the one with a Liberal and the other with an SDP candidate. Martin Thomas (now Lord Thomas of Gresford) and I were chosen as the two candidates and we agreed that, as I was the more fluent Welsh speaker, it would be appropriate for me to contest Clwyd South West which included parts of the Glyndŵr District Council area. Hence, my count at the close of election day in 1983 was held in Corwen Pavilion, a cavernous building left stranded after a national eisteddfod and a place where, in company with 3,000 other people, I had once heard Aneurin Bevan sparkle as only he could.

I lost the election to a Conservative candidate by some 1,500 votes. I was bitterly disappointed, a reaction that surprised me since at one time I had been quite reconciled to the loss of my seat. I suppose the explanation is that it was a disappointment at the dashing of newly raised hopes. Hope, it seems, springs not so much eternally in the human breast, but intermittently according to circumstances. Furthermore, reality when it strikes, does so more deeply than one imagines beforehand. I confess that my dismay was wholly personal, rather than dismay at the loss of a seat by the Alliance; dismay is too strong a word for the detached assessment of a political party's failure to win a particular parliamentary seat.

Gradually, however, my equanimity returned as I began to pick up the political threads once again, at first to assist in the eventually successful efforts at merging the two parties of the Alliance to form the Liberal Democrats, efforts pioneered, as I have already said, in Wales. Two of the more public of my political activities during this period were as candidate at two elections, the one a parliamentary by-election at Pontypridd, the other in the North Wales constituency at a general election for the European Parliament. At Pontypridd, the Labour candidate trounced me, but in the European election I came a very creditable second to the successful Conservative candidate.

The coal industry had died suddenly. The eventual death of an extractive industry is inevitable, of course, but for an industry as large, significant and diffuse as coal had been a mere couple of decades previously, its end, when it came, was needlessly bitter and painful. Better strategic leadership on the part of the management when the industry was flourishing, would have prolonged its life sufficiently to ensure that it was able to die gradually and peacefully; better tactical leadership on the part of the union when the industry was languishing would also have eased much of the pain. I have voiced my criticisms of management failings earlier. Criticism of the union is more difficult because the circumstances were more complex. The split that developed in the union was itself the cause of much bitterness. A formal divorce took place in Nottinghamshire, a large coalfield employing many thousands of men and a rival union was born with policies very different from those of Arthur Scargill. In north Wales, a very much smaller coalfield, the divorce was informal and consequently a more messy affair with even greater pressure falling on the shoulders of the local miners' agent.

Ted McKay confronted Arthur Scargill like a David confronting a Goliath and suffered personally for his efforts. I admired his courage and good sense greatly, especially when I compared him with the south Wales miners' leaders who also had the sense to know what was happening, but who lacked the moral courage to reject Scargill's kamikaze policies. North Wales miners have had five agents since the 'North Wales and Border Counties Mineworkers' Federation' was formed. I rate four of them, Edward Hughes, Hugh Hughes, Ted Jones and Ted McKay, as excellent leaders and if I had to choose the best, I would be hard put to decide between Edward Hughes, the union's founder and Ted McKay. After Bersham closed, Ted McKay, who had played a prominent part in the unsuccessful effort to retain one of the headgears at Gresford, yet again showed his worth, this time successfully.

In 1986 Bersham colliery closed, the last colliery to do so in the Wrexham coalfield. A few years previously, many people had been affronted by the local authority's negative response to a proposal to retain one of the Gresford colliery headgears when that colliery closed in 1974, both as a memorial to the miners who had lost their lives there in 1934 and as an acknowledgment of the part coal had played in the life of the local community. When Bersham closed, however, it appears that the Council had become aware of the public's repugnance at its earlier lapse. It did not need a major campaign, therefore, to persuade it to make amends, even if the retention of a headgear at Bersham could hardly have the resonance of one at Gresford. The former miners' agent for the coalfield, who had been a fierce opponent of Arthur Scargill, led successful efforts at persuading Wrexham County Borough Council to purchase the site. This was transformed into a small industrial park, but the main coal-winding headgear and engine-house have been preserved. Their future, alas, was still not assured and a small group of ex-miners and local historians began a campaign to raise funds to develop the immediate area around the headgear and engine-house into an 'interpretation centre' where schools and members of the public could gain an understanding of the part played by coal in moulding Wrexham's character. Fortunately, the headgear and engine-house have now been scheduled as historic monuments by the National Assembly through its agency 'Cadw'. The lack of enthusiasm still shown by our local authority for doing justice to the memory of the local coal industry is difficult to comprehend. One would have expected the Bersham project almost routinely to have had an honourable slice of the Library and Museum Committee's annual budget so that the site could be made into an appropriate historical centre.

There is an irony in all this which arose from a private company's proposal in 2003 to purchase the Bersham pit bank and use the spoil as industrial hard core. The residents of the nearby village of Rhostyllen, however, some of whom live literally within a stone's throw of the bank, have objected strongly to the proposal. Although the bank, when viewed from the village, is covered with an attractive growth of trees and foliage, one suspects there is an element of sentiment based on historical grounds in the desire to retain it as it stands. It so happens that several years previously the Wrexham Council had transformed the unsightly Hafod bank, a mile or so distant, into a nature park complete with trees, vegetation and nature trails, a largely un-sung exercise now begining to fructify. Almost certainly, however, had there been a proposal at the time to remove that bank, no one would have objected. It is not simply the intimate

The Bersham Colliery headgear, a solitary reminder of the North Wales Coalfield, awaits development as part of a heritage site.

nearness of Rhostyllen to Bersham bank that makes the difference, but also the growing public awareness of a need to retain something of the heritage of what was once the region's principal industry. The following paragraph is taken from the web site of the 'Friends of Bersham Colliery':

Coal mining used to be one of the major industries of north Wales, lasting from early times up until 1996 when the last working colliery at Point of Ayr finally closed. Today, however, most of the old colliery buildings have been demolished, shafts have been filled and remains of this important industry are being lost forever. Strangely, as the remains get less, the public interest in industrial archaeology seems to be growing and over the past few years there has been great demand to see the working conditions of our ancestors. However, if you go to the site of ex-collieries like Point of Ayr now, you will see nothing, as all the surface buildings were completely flattened.

Bersham Colliery closed earlier, in 1986, but we were lucky that the actions of local people like Ted McKay managed to preserve the orignal headgear and engine house. These are now the only complete ones left in north Wales and desperately need preserving while we still have time.

It is not just the sentimental nostalgia of people looking back at the coal industry through tinted spectacles that motivates groups such as the 'Friends of Bersham Colliery', but also a desire to ensure that succeeding generations should have a sense of their own history. A profound change has taken place in Wales in my lifetime regarding Welsh history. During my schooldays it was regarded as a non-subject. That attitude now has been completely subverted, as witness the remarkable achievments of Welsh historians during the post-war years and the public demand in Wales for popular literature on the subject. There are, of course, fascinating reasons for the change in attitude, not least the extent of contemporary social, economic, political and industrial change, the latter being most comprehensive in the old coalfields.

The change in my life in 1983 was, of course, considerable. I became more active in areas where previously I had been involved only at the periphery. One such interest was in the work of the Electoral Reform Society, of which I had been a member since the early 1970s and had been elected to its governing Council. The Society was a long established body campaigning for the introduction of a particular electoral system known as the Single Transferable Vote. It derived its income principally from two sources, members' contributions and income derived from conducting ballots for large organisations, mainly trade unions. This latter function grew appreciably following a reorganisation of the Society's management structure in the mid-1970s. Previously, the Society's Council of fifteen members had supervised the staff conducting the ballots. It was an unsatisfactory arrangement because too many individual members of Council felt a need to give instructions, often contradictory, to the staff. The embryonic business displayed the worst features of management by committee. During my period of office as vice-chairman of the Society and at the instigation of the staff, the structure was changed so that ballots were carried out by a newly formed small company called Electoral Reform Ballot Services. The company was wholly owned by the Society but had an 'arms-length' relationship with it. The company has since grown into a flourishing business and now conducts ballots for many types of bodies such as shareholders of large industrial companies, building societies and insurance companies as well as for trade unions. It also carries out ballots for central and local government, for example ballots of parents of school children. The Society's income has grown correspondingly. That fact directed my activities for several years after I had lost my seat.

A charity called the McDougall Trust, of which I became chairman of trustees in 1982, was associated with the Society. The Trust gave grants to research workers in the fields of electoral systems and representative democracy, but its relatively small endowment income, when divided into a dozen or so annual grants, was being used to little effect. The Electoral Reform Society had for some time produced an annual news-letter giving a cursory survey of electoral developments. I proposed to the Society that the Trust should be responsible for producing the news-letter, my intention being to concentrate its limited financial resources on the task of developing the news-letter into a quarterly journal of standing. That has been achieved and *Representation* is now a major journal in its field, having a world-wide circulation and receiving unsolicited articles from leading academics and practitioners of five continents. The development was facilitated by a financial arrangement with the blossoming Electoral Reform Ballot Services.

I had accepted the responsibility of chairing the Trust on the condition that a young graduate employee of the Society would be seconded to work full time for the Trust as an administrative assistant. It was an inspired choice and Paul Wilder, the young man in question, is now the managing editor of *Representation* and is recognised as a leading authority on electoral systems and representative democracy. For several years I attended the London office each week, sometimes for one day, at other times for two or three days. The work of chairing the trustee and editorial board meetings — we gathered together a small but distinguished editorial board — commissioning contributors, writing editorials and an occasional article, proof reading and so on became ever more time consuming. It was highly satisfying, however, not least because it was happening during a period of considerable public interest in electoral systems. Major reports were being commissioned, notably by the Labour Party (Plant Commission) and the government (Jenkins Commission). I wrote a critical assessment of the Jenkins Report, based on inside knowledge shortly before it was published, which resulted in a slight chill manifesting itself in my previously warm friendship with Roy Jenkins. The following are the opening paragraphs of my editorial, written shortly after the publication of the Report:

> Change in Britain's social culture during the second half of the twentieth century, for a host of reasons, has been dramatic. Change in her political culture has been considerably less so. Consequently, the

two cultures, to use an ugly modernism, are out of synch; they do not mesh. That fact lies behind the demand that the country's political institutions be modernised to meet the requirements of a society where 'Jack is as good as his master'. In political terms this translates into making parliamentary democracy something more, much more, than the opportunity to 'throw out one lot and put another lot in'.

The present government, therefore, deserves praise for embarking on a programme of constitutional reform. Like many people, it is clearly aware that the existing polity is unsatisfactory. What is less clear, however, is whether the government appreciates how deeply reform must penetrate if British democracy is to reach a level adequate for the society it aims to serve.

The seminal reform involves the political party. Any number of seemingly radical changes in the existing machinery of the country's parliamentary government would be woefully inadequate if the nature and role of party as prime mover were to be left unscathed. It is that reform, however, which our politicians resist fiercely and unscrupulously. They know that party is the linchpin of their own political involvement.

That is why the establishment of the Jenkins Commission was, potentially, of enormous importance and why the four criteria laid down in the Commission's terms of reference were to be welcomed so warmly. Unfortunately, it appears at the time of writing (September 1998) that a fifth criterion has been introduced which is proving decisive. It is also undermining the importance of the exercise. That criterion is the insistence that, whatever the Commission recommends, must be 'feasible', or less euphemistically, acceptable to the government. The extra criterion raises issues ranging from the profound to the shallow, from so-called political idealism to so-called political realism, from moonshine to sophistry; worst of all, it compounds the fraud already covert in the referendum exercise. The fraud lies in the fact that the alternative electoral system when it appears on the referendum ballot paper will have been chosen by the Commission, solely from the point of view of party at the expense of that of the electorate. The choice will have been rigged before the public can express its view and before any serious public discussion takes place on its merits. Two systems chosen to represent both points of view would have resolved the dilemma.

The article continued in much the same vein to disparage the work of the Commission in its seeming subservience to the prejudices of the government and, of course, inevitably implied doubt as to the political integrity of its chairman. I ended the editorial article with the following broadside:

> When a radical, indeed revolutionary, opportunity occurs, firstly to question Britain's political culture and the hegemonic role of the private institution of party within it and then to suggest a means of democratising that culture, the opportunity is nobbled, seemingly by common consent, before it can be grasped. The oligarchs are indisputably in control. The failure to challenge that fact, not the algebraic subtleties introduced into the recommended system, will, one ventures to forecast, be the historic indictment against the Jenkins Commission. Tactical political considerations will have undermined what should have been a report of great significance. Public understanding of Britain's democratic problem will remain minimal and the irony could well arise of a weak, fabricated cause, in any case being trounced by dissident government voices.

Jenkins's view, that, whatever else his Commission did, it had to ensure its final recommendation was acceptable to the government, was wrong on two counts. Firstly, it ignored an essential democratic requirement by assuming that the ultimate criterion for choosing an electoral system is that it should be fair as between political parties. That is too narrow a criterion because it is less than fair to the voter. How is one to vote for a preferred party whose candidate one disagrees with profoundly on, say, capital punishment, devolution and membership of the Euro?

Perhaps I can put the matter vividly by referring to a question I was once asked when I addressed an audience of schoolchildren. A brave young girl asked "Do you have to be good-looking to be an MP?". Out of the mouths of babes and sucklings comes forth wisdom.

During the referendum campaign on whether the U.K. should remain a member of the European Community (as it then was), a number of well known faces appeared on our television screens. On one side of the argument were Enoch Powell, Peter Shore, Neil Marten and Tony Benn, while on the other side were Ted Heath, Roy Jenkins, Joe Grimmond and Willie Whitelaw. Many people surely voted on what was a difficult and complex question by assessing the characters of the proponents of each side. It seems the 'Yes' ones were better looking!

The ability of voters at an election to choose between a number of candidates of the same party, produces in the long term a significant influence on the character of the party. Most notably it militates against extremism as the party comes gradually to reflect more sensitively voters' assessments of the characters of individual candidates. The classic example is that of the Republic of Ireland, a country which at its birth in 1922 was faced with a civil war and the loss of 5,000 lives, but which years later was sufficiently at ease with itself to maintain a successful 'social contract' that led to economic prosperity. Ireland today, with the exception of Luxembourg and its special circumstances, is the wealthiest of all 26 members of the European Union.

The second error on Jenkins's part was his conviction that the government would in any case put in place the electoral system he recommended. Hence the historic indictment I have referred to above. The real debate is not the one addressed by Jenkins but one of whether an extension of democracy should be regarded as imperative. There are many people who believe that it should. The following passage by Professor John Dunn speaks for an increasing number. He is referring to a statement by an American feminist which, he says:

> ... carries the voice of democracy across the ages: the demand to speak for oneself, to be heard and to make what is said effective in the texture of lives lived together. That voice has never gone unchallenged and it

has often been very thoroughly suppressed. But two and a half millennia after Kleisthenes it is clearer than it used to be just how hard it is to keep it suppressed. The democratic hope is that, for as long as there continue to be human beings, it will never again be silenced.

Despite the satisfaction of firing off broadsides in the slowly ripening constitutional debates, I found as I got older that journeying each week to the office in London was becoming increasingly burdensome. Also, by 1999 the editorial board of *Representation* had well and truly established the journal as one of the major journals in its field. Thus shortly before the turn of the millennium I retired gracefully. My hobby now, other than that of washing dishes, has been to undertake the close study of contemporary poetry that I had long wanted to make.

There is a Welsh proverb — 'The old know, the young surmise' — which I have come more and more to lean on as I have grown older myself. I suppose that I rely on it as a valid excuse for being less and less concerned with the trivial burdens of everyday life and being more and more concerned with occupying a retreat amidst the eternal verities expressed by poetry of the first rank. I have long had an interest in poetry and can remember occasional lines of verse from my primary schooldays, lines such as "The Assyrian came down like a wolf on the fold," "The road was a ribbon of moonlight crossing the purple moor when the highwayman came riding, riding up to the old mill door," and, of course, "Mary call the cattle home across the sands of Dee," a line, incidentally, that I was thrilled to see engraved under a coloured glass window depicting the estuary when the Bersham Colliery committee visited the office of John Summers' steel works for lunch.

As I grew older, the interest deepened and became, I trust, more discerning, both in English and Welsh poetry. It has always struck me as odd, however, that in matters poetic I have found contemporary offerings more appealing than those of the greats of past centuries, while in music the opposite holds. I find modern music much less appealing than that of the period ranging from the baroque to, say, Schumann and Brahms. Another of my peculiarities is my failure to appreciate some great contemporary poets e.g. T. S. Eliot, while revelling in others e.g. W. B. Yeats. In Welsh, Gwenallt fails to stir me, while the cousins Williams Parry and Parry-Williams both strike twelve. But in English language poetry R. S.Thomas stands supreme. I am the proud possessor of every book of poetry he has published, from *Stones of the Field* in 1946 to *Residues* published posthumously in 2002. As befits a critic manque I have taken to writing short monthly articles in my old age for my *papur bro*, dealing with various aspects of R. S. Thomas's poetry. On one occasion, however, I reverted to firing a broadside, not in order to defend the poetry, but to defend the man.

R. S. Thomas had made a speech in which he advocated pasting notices in the Welsh-speaking heartland telling non-Welsh-speaking immigrants that they were not welcome because they were destroying the local culture. The following morning the police announced that they were 'making inquiries' into the circumstances of the speech, implying that a prosecution was being considered. I was stung into writing in reply a long article for the *Western Mail* newspaper headlined 'British justice in the dock'. It began uncompromisingly: "British justice is hardly the envy of the world: on the contrary it has become something of a sick joke. The pressures which have deformed the judicial system and brought about this pitiable state of affairs have been imposed in turn and in varying situations by the government, the judiciary and the police." The article then quoted examples from the three institutions, concentrating in the case of the Welsh police on numerous manifestly prejudiced actions in 'Welsh language cases'. I argued that in an explosive language situation, as it was at the time, we had had too many examples from the police of a less than balanced approach to the sensitive political issues involved. The article ended:

"The emerging picture is of a police leadership antipathetic to the Welsh language and all efforts at fostering it. Mechanistic interpretations of the rule book for what look suspiciously like perverse reasons do not serve the cause of justice. This cause suffered a grievous setback in Wales nearly 20 years ago when the supposedly randomly chosen jury in a 'language case' at Carmarthen was for the most part composed of people with names like Arbuthnot-Bodger or Noddington-Smythe with not a Jones, Edwards or Williams in sight. A positive act of discrimination from the police in Wales in favour of the language would now do something to restore the balance in favour of justice." I do not know whether the article had any effect on policing policy; at least, no statement followed that 'a man is helping police with their inquiries'.

In recent years I have lived a quieter life, devoting some time to writing my autobiography — *Dan Loriau Maelor* (Under Maelor Floors) — and latterly engaged upon translating that 'masterpiece' into English. I hope now to indulge myself for a few more years writing profound insights into the poetry of R. S. Thomas for the benefit of my Rhosllannerchrugog fellow parishioners.

APPENDIX I

Why Electoral Reform

The following is the text of a pamphlet written by the author for the Fabian Society in 1980.

Democracy is today a freely used word; it is at the same time a difficult one. Mass-democracy presents even greater difficulties. Nevertheless the effectiveness of its mass-democratic institutions must be a paramount consideration for the citizens of a country whose most significant political development during the twentieth-century has been the erosion of its formerly hierarchic social and political structures. Britain today has become a laterally structured society in which Jack is as good as his master. At long last the unique 300-year-old continuum of the country's ruling class has been ruptured bringing to an end the seemingly effortless stability and success, which had characterised it. In the meantime extraordinary problems have arisen impairing the effectiveness of Britain's political institutions.

Problems of adaptation present themselves especially in respect of two essential characteristics of mass-democratic government: firstly that it depends on a sufficient degree of consensus which can be represented existing in society and secondly that its leaders should trust the people sufficiently. Neither characteristic, each of which complements and stimulates the other, is convincingly demonstrated in Britain today. The shortcomings are particularly grievous for Britain because of her unique tradition of unfettered parliamentary sovereignty — the 'very keystone' of the unwritten constitution — whereby parliament is free of the encumbrances of a written constitution, constitutional court, separation of powers, federal structures, delegated membership and almost, one might say, bicameral prudence. To justify this somewhat extraordinary constitutional arrangement, society must at least feel that parliament truly represents it and can be trusted.

An additional problem is that British parliamentarians, conditioned slavishly to follow outmoded practices some of which today are aberrations, seem to be instinctively prejudiced against these two essential characteristics of mass-democracy and to be determined to prevent their being established in any meaningful degree. For Britain to regain her self-assurance and poise therefore, it has become necessary for the British people, despite the waywardness of their political leaders, to insist on their proper democratic entitlement.

Two common myths, held against the weight of all the evidence, must be demolished initially if significant advances are to be made. The first is that the British parliamentary system of democratic government is the finest in the world. Nowadays perhaps, in the face of its more obvious shortcomings, some people shamefacedly might concede let us say, that it is served by parliamentarians of less than the highest calibre, but nostalgia for past glories still persuades them of the system's continuing superiority. The myth draws sustenance from many sources. An example is the melange of parliamentary flummery on which it feeds, the archaic ceremony and procedure, sentimental nostalgia about the Mother of Parliaments and the country's long history of stable parliamentary democracy, wishful thinking about our effortless constitutional supremacy — the easy flexibility of an unwritten constitution, that gentleman's agreement denied to lesser mortals — and the commonplace snobbery evoked even today by the idea of gallant if hardly patrician amateurs muddling through successfully in the end. Or again there is the more direct influence of luddite politicians determined to retain the system under which they were apprenticed to their craft and which has served them well. Many of them with their own tributes are only too anxious to humour a national proclivity in parliamentary matters dangerously predisposed towards self-congratulation.

The second common British myth is that electoral reform while no doubt desirable in itself and worthy of support, is of marginal political significance; that it is merely a do-gooding, fuddy-duddy, middle-class thing, a Liberal whimsy concerned with arithmetic and best left to clever people in colleges to argue about. The established politicians, however, appreciate that electoral reform is political dynamite and oppose it implacably for that reason while at the same time nurturing the myth by pretending less vehemently to disparage electoral reform either as an irrelevance or as perverse, foreign obscurantism.

It is important to demolish the first myth because a causal relationship can now be established between the shortcomings of Britain's parliamentary system and her chronic decline. The importance of demolishing the second arises from the fact that introducing an appropriate electoral system incorporating a much stronger democratic bias is probably the single most effective practical step one can readily take which would initiate radical qualitative change for the better in the parliamentary system. The aim of this pamphlet is to justify both those claims. Before considering these political issues, however, it might not be inappropriate first to look briefly at some factual and quantitative aspects of the present British electoral system.

British Electoral Arithmetic and Its Aberrations

The British electoral system, like universal suffrage and the franchise itself, was not established in antiquity and there are no historical grounds for regarding it as sacrosanct. Prior to the 1884 Reform Act, the majority of constituencies were multi-member and even under the 1918 Representation of the People Act, 13 constituencies had two members of which all were not finally abolished until 1950. In addition, in the multi-member university seats (Oxford, Cambridge, combined English universities, Scottish universities) which also survived into the post-war era, candidates were elected under the Single Transferable Vote (STV) system of proportional representation.

Nor is there an international consensus for the British system, thereby suggesting that it is overwhelmingly attractive. Out of some two dozen or so leading western democracies, only four — Canada, New Zealand,* the USA and South Africa — operate our simple majority system and some of these countries have other constitutional balances (separation of powers, federal structures, constitutional courts, written constitutions, etc.) which ameliorate the adverse consequences of British-type electoral arithmetic.

In Britain the system has in fact resulted in comparatively short-lived governments. Between 1964 and 1974, largely because of the waywardness of external events, we had little of either strong or stable government. Four elections in ten years, providing an average of 30 months a government, was even worse than the average of 35 months between July 1945 and October 1974. A more seriously debilitating result of the system, however, is that since 1935 neither of the major parties has been able at an election to muster over 50 per cent of the votes cast let alone 50 per cent of the electorate, yet they have formed governments with large majorities in the House of Commons. Indeed, on two occasions since the war, a party which had

---

* New Zealand now has a different system.

received less electoral support than its main rival actually held a majority of seats and formed a government. One could well argue in a Fabian tract that the course of British history might have been very different if, in 1951 for example, the Labour Party with its highest ever vote, a figure never again achieved, had won its proportionate share of parliamentary seats. In fact Labour, with 48.8 per cent of the vote, returned 295 MPs and the Conservative Party, with 48.0 per cent, returned 321 MPs to claim a substantial parliamentary majority.

The concept of a 'mandate to govern' much trumpeted by party leaders after successful elections, is clearly disingenuous and at best no more than a claim to exploit a perverse set of rules. At worst, as will be seen, it has become, under the British system, a licence under which extravagant and simplistic appeals to the electorate reduce politics to a cynical game of goodies and baddies. The bias in the system is in fact profoundly anti-democratic. Neither major party is concerned with trusting the people or with the credibility of its policy. The aim is to cultivate a dichotomy of interest expressed by two parties, based largely on sectional and class differences and then simply to wait for the swing of the pendulum when 'our turn will come'. It is this heightened and frequently unreasoning partisanship on the part of the politicians, and the stunted application of the concept of governing with the consent of the people, which is at the root of the public cynicism surrounding politics and politicians in Britain.

The phenomenon of large numbers of wasted votes, votes which have played no part in choosing the final representation either because, in a particular constituency, they are given to a minority party, or because they form part of an excessive majority of the dominant party, also helps in producing frustration and ultimately cynicism. The mood is reflected in the arithmetic, by the large number of abstaining electors and the declining proportion of votes received by the two major parties, despite the ineffectiveness of the system in sustaining a three party House of Commons. The turnout at the general election of 1950 for example was 84.0 per cent, whereas in October 1974 and May 1979, the figures were 72.8 and 76.0 per cent respectively. Even the 1950 figure compares unfavourably with the 90 per cent or more nowadays achieved in several continental countries (apart from those where voting is compulsory) using systems of proportional representation, where a much greater proportion of the votes cast are used to effect. The most recent British administrations, the Labour government of 1974 and the present Conservative government, were elected respectively by 27.8 per cent and 33.3 per cent of the electorate.

The combined Labour-Conservative share of the total vote (not electorate) in October 1974 was just 75 per cent. That compares with the period 1931 — 1970 when it averaged 91 per cent and never fell below 87 per cent. From a Labour point of view, however, the most starkly chilling comparison is between its vote in 1951 and 1979. The electorate increased during the period by 5.7 millions from 34.6 millions to 40.1 millions while the Labour vote fell by 2.4 millions from 13,948,605 to 11,457,079.

Another important aberration of the British electoral system, is the discrimination exercised against minority parties and their supporters, seen at its worst probably in the February 1974 general election when the Liberal Party was rewarded with 14 parliamentary seats for its 6,063,470 votes. Each of the two main parties at that election had less than twice as many votes as the Liberal Party, but captured more than twenty times as many seats. Any political party, which claims to support a democratic system of government based on parliamentary representation and, at the same time, refuses to remedy so gross an injustice, cannot deplore criticism of its own lack of idealism and morality, nor complain when the democracy itself begins to show symptoms of the cancer at its heart. Nor, for that matter, can a politician claim to be a socialist as some do, including members of the Fabian Society, who cannot see that a socialism which does not struggle against abuses is depriving itself of its *raison d'etre.*

The abuse of the franchise is bad in itself, but even worse are the consequences of that abuse. Two in particular need to be drawn to people's attention. Firstly, a feature of British political life now seems to be that in large parts of the country a single party holds a permanent monopoly of representation. For example, in the south-east region of England from Kent to West Sussex, in the south from Berkshire to Dorset and in the south-west from Avon to Cornwall, the Conservative Party, which received about 54 per cent of the vote in 1979, holds 107 out of a total of 116 seats. There are 1.5 million Labour voters and 1.2 million Liberal voters in the whole region, some of whom would have to travel 100 miles to contact their nearest Labour or Liberal MP. The phrase 'two nations' has acquired a new and dangerous territorial connotation, which would never have entered Disraeli's mind.

Secondly, Lord Acton's dictum about power tending to corrupt has been confirmed on a number of occasions in recent years, especially in the field of local government when monopoly control enjoyed by both main parties has been well established. Caucus rule untrammelled by effective democratic restraint has been given its head in too many areas for the good of democracy.

Finally, there is one other 'factual' consequence of the British electoral system worth noting. An elector, if he chooses to vote for a particular party, is unable to choose between individual candidates from that party. If his party's candidate, chosen usually by a small group of party activists, happens for example to represent a wing of the party not to his liking, then the elector's dilemma is a difficult one.

What Kind of Electoral Reform?

Electoral reform is frequently regarded as being synonymous with proportional representation, the implication being that the prime or even the only aim of reform should be that a political party be awarded seats in an assembly proportionate to the number of votes it received at the election. This mechanistic view, however, despite its virtues, is a limited one, chiefly because an exclusive preoccupation with proportionality is bound to leave the voter's options too closely circumscribed. The elector's dilemma mentioned in the previous paragraph can be as pronounced with electoral systems striving for absolute proportionality as with the present system.

In Israel, for example, candidates' names do not appear on the ballot paper; only those of the political parties do so and a Labour supporter would simply vote for the Israeli Labour Party. The party is then allocated a number of seats in the *Knesset*, proportional to the number of votes it has received in the one national constituency. The system achieves almost complete proportionality between parties but, it can be argued, convincingly, that this quantitative achievement does not justify the qualitative decline in the democratic nature of the representation, since the actual individuals who sit in Parliament are nominees of the party machine, thus depriving the ordinary voter of any influence he might otherwise have had in deciding this key democratic function.

This is an important principle connected, ultimately, with the quality of the democracy it inspires. A democratic electoral system should enable the voter, as far as possible, not only to support the political parties he prefers but, also, to choose the individuals from those parties who in fact constitute the parliament. Indeed, the system should go further. While in practical terms the political party is a convenient, perhaps essential, vehicle of representation, it should not be exclusive. One could visualise for example, a feminist who was more concerned with electing women rather than voting a party ticket.

The electoral system, therefore, should be designed to accommodate such essentially democratic aspirations as well as achieving party proportionality and a balance has to be struck between the two aims. It is here that the democratic characteristics — trusting the people and the existence of a degree of consensus — have their roots. The ideal electoral system enables both characteristics not only to stimulate each other but, also, to develop the subtle and complex political inter-dependence of a genuine mass-democracy, which is at the same time a decisive governing system.

The stark alternatives of British politics are a consequence of an over-developed party exclusivity brought about, not least, by the dichotomising bias built into the electoral system. For this reason, preferential voting allowing voters the freedom just described is desirable, despite the fact that it may lead to a slight loss of proportionality. Reform of the electoral system should aim beyond strict party proportionality although, clearly, greater proportionality than exists at present is essential. Achieving this fine balance between greater discretion for the voter and proportionality for the parties, should be central to electoral reform. That is why a comparative assessment of the various available systems is of much more than academic interest. Furthermore, the argument that, because any system of proportional representation is better than existing electoral arrangements, the choice of system should be made on the grounds of which one MPs are most likely to accept, begs a crucial question, namely whose interest the system is designed primarily to serve, that of MPs or that of the democracy itself?

Systems of Proportional Representation

There are broadly two systems of proportional representation, which are commonly accepted as being appropriate to British circumstances, although there are many adaptations of each. They are the 'multi-member' system with its preferential voting and the 'topping-up' system. Confusion about the relative merits of the two arises from the fact that they are sometimes viewed from different standpoints; that of the MP and that of the voter.

Some MPs, who are prepared to accept the need for electoral reform, favour the topping-up system and decry the multi-member system. There is a jealous resentment at sharing a constituency with other members, which may be rationalised by stressing the importance of an alleged personal link between a member and his constituency that can be forged only if the constituency has a single member. On the other hand, evidence is strong that citizens who have elected MPs under a multi-member system are glad to have the opportunity of choosing any one from a number of MPs in their constituency to deal with problems.

There are many similar 'technical' advantages to be had under the multi-member system, such as the greater proportion of women or blacks likely to be elected under it who would all rank as MPs of equal standing, but the true merit of the system is incomparably more important. It is that the system gives the voter more discretion in deciding the nature of his representation and, thus, indirectly of his democracy. Not only is a much higher proportion of the votes cast used to some purpose, but the individual voter can express his preferences between two or more candidates from different wings of the same or any other party. Over time, he will not only shape the character of 'his' party, but it in turn will more sensitively respond to the subtleties which the voter with his greater discretion can now express. A doctrinal party like the Labour Party, if it is to remain in business will be obliged intellectually to regenerate itself — a process, which in turn will lead towards nurturing consensus. The process is vital to the health of what is, at present, an excessively polarised British politics wallowing in the dogma of 50 years ago.

The Quality of a Democracy

The foregoing brief look at some technical and quantitative aspects of British elections can hardly have concealed the real issues. They are qualitative ones and the mechanics of elections become important only because of their influence on the quality of democratic government. The demand for electoral reform grows inexorably, because government in Britain today is demonstrably capricious, divisive and even undemocratic. It fails primarily in the democratic essentials of trusting the people and fostering a degree of consensus. Indeed, the British system of parliamentary government seems today as if calculated to divide the British people and to produce a maximum of antagonism between two dominating sections of society — Big Labour and Big Business — which are allegedly in conflict with each other.

Before considering these defects in greater detail, however, the causal connection should be clarified between the electoral system and the quality of British democracy. Perhaps one of the most succinct admissions that the connection is a direct one, was that quoted by Professor H. W. R. Wade in his 1980 Hamlyn lectures.

> I cannot help quoting, since it reveals the situation so candidly, the guidance issued several times in 1976 and 1977 by the General Secretary of the Labour Party, urging that Labour supporters should oppose proportional representation as the method of election for the European Parliament. His argument was that it would then become difficult to resist pressure for proportional representation in the British Parliament and he was reported as saying: 'Proportional representation means coalition government at Westminster on the lines of our European partners and it is goodbye then to any dreams or aspirations for a democratic socialist Britain'. There could hardly be a more honest admission that the party could not carry out its policy if the voting system fairly reflected the wishes of the electors and that it must rely on the possibilities, indeed probabilities, of what the Blake Commission called 'flagrant minority rule'.

There are probably as many definitions of democracy as there are of socialism and thus one man's 'dreams or aspirations for a democratic socialist Britain' might not necessarily be the same as another's who also regarded himself as a democrat and a socialist.

However, if one takes democracy simply to mean no more than the endorsement through the ballot box of the broad policy proposals of a government and putting aside questions of participation and representation to influence that policy, the Party Secretary's admission is a devastating commentary on the party's attitude to democracy. But the admission is even more ominous and malign than might appear at first sight.

The editorial in *The Guardian* newspaper of 16 June 1980, discussing the then current constitutional controversy in the Labour Party, together with the Party Commission of Inquiry's newly published proposals for strengthening party democracy, boldly proclaimed that 'The electorate is Labour's final judge'. The article went on to argue that 'the ultimate test' of the Commission of Inquiry's recommendations was whether they would strengthen or weaken the party's appeal to the electorate the next time round. That may have been so, but only in the limited sense of what was electorally expedient for the Labour Party within the existing system. The real issues facing the country — 'the ultimate test' — are broader.

One accepts, for argument's sake, that the basic issue convulsing the Labour Party in recent years has been that of democracy. It is here that the question arises of whether *The Guardian's* proclamation was not an over-simplification of some significance, or whether in Britain the electorate really is the final judge. The evidence is now overwhelming and well documented that the electorate, at best, is less influential in that role than it should be in a democracy and, thus, incidentally more cynical and that at worst it has become irrelevant. It has already been pointed out, for example, that on two occasions since the war a party has gained a majority in the House of Commons and, consequently, formed a government, although another party had received greater support from the electorate, while governments elected on minority votes have now become a permanent British peculiarity.

However, the cancer is deeper-seated than might be suggested by a couple of arithmetical aberrations. The unhappy circumstances of the Labour Party controversy — *The Guardian* article's subject matter — arise ultimately from the fact that Labour has become a doctrinal party without a doctrine. It is the intellectual sterility and barrenness that cause most concern to 'democratic socialists' conscious that 'Labour is nothing if not a crusade' and anxiously seeking a credible contemporary ideology to crusade for.

The Party General Secretary, however, was content in the knowledge that there is really no need for a valid doctrine, or even a set of credible policies, to gain the support of a majority of the electorate. Hidebound party activists know that under the British electoral system their turn will come, if not next time round then the time after. The swing of the pendulum is a certain feature of that system. Here lies the malign nature of the Party Secretary's advice. In its cynical repudiation of the need for intellectual regeneration, it panders complacently to the simplistic rhetoric of the reactionary and the atavist. His advice was an admission not only that the 'democratic socialism' being offered is unattractive to the British people, but that the Party knows this and is content to let it be so. In short, the Party exists for no other democratic purpose than to get itself elected by exploiting the perversity in the rules.

It is here that the democrat arrives at his truly 'ultimate test'. The test can be defined succinctly. The real threat to democracy arises when it is no longer necessary for policy to be credible. The causal connection between the electoral system and the quality of British democracy is thus manifested. More worrying still (given the idiosyncratic nature of the country's constitutional arrangements) is the fact that it would not need a great deal more cynicism than that flaunted in the Party Secretary's advice, for British democracy to be immediately under a grave direct threat arising from an imprudent exercise by Parliament of its sovereign power.

Historical Change

A sceptical response to this argument of course, would be to ask how Britain has succeeded over the centuries in maintaining her stable democracy, which has been the envy of the world?

The short answer is that her electoral system at anyone time reflected social and political reality to best advantage and that it is precisely this, which is no longer the case. The history of England has been characterised by Perry Anderson as being that of a country enjoying a unique continuum in its ruling class. From the Civil War onwards — itself hardly revolutionary by French standards — the historical process contrived to produce a ruling class which, as an amalgam of established agrarian aristocracy and newly emergent manufacturing *bourgeoisie*, was not only peculiar to England but provided the basis for a rare political stability. The political balance, enjoyed in the England of the nineteenth-century, would hardly have been realised if the composition of its ruling class had suffered from the discontinuities common to many other countries. Furthermore, the imperialist tradition, reaching its climax during the latter part of the nineteenth century, contributed to the sense of undisturbed and easy superiority and reflected itself in the unabashed jingoism of the turn of the century. Geography too played its part in sparing the island country from the traumatic experience of an invading army. Thus, the continuum was consolidated and the national psychology set in its distinctive consensual mould of superior, chauvinistic conceit.

It was a psychology conditioning Englishmen to a world where Britannia carried the white man's burden across an empire on which the sun never set, where a quarter of the world's population were grateful British subjects, where the phrase 'the thin red line' somehow transformed brute imperialism into the inspiring chivalry of amateur gentlemen practising the virtues of *noblesse oblige*. In this world, aristocrat and manufacturing bourgeois, hybridised during the long continuum and not a little helped by the peculiar English invention of the public school, together provided the imperial success which the new British state used in its mystification processes, so that the proletariat became willing and docile partners in the continuous development of capitalist Britain. The consensus within the minority ruling class was faithfully reflected by the burgeoning proletariat, at least for a little while longer.

During the latter half of the twentieth century, however, it has all come to an end — the success, the power, the imperial rôle, the tacit consensus; — to all appearance within a generation. It is a bitter pill to swallow and all the more difficult, therefore, to make the substantial adjustment towards mass-democracy and the development of new skills and institutions required for its effective government. The inertia is at its greatest, the traditions most entrenched in Parliament, that ultimate repository of power at the apex of the hierarchy, upon whose sovereignty has rested the constitutional tradition of the United Kingdom, whose privileges have been sacrosanct, whose authority absolute, whose voice has decided the fate of continents and where clashes between the front benches have been sufficient acknowledgement of democratic pretensions. The accretion of such complete power by Parliament, extraordinary though it appears today, was a natural consequence of the stability and success provided by a ruling class that had remained a small minority of the population. It is noteworthy, for example, that even after the great industrial leap forward in the late eighteenth and early nineteenth centuries, the Reform Bill of 1832 carefully limited the extension of the franchise to the new manufacturing bourgeoisie only.

One consequence of that stability was the unwritten constitution. There was never a post-revolutionary moment, nor one after a war of independence, or *coup-d'etat* or, even, secession when the Englishman had to sit down to pen his new constitution. The British Constitution 'just growed'. There were no extra-parliamentary estates of the realm to cause difficulty. The crucial political requirements were met, that a consensus existed in what was a small exclusive ruling society and that parliament in fact represented it. Indeed in 1850 half the members of the House of Commons had blood relations there. Contemporary society, however, is not that of the nineteenth-century although the last vestiges of the closed consensual circle that constituted the establishment of that time, persisted into the post-war period when, for example, leaders of the Conservative Party still 'emerged' into being.

Radical constitutional reform is now urgently needed to reflect a new society and its masses. The key to this process lies within the electoral system. A seemingly minor piece of the old machinery — the simple majority system of election which, rather like a show of hands might have been adequate for electing a parliament at the end of the nineteenth-century — is clearly unsuitable for a modern mass-democracy which will not function adequately if the political intention is merely to replace a lumpen-proletariat by a lumpen-graduariat! The plain fact is that the electoral system no longer reflects society to advantage — indeed in its failure to adapt to modern requirements it has exercised a malign influence on British parliamentary democracy both in theory and in practice.

Theoretical Objections

In theoretical terms the very concept of a supreme parliamentary authority, constrained by neither written constitution nor constitutional court, directing the affairs of a modern highly centralised unitary state, is itself hardly reconcilable with that of a full-blown participatory or even representative mass-democratic society such as, one assumes, social democrats aspire to (one uses the phrase social democracy since democratic socialism has become altogether too ambiguous, the noun having the adjective by the throat!). The anomaly is compounded when the executive, represented in practice by at best half a dozen members of the inner cabinet, dominates Parliament through its highly developed whipping system, the extraordinary effectiveness of which is itself traceable to the electoral system and the dichotomous nature of British party politics. More ominous still, in the case of the Labour Party is the increasing erosion of the representative nature of the MP and the shift of power quite openly from Parliament to the party.

There has thus been a clear failure in post-war years, to adapt the parliamentary institutions and the political structures of the state to the needs of mass-democracy and the representation of the people. Instead, there has been a shift of power towards the extra-parliamentary agencies of government, managers, unions, the media and, most recently, party. Any attempt to resolve the dilemma requires at the very least, that representation should be as true a reflection as possible of the general will of the people and not of sectional interests and should be designed towards fostering such a general purpose. We have already seen, however, that this minimum but seminal requirement is completely subverted by the existing simple majority system used in British elections. It is clear, therefore, that a powerful argument exists in theoretical terms for radical change.

Practical Objections

The damage done, in practical terms, through an outmoded political structure, buttressed by an undemocratic electoral system, is even more obvious and ubiquitous. The one heartening sign, amidst the gloom of Britain's chronic post-war relative decline, has been the growing realization that the roots of the problem are not in economics and that the decline will not be reversed by a government simply adopting technically 'correct' economic strategies. There are now many references in the literature to deeper-seated sources of infirmity.

Bernard Crick, for example, as long ago as 1964 was pointing to more subjective but no less real influences:

> Britain today suffers under the burden of three native curses: that of amateurism, that of 'inner circle' secrecy and that of snobbery. All three seem to debase both the quality of political life and the energy of economic activity. The unreformed Parliament is more than a symbol of these things; it helps to perpetuate them by the most effective of all forces in politics and society — example; if Parliament were reformed, the whole climate of expectations could change, much of the sweet fog we muddle through might lift ...
> [Quoted by Tom Nairn in *New Left Review*]

The 'sweet fog' has since been dissipated by straightforward disenchantment. Roy Jenkins, when he left Westminster to become President of the European Commission, expressed the view that 'When all possible qualifications have been made, there can be no doubt that the British political system has failed adequately to promote the long-term interests of the British people — not merely over the last 20 years, but over a much longer period. In my view, there can also be no doubt that that failure has been due, not merely to obdurate circumstances, but to some features of our system of government and politics and to the conventions and assumptions which underpin it' [*op cit*]. Dennis Kavanagh writing at the end of 1978 refers to criticism focussing no longer on economics and society but on "... the political institutions, particularly the workings of the two-party system and the sovereignty of Parliament". Finally, Tom Nairn in a comprehensive yet succinct paragraph expresses more radically the now growing agreement:

> So it would be more accurate to say that the nature of the state is the proximate cause of the British crisis. It is our constitution, our political and administrative system and an associated penumbra of civil hegemony, powerful yet hard to define, which maintain society on its hopeless course ... What is this nature? ... The unwritten constitution

reposing sovereignty upon the Crown-in-parliament rather than the people; a two-party political order placing stability before democracy; ... [*op cit*]

It is this failure to transfer sovereignty to the people, which is at the heart of the matter and it is here that a start must be made on the cure, complicated though the sickness may be. And the first move must be in the matter of electing a parliament, the practical first step towards more comprehensive reform. It is significant that the immediate symptom of British democracy's morbidity, is the low esteem in which the electorate holds Parliament and the cynicism with which it regards politicians. It is certainly not too fanciful to argue that parliamentary shortcomings have themselves been a major stimulus to the weakening of morale, the collective loss of will and the political cynicism now plaguing British society.

The Simple Majority or First-past-the-post system, converts marginal differences in the numbers of votes cast for parties at an election into significant differences in the numbers of parliamentary seats they hold. The extraordinary probability — there is in present British circumstances an almost actuarial certainty to it — that if three parties were respectively to receive 34, 33 and 32 per cent of the votes, then one party could be awarded 350 seats and another only 50 seats, is made even more bizarre by the possibility that the party with the largest number of votes could receive the fewest seats. Thus, by its very arithmetic, the system sustains the dichotomy which for so long has been, at least apparently, a feature of the House of Commons and which now, in the absence of the nineteenth century basic consensus, is real as well as apparent. Difficulties are bound to arise in any modern industrial state, especially where government has an almost absolute constitutional dominance, if small changes in national sentiment produce such capricious changes in representation. The immediate practical consequence is the stridency introduced into the political process. It is a kind of inverse to the law of diminishing marginal utility, with parties ever more outrageously outbidding each other for the last one per cent of the votes.

This has led to a depreciation of the franchise. Universal suffrage has turned out to be no more than a quasi-democratic veneer laid over an old oligarchy. The roots of the present-day British malaise are bedded in this deceit. A modern advanced state, depending on the initiative, skill, professionalism and responsibility of its citizens has no role for a lumpen-graduariat passively accepting whatever lot its betters in their capricious ways, provided for it as its nineteenth-century proletarian grandfathers were obliged to do. The need, instead, is to develop a role for a mass-citizenry, displaying the authority, responsibility, self-discipline and assurance that membership of a true democracy demands.

To this end, the necessary degree of consensus about basic objectives and the country's destiny has to be fostered by the political system. In Britain, however, two major parties are obliged to vie with each other at elections, pandering to the masses with policies of 'bread and circuses'. The syndrome is established, of simplistic and open-ended demands from the voters for all manner of goodies on the one hand and cynical promises from would-be rulers on the other, to deliver the moon in return for a few votes every four or five years. The whole thing is profoundly anti-democratic. Any sense of mass-democratic participation, by citizens shouldering heavy but creative responsibilities, difficult though this may be to engender, is profoundly discouraged. In short, the transition from oligarchy to democracy has been bungled and made more difficult by the electoral system.

In addition, the system has imposed an immobility on the House of Commons itself. Here a stylised adversative posture remains sacrosanct — a kind of bedraggled and rather pathetic virility symbol, for romantic sentimentalists hankering after past gladiatorial glories, without realising that this is a luxury to be afforded only when a basic consensus exists. The two sides of the chamber are occupied by parties, each of which vows, when in power, to undo what was achieved by the other when it in turn held power. The posture with its premium on the simplistic at the expense of the meaningful has become a major stultifying influence on British attitudes.

It is not simply that British Members of Parliament are conditioned by the system into seeing the political issues in the starkest terms, but that in addition it accentuates and perpetuates divisions, thereby promulgating facile solutions to unreal problems. That is why the real issues are not tackled. They are to do with the political and social structures of the state, the democratic involvement they beget and the political leadership they inspire. It is why the Labour and Conservative Parties, not simply at their fundamentalist extremes but at their centres, are reactionary parties fighting the irrelevant battles of long ago. It is also why the British people are denied the political leadership to which they are entitled. Anyone who would question the foregoing has only to listen to debates in the House of Commons where politics is still the old battle between the haloed angels on our side who can never do wrong and the horned devils on the other side who can never do right. One refrains from commenting on the superficialities of style that have developed in what passes for debate — the insensitive crudeness and the callow prejudice merging occasionally into baying infantilism.

What follows inevitably is that the British people scornfully drift into ever-greater depths of cynicism. Even more deplorably they have to suffer the degrading spectacle of the party in opposition blaming the party which happens at any moment to form the government for all the complex problems of inflation, unemployment, low growth, lack of investment, poor public services and so on, which have bedevilled their country for so long. There are numerous parliamentary examples of this cynical and cavalier approach to the political proprieties even on matters of immediate practicality. Ieuan

Maddock has spoken of the Tweedledum-Tweedledee attitudes on policy where the opposition party not only opposes government policy but commits itself to reversing it at the first opportunity despite the fact that Parliament may be dealing with an issue whose effects spread over many decades. Steel is but one example out of many of an industry that has suffered grievously from this parliamentary gamesmanship.

Conclusion: Alienation in a Democracy

At the theoretical core of the British system of parliamentary democracy, is the representative role of the Member of Parliament. Here was the justification, not only for granting Parliament its absolute authority, but also for the increasing dominance of the Commons within the parliamentary trinity. It was an adequate justification during the nineteenth-century, because representation adequately reflected the basic consensus within a governing class. Thus were nurtured the moral leadership and growing self-confidence of nineteenth-century Britain which, in turn, together confirmed the consensus even further and imposed its ethos on the proletariat.

Britain's position today is different. Parliamentary representation is inadequate, not merely in that it neither represents nor nurtures a consensus, but in that it does not even strike a reasonable balance between political parties and their support in the country. Thus, in contrast to the past, it promotes divisiveness, weakens leadership and erodes confidence. There is neither a self-confident governing class certain of its own mores, nor a popular leadership deriving its momentum from the common will it has succeeded in stimulating.

British decline is therefore compounded and the country's problems become intractable. There is a striking passage towards the end of Raymond Williams' novel, *The Fight for Manod*, a senior British civil servant is speaking: "The whole of public policy," he said emphatically, "is an attempt to reconstitute a culture, a social system, an economic order that have reached the end, reached the limits of viability. And then I sit here and look at this double inevitability: that this imperial, exporting, divided order is ending and that all its residual social forces, all its political formations, will fight to the end to reconstruct it, to re-establish it, moving deeper all the time through crisis after crisis in an impossible attempt to regain a familiar world. So then, a double inevitability: that they will fail and that they will try nothing else".

The passage captures the British predicament. If a remedy is to be found then a new approach has to be adopted. There are of course a whole range of economic, social and historical facts and myths that mould the attitudes, aspirations and beliefs of the citizen. These latter will not be changed overnight, so that Britain's new role might more readily be found and accepted. The first step, however, is clear; it is that 'the divided order' should be reconciled, that a basic consensus of all the people should be fostered, that democracy and the more difficult concept of mass-democracy be accepted as reality. In short, the people must be represented as faithfully as possible and that means, in the first instance, an appropriate electoral system. Only then will the nineteenth-century's virtuous circle of parliamentary democracy begin to be re-established in a contemporary Britain where consensus strengthens confidence, which in turn accepts change.

The majority of our present political leaders will have none of it. Their way is that of the former general secretary of the Labour Party, with his predisposition for the elitist rule of the party caucus and the burgeoning of the apparachik. It is bound to fail because it produces an alienation within society. Here is the root cause of our failure to reverse British decline.

Electoral reform will not produce miracles overnight. It is no more than a key, which will open a number of doors. When these are opened a process of change can be initiated in our political system which will be cumulative and which can reach out at the national psyche. At least, within a reasonable time, the country will be more truly a democracy. The democrat's faith is that the democratic way is also the effective way.

APPENDIX II

Glossary of Mining Terms

Air lock A metal chamber enclosing the top of an upcast shaft to prevent air short-circuiting to the fan drift.

Air doors: Sets of double or treble doors in a roadway connecting intake and return airways underground.

Arch: A steel frame for supporting the roof and sides of roadways (tunnels).

Bank: A term used colloquially for the colliery surface: it includes all the buildings associated with the colliery. For example, a man employed in the washery would be working 'on the bank'. The literal bank of colliery waste was called the tip.

Banksman: Man employed loading and unloading the cage at the pit head i.e. on the bank.

Bar: A length of half-round timber or corrugated steel held against the roof by a prop at each end.

Bind coal The top part of a seam deliberately left as a roof supporting friable strata above the seam.

Bonyn & Brigyn Welsh terms denoting fissures in the coal seam. A bonyn heads downwards away from the faceworker, a brigyn upwards.

Brake: A steep tunnel along which ran an endless steel rope. Full drams were attached to the rope at the top. As they descended under the force of gravity, empty drams were hauled up from the bottom. The speed was controlled by a brake (hence the name).

Brattice: A partition to direct the current of ventilating air into recesses in the roof where methane (being lighter than air) accumulated. It usually consisted of hessian cloth.

Byeman: An experienced workman employed on skilled mining work not directly involving coal production, e.g. enlarging roadways. The work was usually done on the night shift.

Capping: Cutting six feet of the end of a winding rope and recoupling it to the cage. This had to be done every six months as a legal requirement. The rope itself had to be replaced every three years.

Cap and Bell: An arrangement in the headgear of uncoupling the cage from the winding rope in the event of an overwind.

Casting: Term for shovelling coal more than once in order to reach a conveyor belt or dram.

Checkweighman: A man employed by the workmen to check that drams of coal are weighed accurately by the company weighman; a personification of the distrust felt originally between workmen and 'the owners', the latter, in my childhood, being a term of abuse.

Chock: A roof support built of blocks of hard wood laid squarely across each other. Metal 'chock releasers' were incorporated for dismantling the chock when necessary.

Cleat: A wooden block a few inches thick set between a steel prop and a steel bar.

Company Man: A workman not paid by piecework, also called a 'day-wage man' or 'dataller'.

Damp: A gas other than air, commonly methane (called 'firedamp'), but after an explosion, other noxious fumes (called 'afterdamp').

Deads: An area of a mine from which coal has been extracted.

Deep: A tunnel running downwards.

Deputy: Also called a fireman. The man in charge of a 'district' in a mine. A district, in strict legal terms a 'deputy's district', had to be in size such that it could be examined by its deputy within a period of 90 minutes. The post was one of considerable authority and responsibility.

Dial: A simplified theodolite (often called a 'miner's dial'), hence the term 'dialler' for a colliery surveyor.

Dirt: All broken strata other than coal.

Doggy: A man in day-to-day charge of 'the haulage'; his work was principally ensuring the soundness of the underground rail tracks.

Dram: A waggon running on rails. When filled with coal it became, in some collieries, a paitch.

Appendix II: Glossary of Mining Terms

Drift: A tunnel crossing the strata from one seam to another.

Fall: A collapse of roof.

Fault: A geological displacement of the strata. Small faults could be negotiated without loss of output. In extreme cases faults of up to 7 or 8 feet running square to the line of advance of the face could be carried with some difficulty.

Flat: A level roadway with two parallel rail tracks whereby 'journeys' (trains of drams) going in opposite directions could pass each other. (See Haulage)

Gob: The area 10 or 12 feet behind the coal face where the coal had been extracted and the roof allowed to collapse. Also known as the 'waste'.

Haulage: Coal was transported to the pit bottom by a combination of conveyor belt and 'rope haulage,' i.e. drams running along rail tracks. The term haulage applied to the latter. A 'lad' (haulage hand) was said to be employed 'on the haulage'. There were three types of rope haulage: direct rope, endless rope, main and tail rope. Direct haulage was used on dipping roadways to haul 'journeys' up, or to lower them down. For main and tail haulage, the rope ran the whole length of the road and was attached to each end of the journey (having run round return pulleys). The advantage of both these types was that only a single rail track was required. Endless rope haulage, by far the most common, had the rope, to which drams were lashed on and off, running the whole length of the road over two tracks.

Holeing: Undercutting a coal seam by handpick.

Hooker: Workman in charge of loading and unloading the cage at the shaft bottom.

Intake: A roadway carrying ventilation air from the shaft bottom to a coal face.

Journey: A train of drams.

Kench: A place where the cross sectional area of a roadway was being enlarged. The men employed on the task were called back 'rippers'.

Lagging: Timber planks placed between steel arches and the strata.

Lamp: There were two types — oil hand lamps (the traditional Davy lamp) and electric cap lamps, the first used for gas testing and the second for illumination.

Linesman: A surveyor's assistant who, as a roadway advanced with the face, extended a chalk line marked on the centre point of the arch so that the road did not deviate from its true course.

303

Lock:	A metal rod thrown between the spokes of a dram to bring it to a halt.
Lodgement	An excavation in the pit bottom area for holding water pumped to it from various places underground. The water was then pumped to the surface.
Moll:	A type of arch sitting on chocks on each side of the road.
Pack:	Walls of stone built in the gob as the face advanced and filled with rubble.
Pit Bottom:	The area around the bottom of the shaft where drams were marshalled as they came off the cage, or prior to being loaded onto it. The pit bottom could extend for 100 yards from the actual shaft bottom.
Play:	To be off work.
Pot:	A ball of stone, smooth like a pebble but much larger, set in the sedimentary rock roof. They were dangerous as they could fall unexpectedly if they happened to be between roof supports.
Prop:	A roof support, originally of wood, then steel and finally hydraulic supports. The props were set either individually under a 'lid' or in pairs under a 'bar'. Wooden props were spruce, bars were larch. Metal bars were of corrugated steel. At Ifton colliery on the southern edge of the coalfield, the term for a prop was 'tree'. The Welsh term at Hafod for a 'prop and lid' was 'fforch a hetri'. The word 'hetri' does not appear in the dictionary and one sumises that it derives from the other meaning of tree in English (the crucifixion cross); hence a 'tree' set across the head of a prop as a 'lid' — a head tree. The Welsh for Oswestry (Oswald's Tree), a town not far from Ifton, is Croesoswallt (Oswald's Cross).
Return:	A roadway carrying ventilation air from the face to the shaft bottom. There is a poem by Huw Menai, a miner in south Wales, called 'Back in the Return'. The poem begins:

> Where shall the eyes a darkness find
> That is a menace on the mind
> Save in a coal mine, where one's lamp
> I smothered oft by afterdamp?

	The poetic licence is startling. Afterdamp contains carbon monoxide. Something other than one's lamp would be smothered. A return is also called a 'wind road'.
Ripping:	Enlarging the roadways leading to the face. The front ripping was done each time before the face 'turned over' i.e. advanced after the cut coal had been cleared. Back ripping (the work of byemen) was done to enlarge the roadway some distance from the face after it had been squeezed by the pressure of the strata.

(A) Rope: Each traverse of the shaft by the cage was a 'rope'. A compulsive managerial question at the end of a shift was 'How many ropes have you had?'.

Screens: A place where run-of-mine coal was riddled into various sizes and large lumps of stone were removed.

Shotfirer: An official charged with blasting the cut coal. The following poignant words are taken from a poem written by an anonymous poet after the Gresford disaster and made famous by the pop group The Henesseys:

> If you fire that shot,
> The deputy Tomlinson cried,
> We'll all be blown to hell,
> And no one can say that he lied.

Sonni: The term used in Hafod for a stationary engine driving a haulage rope. It derives, no doubt, from a large engineering firm of the 19th century named Sawney.

Splicer: A man employed splicing the numerous steel ropes. The craft was jealously admired. At the Rhosllannerchrugog National Eisteddfod in 1945 there was a hotly contested rope splicing competition.

Sump: The bottom of the shaft below the bearing girders onto which the cage is loaded.

Washbox: A large pulsating container full of water at a prepared viscosity into which the run-of-mine coal was loaded. The heavier stone separated from the lighter coal.

Wicket: The length of face a collier was required to 'clear'. The term had gradually been superseded by 'stint'.

Winding engine: The large engine used to wind the cages through the shafts. After nationalisation steam engines were gradually replaced by much less glamorous but more sensitive electric engines. Governors regulated the speed as the cage neared its terminus thus making overwinds much rarer.

Index